E

Who Says You Can't Go Home?

B. LOREN

Who Says You Can't Go Home?

ISBN: 9798596091335

DEDICATION

The desire to write my story was created by so many friends and family over the years that said, "You really should write a book!" During my 28 years in direct sales, I was asked many times to share my story again and again. The story I shared was a Readers Digest version, of course! It seemed redundant to me, but I learned that sharing it helped others believe in themselves more and inspired others to never give up. I believe a life worth living is a life to be shared! My husband has been an enormous inspiration and support in helping me solve the mysteries of where I came from and who I belong to! Without him, there would be no answers. My partner in this adventure, Peggy Sue, is not only a constant part of every bit of my life, but she is an integral part of this process - since she's the expert in terms of everything involved in writing a book. I am forever indebted to her! While sharing the pieces of my life with both friends and strangers is uncomfortable and terribly intimidating, my goal was to release it by putting it on paper and share it with those it may help.

To Our children - Ryan, Cameron, James, and Taylor - I love you with all my heart. My role as a mother has always been my reason to persevere. To Peggy Sue - the connection, trust, respect and love I have for and with you is larger than life itself. I believe you were the very first blessing God gave me. He knew I needed you by my side throughout my life. To my husband Jim - you are my world, you are my heart, you are my everything - now and always. You are truly my soul mate. This book is dedicated to each of you, as well as those members of my biological family who tried to find me and to those that welcomed me with open arms when we finally connected! I also want to recognize members of the family I believed I belonged to - those that treated me well, those that loved me, and those that still accept me as family even though we're not related by blood after all.

This is my life - good, bad, beautiful, and ugly. It took me 15 years to write it. I pray that it touches you in a positive way. Thank you!

CONTENTS

"You own everything that happened to you. Tell your stories. If people wanted you to write warmly about them, they should have behaved better."

— Anne Lamott, Bird by Bird

B. LOREN

CHAPTER 1

My Reason for Everything – My Boys

It was the day after Christmas, 2008. It was such a great holiday that year! No drama, no arguing; that's a big deal with my 21 and 18-year-old boys! We had Christmas Eve dinner together and then watched my favorite holiday movie, It's A Wonderful Life.

Cameron seemed to pay more attention to the storyline this time. His years in acting school had ignited an interest in old movies. Ryan watched, as he did every year, just to appease me. I didn't go overboard with gifts this year, which was unusual for me. They understood that their college expenses and my income weren't quite keeping us in the lifestyle we had become accustomed to. I knew in my heart that they would eventually graduate and be successful and then get married and have babies and I'll be the "cool grandma" that travels and brings the grandkids gifts from countries all over the world like Aunt Jenny on the Brady Bunch!

These two were my life and they had been since the day they were born. They were my chance to get it right—to be the parent that would leave them with happy childhood memories and not trauma. I would later learn that memories are seen through different lenses for each person. I did more damage than I thought.

After Ryan made a wonderful breakfast and Cameron cleaned the kitchen, they began their ritual of packing to go to their Dad's house for the remainder of the holiday. It was that time again. Joe and I were married in 1987 and began a family together later in 1987. Our marriage didn't make it. My biggest lesson during that time was that sometimes love just isn't enough. Sometimes the relationship is for a season or a reason, but not for a lifetime. The relationship with the children, however, is a lifetime.

My children will always have both parents, no matter how difficult it can be. They will get the best we can both offer as long as I have anything to say about it. For Christmas day, they get to join in the big family holiday that their Dad can provide. I love that they have family and tradition like that with him. They'll be surrounded by a big loving family with their Dad and Vickie, their stepmom of the past 13 years. They'll be joined by grandparents and aunts and uncles and cousins and dogs and all that wonderful family stuff. They'll have great food because Vickie is an amazing cook and so is their grandmother, Delores. They'll be surrounded by more love and that's the best part.

As for me, I loaded up my car with gifts and the pies I made for the holiday dinner and I drove over to my latest boyfriend's house. I had been seeing him for a few months. He was a great guy with 3 beautiful teenage daughters. I couldn't quite figure him out, but I enjoyed myself with him most of the time. He was surely not Mr. Right, but he was Mr. Right Now.

I had been here before and it wasn't a good feeling knowing that there would be an end, but it is what it is. The end would be coming soon.

Same story. Different face.

It must be me. I am the common denominator. At 44 years old, you would think I would have figured it all out by then. I'm usually not a slow learner...except when it comes to men.

On this particular day, I woke up feeling melancholy. Why? I hated this feeling and it made me upset that I could feel this way when I have so much to be grateful for. Who would have imagined that I could live a life like I do after the childhood I had?

I have a beautiful home across the street from the Chesapeake Bay. I can watch the water from where I sit in my home. I have 2 wonderful, beautiful, intelligent, healthy sons pursuing their education in college; something I always wanted to do, but never got the chance. I have my own business and I work when I want, how I want, and with whom I want. I earned a six-figure income without a college degree and while working an average of 40 hours or less per week. I was single and still marketable and as Cameron told me before he left for college, I had no limits as to what I could do. Maybe that's the problem.

Maybe I was so used to limits and trying to defy them that I didn't know what to do without them? Nah, that's not it. Maybe it was the big black depression that sneaked up on me every now and then and then grabbed me from behind to drag me into the darkness?

Not this time. It felt different.

Maybe it was just that I needed a new plan. For 21 years I had defined myself as a mother. I'll always be a mother and I've loved that title more than anything in this world. But at this point, my boys don't need that kind of mother anymore.

Cameron was away at college in New York and absolutely loving it. Ryan was in his fourth year at a local college while working and living at home with me. I didn't see him often and when I did, we were usually just passing each other. He loved to tease me about not cooking for him, but I never knew when he would be here, and he didn't eat leftovers. I knew he was going to be leaving again soon and I was fearful that he would fall back into old unhealthy habits. I had to dig deep to trust him and to believe that he was growing up and I had to stay positive. I had to try to stop controlling things. Let things happen. I needed to have faith that even if bad things happened, there's a reason and a lesson to be learned.

Look at all the lessons I've learned along the way.

The new plan for me? How can I make a new plan when I've exceeded every dream I've ever had? What else is possible? The only thing I felt I was missing was a husband and I didn't know that I really wanted one of those! It was just too much trouble, it's too much compromise, it's a thankless job and it always ends ugly.

Sure, I'd love to have that fairy tale relationship, but honestly, does it really exist? If it does, it's not like anyone I've ever had or even ever seen. None of my friends are in a relationship that I would want to be in. Yeah, I've been in love a few times and it felt wonderful...for a minute. Ok, that's not completely true, but I do think I fall in love too easily. My heart begins doing the pitter-patter thing, he makes me laugh, touches my face and hair and then he kisses me, and I'm done! As long as the kiss is good, the fairy tale has begun! But, unlike the stories and movies, all the crap that follows will lead the story to a fiery explosive end!

I was the only person I knew who had three failed marriages at my age. On top of that, I've been engaged three other times to three different men! Throw in all the "Mr. Right Now" guys and it was enough men to fill a football team, all in search of the right one.

I will never settle for less again.

Self-help books, advice, mentors, friends, and many therapy sessions over the years have blamed my childhood experiences. They say it's because I never had proper role models and my view of love was distorted at a very early age. Perhaps distorted isn't quite strong enough. The term "dysfunctional" doesn't seem big enough to describe my childhood either. Words like criminal, irrational, and chaotic seem to fit a bit better.

But I think that's a cop-out. I am who I am today in spite of my childhood, not because of it. I am responsible for who I am today. I refuse to point the finger instead of using all the lessons I've learned to make myself a better person. I am, have been, and always will be too hard on myself. That's the way I want it. I want to stand on my own two feet with my head held high. No one will ever take credit—good or bad for who I became. It's all on me.

There are, however, many characters who took part in molding me. I'd like to share my journey with you. My hope is that my story touches you in a way that makes you feel better about your own life.

CHAPTER 2

Gail – 1964

Gail was my Mom. She died when I was 10 months old. I was too young to know her, of course, and I never got straight answers as to how she died until much later in my life. I spent most of my younger years resenting her terribly for leaving me. I believed my life could have been so different if she had stuck around. I always longed for a mom and my Dad, Paul, certainly provided many girlfriends and wives to assume the role, but those that I remember just couldn't fit the bill.

I gravitated toward all the moms of my friends and boyfriends throughout my childhood. Some teenage relationships lasted longer than they should have just because I loved their moms so much. I learned recipes, driving skills, make-up, fashion, and even relationship advice from spending more time with their moms than I did with them. Even with my friends, I would follow their moms around in the kitchen and talk to them like I was their child, but I was always respectful. Friends' moms took me into their lives and even took me shopping for my prom dresses.

Gail clearly had issues. From the stories I've heard and believed for the first 35 years of my life, she came from an alcoholic family in Worcester, Massachusetts. She was young and beautiful and completely uncomfortable in her own skin. She was married at a very young age and had two children, both boys, Dale and David. Since this was before my time, I don't know the reasons for the demise of that marriage, but her husband was awarded custody of the two small boys at the divorce. Because this was the early 1960's, it was very unusual for a woman to lose custody of her own children. Whatever the reasons, she was devastated by the loss and never got over it.

At some point, Gail met a stranger passing through town by the name of Paul. He was traveling through Worcester with some buddies after they stole a car to drive north in search of jobs. She had just recently gone through her divorce and custody battle and was a very sad young woman. Paul fell for her immediately and decided to stick around town to win her heart. He was very handsome and very charming, and he was pretty cocky too. Unfortunately, his time hanging out with her was shortened by the police finding him and his buddies and putting them in jail for stealing the car that got them there.

My understanding is that Gail would visit him in jail and waited for him to be released. She clearly had a "bad picker" just like me. At some point during that time, I was born.

After Dad was released from jail, he convinced Mom to move to Baltimore with him. He promised to marry her, and he promised to help her regain custody of her two sons. I was always told that my Mom was a very weak woman, but I'm not sure I believe that. This had to have been a moment of incredible strength for her. She was leaving her home, her family, and her two boys to start a new life in a new city with a new man and a baby.

She had a goal and she was going to do whatever she had to do to get her boys back. She must have had moments of believing there was more for her, and possibly a better life for her children.

Once arriving and settling in with a rented home in South Baltimore, I can't even guess what was going through her mind. She learned that Paul had no money. She learned that he was controlling and angry and had no intentions of following through with his promises. He took her to the courthouse in Baltimore to be married but she refused. They argued intensely, she confronted him on his lies, and he demanded that she at least wear the wedding band so his family would believe they were married. She did. Within just three weeks of arriving in this new city, he beat her unmercifully. She swallowed a bottle of pills. She passed away just over one month after her 21st birthday.

The questions that I asked, again and again, were always either answered with vague answers or unsure responses. This led to my lifelong obsession with finding out the truth.

CHAPTER 3

Tessie – 1965-ish

Dad was a very handsome, very charming 21-year old widower with a baby girl. He was basically irresistible. A young woman from the neighborhood was already enamored with him, and he was on the prowl for someone to take care of this child. To this day, I don't understand why he wanted to keep me. He could have given me to my Mom's mother. He could have let one of his many married sisters raise me—several of them made the offer. He had so many options, but, as I learned later, it was all a game for him. He would never, ever tell me the truth.

Tessie was a wonderful, loving woman and she adored me, almost as much as she adored Paul. When they married, she became the person totally responsible for taking care of me. She planned my christening and prepared all the details, including the party to follow. Paul didn't bother to show up. She didn't know where he was, but that was nothing new. He often disappeared and had no explanation. When she pushed for an explanation, he got angry and violent. She didn't push often.

The marriage was a painful disappointment to her. She was a good Catholic woman, and she did whatever necessary to keep her marriage and to keep me. When she announced to Paul that she was expecting a baby of their own, he seemed very happy. She believed this could be a great thing for their marriage and she was excited to welcome her own new child into the family. A new little life would certainly bring joy and she was excited.

Several months later, however, there was a knock on the door. A 14-year-old girl was standing in the doorway. The child's name was Alice, and she was pregnant. She had come to tell Tessie that her mother had kicked her out because she was pregnant, and Paul was the father.

I cannot imagine how devastated Tessie must have been. To find out that another woman, or rather a 14-year-old child was pregnant at the same time as she was with Paul's child. How surprised do you suppose he was when he came home that evening to find both his pregnant wife and his pregnant child mistress making arrangements to share a home?

Yes, Tessie was that magnanimous that she agreed to allow Alice to live at her house while she carried the child and until she found other arrangements. Paul was relegated to the sofa.

Alice stayed for quite a while, but not through her entire pregnancy. She was gone before Tessie gave birth. Tessie stayed married to Paul and when the new baby was born, she named her son after Paul, in spite of all he had done. A few months later, Alice gave birth to a child she named after Paul as well. He now had two sons, born just months apart, named after him, from two different women.

The marriage to Tessie ended and I don't know what the final straw was. I hope it was because she had enough and decided to put her son and herself first and stop putting up with Paul's behaviors. I don't remember daily life with her, but

I do remember her sweet spirit. She was always good to me throughout my childhood, whenever I would see her. She didn't deserve to be treated the way she was, and I know that she eventually found the love of her life. I'm so glad about that. If anyone deserved happiness, it was her.

Her son, Paul Wayne, was not an active part of my life because our Dad was an absentee parent to him. Dad kept moving forward as if it had never happened. He didn't even pay child support. I stay in contact with Tessie and with Paul Wayne through social media and Tessie and I have shared lunches together now and then. We have kept a place in our lives for each other.

CHAPTER 4

In Between Wives

Dad was not the type of man to be alone. There were many other women in-between his marriages. I don't remember all of their names. We moved a lot too. Dad always rented homes and would argue with landlords until we were evicted. He was a factory worker who lost his job for stealing. He then became a taxicab driver. He had seven brothers and sisters.

There was Aunt Betty and Uncle Dave: Aunt Betty was the local President of the Elvis Presley fan club and there were Elvis statues and memorabilia all over her house.

There was Aunt Dottie and Uncle Lee: Aunt Dottie was very, very religious and Uncle Lee was always angry.

There was Aunt Daisy and Uncle Mike: they were the most fun couple.

There was Aunt Patsy and Uncle Robert: they were both deaf and Aunt Patsy taught me sign language. She was always the sweetest person ever.

There was Uncle Billy and Aunt Sharon: they got divorced and then he married Aunt Linda.

There was Aunt Shirley and Uncle Ed: I spent more time with them than any of the others, along with their 7 children.

And there was my favorite, Uncle Gene and Aunt Peggy. Uncle Gene was in the Air Force and he was rarely around because he lived in either Utah or New Mexico. He did always bring me gifts when I saw him though.

The family helped a lot with taking care of me. I often spent the night or many nights at one of their homes. At some point, I lived with Uncle Billy and Aunt Sharon, Uncle Billy, and Aunt Linda and Aunt Shirley and Uncle Ed. I also lived with Aunt Dottie and Uncle Lee and their 3 children. Their daughter, Doris, was not only my cousin, she was my best friend. I looked up to her and wanted to be just like her. It felt like a family when I lived there, but it was odd because I knew I didn't belong there. That sense of not belonging would follow me for the rest of my life.

Dad would show up once in a while, but I would go for long periods of time without seeing him. My fondest memories of this time period were when Doris and I would put together performances for the family. We would sing and act and dance and sometimes the neighborhood kids would stand outside the back fence and watch us too. It was so much fun!

For reasons that had not been determined yet, I was a habitual bed-wetter until I was 18 years old.

It was just about every single night and it was long before they had "pull-ups" for children. Aunt Dottie bought celebrity posters for Doris and I. Doris got David Cassidy and I got Donny Osmond!

But as Doris excitedly hung her poster, I was told that I could have mine when I went for 2 full weeks without wetting the bed. I never got that poster.

Uncle Lee was disgusted by it and many family members believed that I was just too lazy to get up in the middle of the night to go to the bathroom. Did they think I enjoyed waking up in a puddle? I was punished constantly and when that didn't work, there was the morning ritual of being laid across Uncle Lee's lap at the kitchen table for a beating with the switches off the tree in the back yard.

I remember one Saturday morning as I was sitting on the floor watching cartoons when Dad came to visit. When he hugged me, I winced in pain? He lifted the back of my shirt and saw the raw switch marks and a huge argument ensued between him and Aunt Dottie. I was taken away from Aunt Dot and Uncle Lee that day. I thought my Dad was my knight in shining armor. He saved me from those terrible switch beatings. I would learn later that those were the least damaging wounds I would have to live with.

The sequence of where I lived and when I lived there is so questionable to me. I was moved and placed into so many different homes and I'm not sure which order it all fell in. There are also gaps in my memory. I decided that if my mind chose to hide memories, based on the memories I do have, I don't need to dig that up. What I remember is bad enough. What follows is what I believe to be the proper order.

At some point, I was taken to stay with a much older couple, to be known to me as Mom Ann and Daddy Frank. I don't know what their relationship was to my Dad, but I know they weren't family. They lived in a teeny, tiny house and they welcomed me to stay with them. They were quite wonderful to me. By that point in time, I was not only timid; I was terrified of making mistakes. I'll always remember the morning I knocked over a glass of milk on the kitchen table and I ran to the corner of the kitchen covering my head and repeating over and over that I was sorry. I could see the concern in Mom Ann's eyes as she comforted and told me it was ok. It really was ok. At this home, I had nothing to be afraid of.

One day Dad came to get me. He packed all my things and we got into his car and drove. Our destination was Nashville, Tennessee. When we arrived, we pulled up to a house and I was introduced to a woman, whose name I do not remember, and her two children. Apparently, this was Dad's new girlfriend, and this was our new home. I was now 5-years old and had not been enrolled in kindergarten.

My time there is foggy. I don't remember if it was happy or not. I remember having baby chicks at Easter and they had been dyed in different spring colors. There were a bunch of them, and I remember laughing and chasing them around the yard. My only other memory was the day Dad and his girlfriend dressed me in a pretty blue dress and fixed my hair with curls. Dad took me to a motel. There was a man waiting for us in one of the hotel rooms. Dad sat me on the unmade bed and the man took pictures of me. In retrospect, I find this disturbing. What were the pictures for? Was he planning to sell me?

My only other memory of that time was the day Alice showed up at the front door and everything changed again.

CHAPTER 5

Alice -1970-ish

After moving from Tessie's house, Alice had her baby boy, Paul Robert, and went on with her life, until she lost custody of him within his first year. His crying was apparently getting to her, so she picked him up out of his crib and threw him across the room. Social Services put him into a foster home. Alice had gone to visit the foster home and was convinced that they were doing more damage to him than she did, and she wanted to get him back. She believed the only way she could regain custody would be to get married and prove that she had a more stable home. She wanted Dad to come back to Baltimore and marry her.

Once she found us, we packed up again and moved back to Baltimore. Dad and Alice were then married and "Little Paul", as we called him, came back from the foster home shortly afterward.

At 7-years old, I was finally enrolled in school and went right into the first grade without having attended kindergarten. I was behind one grade and was the oldest in my class. I was a very shy and very quiet child. I didn't make friends easily because I was very insecure. I knew that I would be picked on if anyone found out I was a bedwetter, so I didn't accept any sleepover invitations. This new family situation was to be my first real memory of anger and violence.

Dad and Alice didn't bicker; they screamed and threw things at each other. They wrestled to the floor with fistfights, often knocking over tables and lamps and there was usually blood. One time I remember distinctly was when Alice picked up a living room chair, which was very heavy, and threw it at Dad. Every time it started, I would find a corner and curl up into a ball and make myself "disappear".

I became an expert at disappearing. I developed the ability to step outside a situation and believe that I had truly disappeared, and I was safe. When I would step back into reality, the drama was usually over, and they would be making up. That usually meant they were heading upstairs and leaving me to attend to Little Paul. This was their version of love...dysfunction at its best.

I spent my days in school and then came home to watch television. It was my favorite pastime. When the TV was on, I could hide there. I often pretended to be Jeanie in "I Dream of Jeanie" and my favorite thing was to pretend to be one of the kids on the "Brady Bunch". If I was awake, I was watching TV.

Alice had a best friend who visited often when Dad wasn't home. Her name was Roma. Roma looked, acted, and dressed like a man. She and Dad didn't get along, apparently. I was told by Alice to never let Dad know that Roma came to visit. I did as I was told and kept my mouth shut. I didn't mind having Roma around. She kept Alice smiling and I could relax when she was there.

Alice didn't really like me much. She didn't want to raise another woman's child, even though that woman had passed away. She was a very angry young woman and I was always in trouble for something. Whenever she was mad at Dad, which was often, she would take it out on me. Still a bedwetter, this was the easiest way for her to justify my punishments. I did my best to avoid her and thought that if I could just disappear into the TV, she would forget I was there.

Little Paul was a quiet little boy who just sat on the sofa and barely spoke. He didn't even play as other little boys did. He just sat and stared at the world with a look of fear on his little face all the time. I often wondered what was going on in his little mind. One day I came home from school and immediately sat in front of the TV to watch my favorite afternoon shows like I always did. Alice was angry again, so I stayed quiet. I tuned out the outside world and stepped into my TV world. I didn't see or hear anything going on around me when I did this.

Apparently, Alice had yelled into the living room for me to bring her something. I didn't hear her. Little Paul was sitting on the sofa, just staring, as usual. Angry Alice came charging into the living room, full of rage and furious with me for ignoring her. She grabbed me by the back of my long hair, picked me up, and shook me around while screaming at me. She then threw me to the floor, face first.

The coffee table stopped my fall.

My forehead had gone into the corner of the table and blood was gushing everywhere. When I saw all of the blood, I was terrified and began crying loudly. I looked up to see Little Paul, still sitting in the same spot, still staring, not moving and I could see the terror on his little face. He didn't say a word or shed a tear. I think he was in shock. Alice grabbed me by both shoulders and yelled into my face, "If you tell your father what happened here, I will kill you. Do you understand? I will kill you!"

This is not an exaggeration. Those were her words. Now I know that there are a lot of things that I don't remember, but this was huge. I can still remember that moment as if it happened yesterday. I had no intention of telling my Dad because I believed she would truly kill me.

I was rushed to the hospital by ambulance and got plenty of stitches on my forehead. After the wound healed, I had a huge scar across my forehead and part of it ran down past my left eyebrow and into my eye socket. My father said I was lucky I didn't lose my eye. He told me this because he believed I tripped and wanted me to be aware that I should be more careful. That scar will always remain on my face as a reminder to me of the evil in this world.

Something happened to my spirit that day. I suddenly felt that I was no longer just a child in the first grade. I had to do something. This woman was scary and crazy, and I had to protect my Dad and me. I couldn't tell him just how evil she was, but maybe I could cause a bit of a stir. I knew how angry Alice could get, especially when she was arguing with Dad. She was also extremely jealous, especially when it came to Tessie. She didn't know that Dad took me to visit Tessie sometimes. It was our secret and he told me to never tell her or I wouldn't be able to see Tessie anymore. I decided that this was my way to solve the problem.

One afternoon, I drummed up the courage to tell Alice that Dad took me to see Tessie now and then. As I expected, she lost her mind. When he came in from work, all hell broke loose! Dad was furious with me. He came at me screaming that I had a big mouth and that I had ruined his life. He said he would never forgive me. I didn't apologize. I had gotten exactly what I wanted. We moved out and Alice was never part of my life again.

I was then sent back to live with Mom Ann and Daddy Frank again. That was my favorite place to live! I had solved the problem without any help from adults. I took note of this and realized that I had a power of my own. In my scariest moment, I had figured out a way to change our situation. I had told the truth and gotten the results I wanted.

CHAPTER 6

Anne –1972-ish

Anne was absolutely beautiful. She had beautiful blonde hair, beautiful blue eyes with long eyelashes and she dressed like a movie star on one of the old Elvis movies we watched. When she became Dad's new girlfriend, I was so enamored with her that I wanted to follow her wherever she went. She had no children of her own and she loved me. She was a hairdresser who went to women's homes to do their hair at their own kitchen tables.

On Saturday mornings, she would take me with her. I would sit in front of the ladies' TVs and watch my cartoons, while she made them feel beautiful. The ladies grew to expect me and would have brownies and other sweets waiting for me. It was fun and I got to hang out with Anne. I was proud that people thought I was her daughter.

Anne loved my Dad and I wanted him to marry her. Because I was so enamored by her, I didn't spend so much time watching TV. I wanted to be with her doing whatever she was doing. I started seeing my Dad in a whole new light. I realized that he wasn't the victim when it came to fighting with women, he was the problem.

He was a brutal man. How had I missed this? Anne, unlike Alice, was not an angry woman and she didn't deserve the many arguments they had. She didn't fight back as Alice did. He beat her badly, repeatedly, until she was black and blue. The next day after a beating, she just spent extra time applying her make-up and no one knew what she was going through. My heart hurt for her. She eventually had enough, and she left. I was devastated. I hated that I was going to have to move again and wouldn't see her anymore.

Shortly after this, I was moved back to live with Mom Anne and Daddy Frank again. This time, I stayed there longer than before. Dad came to visit as usual and Mom Anne would give me pennies to go up to the candy store so they could chat with Dad a little without me. As I reminisce, I find it odd that I loved him as I did. I knew he was all I had. Since my mother left me, I had to protect him, and I was so happy when he came to visit.

On one visit, I asked him if he had a new girlfriend. He told me no. I was so afraid he would go back to Alice because he didn't like being alone. I asked him to promise me that he would never go back to Alice again. He kept asking me why I was saying this, and I told him the secret. I told him that Alice had thrown me at the coffee table and threatened to kill me if I told him. He got very angry and ran out the door to confront her. When he returned, he held me and apologized that I had to keep that secret. He told me that Alice was now in a new relationship with Roma! That was officially the end of that saga.

A few months later, Dad came to visit, and he brought someone with him, Anne! She was back! I was so excited to see her! We were going to be a family again! This time, I wouldn't leave her side at all. I was going to make sure she didn't leave again. One afternoon, after an evening of arguing with Dad, I was afraid she would leave again. I asked her if she was going to leave and she didn't answer me. I then asked her if she did leave, would she please take me with her. She stopped and hugged me and told me not to worry.

The 3 of us moved to a new home on Washington Boulevard, which was not so close to our old neighborhood in South Baltimore. We were starting a new life. I learned that Anne had a little wig that she put on the crown of her head and then she teased her hair around it to make her hair look bigger. She put false eyelashes on her eyes and made them really long. She applied her make up so beautifully and she always wore high heels.

Our home had 3 floors. My bedroom was on the 3rd floor and Dad and Anne's was on the 2nd floor. One evening, as I was going up the stairs to my room, I noticed that Anne's bedroom door was open. She was standing in her underwear in front of the mirror with her back to the door. I looked in to see what she was doing, and I saw her take her bra off. When the bra came off, the boobs came off too! I was horrified! She turned and saw the shock on my face in her mirror and laughed hysterically! I told her I couldn't believe that boobs came off like that! She explained to me that not all boobs come off, but since God didn't give her much in that department, she found these fake boobs to make her clothes fit better. She reassured me that my boobs wouldn't necessarily come off once they grew. What a relief!

There were problems arising with visitation with Little Paul and Dad was angry. Alice reported Dad to Social Services for abuse to Little Paul. They came to the house to speak to me. With Dad's permission, they led me into the living room and asked Dad and Anne to stay in the kitchen. They asked me if my Dad ever touched me inappropriately. I pretended to not know what they were talking about. They described in more detail what they were asking, and I pretended to be shocked. I denied him behaving in any way that he shouldn't have. I had to protect him. He was all I had.

After Social Services left, Dad and Anne decided that they were going to take Little Paul away from Alice because she was trying to start trouble and she wasn't taking care of him properly. Instead of doing it legally, Paul walked into Alice's home and just took Little Paul. He brought him home, packed all of us up and we got into the car for a long road trip...to Salt Lake City, Utah. Dad's brother, Uncle Gene, was stationed there with the Air Force. He said we could stay with him until things got straightened out with Little Paul.

School had just ended for the year, so they didn't have to worry about that for the moment. I was very excited to see Uncle Gene. He lived so far away and visited so infrequently. But whenever he was around, he was so sweet to me. He brought me gifts from faraway lands and he once told me that I was his favorite niece.

The road trip was actually fun. I remember stopping in Indianapolis and Dad bought us Japanese jumping beans. That's what I still associate Indianapolis with to this day!

It took us 4 days to get to Utah. We slept in a motel one night and we slept in the car the other nights. I was so glad to finally get there. Uncle Gene and Aunt Peggy lived in a tiny house on the Air Force property and they had 4 children of their own. Needless to say, things were going to be tight.

One day, we took a day trip to the Great Salt Lake. During that time, they still allowed people to swim in the Lake. I remember Uncle Gene trying to teach me how to float on my back. He said that there was so much salt in the lake that all you had to do was lean back and you would just float. But I had other things on my mind.

Out at the other end of the Lake, I saw a big house. Now keep in mind that I was 8 years old. I was sure that Donny Osmond lived in that big house! I didn't care about floating on the Great Salt Lake, I just wanted to swim out to that house and meet Donny Osmond. I swam and I swam, and I swam. The water never got very deep, but it seemed that the house never got much closer. When I looked back to the shore, my family seemed very far away, and I got scared. I also noticed that no one knew how far out I was. No one was even looking in my direction. I decided to swim back and get reinforcements to help me meet Donny Osmond.

When I got back, there was confusion. Everyone was in a tizzy and I couldn't ask anyone for help. It seemed that Dad and Anne got into a terrible fight and Anne left. We all packed up to head back to the house and when we got there, Anne was already gone. She had packed her things and gone to the airport to fly back to Baltimore by herself. She didn't say goodbye to me. And she didn't take me with her.

Shortly after that, Dad, Little Paul, and I packed up and drove back to Baltimore. It was a long, sad trip home. I couldn't help but worry about what would happen to us when we got back. Alice was angry that Dad had stolen Little Paul. Would he go to jail? Alice would get Little Paul back, but what would happen to me? Would they put me in one of those foster homes? Or worse yet, would I be left alone with him again?

CHAPTER 7

Leaving My Body

When we got home, Anne was nowhere to be found. Alice came without drama and took Little Paul back. It was just Dad and me again. I knew what that meant for me.

When Dad didn't have a woman in his life, he looked to me to fill in the void. I don't know when it all started. I just don't remember there ever being a time when it wasn't expected.

I had developed the ability to leave my body, as I explained previously. Living in TV shows was my escape. In the evenings, there was a routine. After dinner, I was to take a bath and put on a nightgown. I was not allowed to wear underwear under my nightgown. We would watch TV and I was forced to lie on the sofa with my back to him. We would watch his shows first; MASH and All in the Family. Then we would watch my shows, Brady Bunch, Carol Burnett, Sonny & Cher, etc.

While my shows were on, he would lift my gown and I would leave my body. I didn't take my eyes off the television ever, but I left my body and took myself away from that sofa.

Sometimes he would come home and fall asleep in front of the TV. I would sneak up to my third-floor bedroom and hope that he didn't wake up. He always woke up. He would stand on the second-floor landing and yell up the stairs for me to come down. Sometimes I would wear pajama pants in the hopes that he wouldn't "bother me".

I never got away with that. He would get angry and question me about why I wasn't wearing my nightgown as he expected. I would then go back to my room and change. Then instead of being able to watch TV, I had to sleep with him in his bed. With nothing to distract me, I would just close my eyes and try my best to leave my body by thinking of my favorite TV episodes.

I knew this wasn't right. I knew it, but what could I do about it?

CHAPTER 8

Moving Again

Dad had issues with the landlord here, just like he had issues with every landlord we ever had. It was simply non-payment of rent. He packed us up and he rented the house next door to Mom Anne and Daddy Frank. Alice was having some personal problems, so she actually sent Little Paul to stay with us for a short time. I really missed him and was glad to see him. He was so different with us than he was with her. Whenever she was around, he was so introverted and so quiet. When he was with me, we played, and we had fun.

One afternoon, Dad invited a lady friend over. They went upstairs and Dad told me and Little Paul to stay out of trouble. The house was very tiny, just a living room and kitchen, with the stairway to the upstairs right in the middle of the two rooms. The cartoons were over and there was nothing on TV. We weren't allowed to go outside, and we were bored. We decided to play hide and seek. We agreed that one of us would hide our eyes in one room, while the other hid in the opposite room, while we counted to 10 slowly. With these 2 tiny rooms, we quickly ran out of options. I had a great idea though.

Since I was a tiny little girl, I realized that I could fit into small spaces and when it was my turn again, I would climb into the refrigerator. Little Paul would never find me, and I would win.

When it was my turn to hide again, I was so excited. As Little Paul counted to 10, I pushed the button on the handle of our old refrigerator and moved a couple of bottles of soda and I climbed in. I fit! I pulled the door just close enough so Little Paul wouldn't see that it was open, but I pulled too hard. The door closed and locked. I did not find the best hiding place after all. I was trapped.

I punched the door, I screamed, I beat again and again on the sides and Little Paul could not find me. He eventually gave up and sat on the sofa to watch TV again. I don't know how long I was in there, but I was unbelievably grateful when Little Paul decided to get himself a drink from the refrigerator. He was quite surprised when he opened the door and I fell out while in the middle of a scream! I was covered with ketchup, soda, and blood from busting all the glass jars inside the refrigerator in my attempts to get out. Dad heard my screams and came running down the stairs. He stopped halfway on the stairs, leaned over the banister with a loose-fitting robe wrapped around him, and said, "I would punish you, but I think you've punished yourself. Clean up your mess." He then went back upstairs to his lady friend, as if nothing had happened. I cleaned up the mess I had made and tended to my own wounds. I was 9 years old.

Little Paul left the next day and Dad had to decide what to do with me since there was no woman to take care of me. Mom Anne was getting older and she was not well. I couldn't go back to live with them. Dad was sure he could win Anne back and that was all he could think about. One night, there was a knock at the door, and it was Anne, but she hadn't come back to stay, she just wanted to pick up the rest of her belongings.

She had gone back to her ex-husband and he was in the car outside waiting for her. Dad was trying to convince her to stay and talk, but she was avoiding him and just trying to get her things. He got really frustrated when his efforts didn't work, and she walked out the door. He ran after her. He reached into the car and grabbed her ex-husband. They started fighting in the middle of the street. Anne was screaming and Daddy Frank came outside to protect me from the situation. Anne's ex-husband ran back to his car and they drove away quickly. Dad grabbed my bicycle from the front of the house and chased the car. Daddy Frank wouldn't let me go no matter how much I cried out. I thought I had lost both of them.

Dad did come back, but not with good news. I never saw Anne again, ever. I don't know what happened to her and I often wish that someday, somehow, I will see her again. I would love that.

CHAPTER 9

Grandma Nettie

A short time after Anne was gone, Daddy Frank came running to our house and said something was wrong with Mom Anne. She had a heart attack and she died before the ambulance could get there. I didn't understand that I would never see her again.

Dad was out of options, so he sent me to live with his grandmother, Grandma Whipp. She lived just a few blocks away from us and she was in her 70s. Her son, Uncle Buck, still lived with her too. He was old too, but I don't know how old. She had one of those old washing machines with the ringer and I used to watch her do laundry. I was terrified of that contraption!

Grandma never ever left the house. There weren't usually prepared meals either. I often had to fend for myself by making butter bread with sugar on top to stop the hunger pains. The house was really dirty, and we had roaches terribly; especially in the bathtub. Uncle Buck always came home from work smelling like alcohol. He was a jolly kind of guy, but he didn't say much. Grandma wanted me to read the Bible, so that's what I did. Each night before I went to sleep, I would read some of the Bible, even though I didn't understand it. I did as I was told.

I finally made a friend in Grandma's neighborhood. Her name was Bubbles. I found that I liked to roller skate and Bubbles invited me over sometimes to listen to records. When I wasn't with Bubbles, I went to my Cousin Doris's house. I tried to keep myself busy and not stay in the house with Grandma and the roaches for too long.

Because the bathtub had roaches, and because there was no real supervision, I didn't take baths often. I had very long dark hair and I didn't wash that either. One day, while I was in my 3rd-grade class, Mrs. Epstein called me to the front of the room. She sat me in a chair with my back facing the rest of my class and forced me to let her brush my hair. I was humiliated. Everyone laughed and made fun of me and I retreated into "invisible mode" again.

A few months later, there was a report of head lice at school. The nurse came to each classroom checking students' heads one by one. I knew it was me. It was sheer torture to watch them search each child's head diligently, knowing that their search would end when they got to me. When it was my turn, the nurse moved one piece of my hair, threw away the tool she was using, and then moved onto the next person. Everyone knew. I was actually covered with lice. Grandma was not happy because this meant having to clean everything in the house; sheets, pillows, clothes, and everything else we had that lice could live in.

I was then bombarded with family members stopping over to inspect what I was and was not doing at home with Grandma. They wanted me to clean. I didn't know how to clean. Grandma was too old to clean, and Uncle Bucky was too drunk. Aunt Dot came over and told me that Doris cleaned all the time and I should try to be more like Doris.

CHAPTER 10

Lula Bell

There was a heavy-set woman with a mustache who was always looking for me in the neighborhood. Her name was Lula Bell. She told me she was a friend of my mother and she was always very nice to me. Dad told me to stay away from her, but she seemed harmless to me. Dad said that Lula Bell wanted to date him, and he wasn't interested. I really didn't understand what that had to do with me, and I decided to not tell him how often Lula Bell approached me. She lived on the same block that my mom and I had lived on when we first moved to Baltimore.

I would often run into her at the park or she would show up outside my school and walk me home. She always had gifts for me: handmade clothes, scarves, hats, gloves, candy, or toys. She was not a wealthy woman by any means, but she made these things for me. I didn't know why she was always so interested in me, but I liked that she was so nice. Sometimes when I was bored, I would go to her house and surprise her with a visit. She would just sit with me and talk, and she always talked about how wonderful my mother was. I often got the feeling that she had something to tell me, but she never did.

With all the moving we did, I lost touch with her. No one told me when she died. I knocked on her door one day and there was no answer. I looked in the window and the house was empty. The next-door neighbor told me Lula Bell had died. I sat on her stairs and cried. She was the only person who ever talked about my mother and as I got older, I had more and more questions, but no one would answer them. Many years later, I found out that Lula Bell had a special link to my family, and she played a part in answering all my questions.

CHAPTER 11

Debbie

Dad didn't visit often. I didn't mind. I was pretty happy living with Grandma, and I avoided thinking about Dad because it brought up very uncomfortable memories that I could not share with anyone. Those times were over for me as long as he stayed away. Then he came to visit. He brought me a heart necklace and told me that I would always have his heart. Then he told me he had a surprise for me, and he would be back the next day. I couldn't wait to see what my surprise was!

When he came back the next day, he had a pretty new friend with him. She looked like Cher Bono and her name was Debbie. She was 18 years old. I was 11. She was just 7 years older than me and she was going to be my new "mom". While she was pretty, there was something sneaky about her and I didn't trust her.

Dad wanted me to spend some time with her and get to know her. The 3 of us went shopping. I did not want to be there. I didn't want to like her, and I didn't want to live with him again. I made the decision right then and there to make sure she didn't like me either!

It was the 70s and she was wearing a pair of hip-hugging bell-bottom jeans with a halter top. Her belly was exposed, and she had really bad stretch marks. I didn't know what they were, but it looked nasty. I pointed at her belly and said, "Yuk! What is that?!" I knew it was rude. She was furious! Mission accomplished. She hated me.

We went into the mall and she and Dad were holding hands and being lovey-dovey. This had all the signs of another new family and I wanted nothing to do with it. We walked by the music section and I saw the new Donny Osmond album. I asked Dad if I could have it and he said no. I pleaded again and again and finally cried and sat on the floor in front of the album rack. I could see anger on Debbie's face as I got my way and Dad bought me the album. I stuck my tongue out at her and our future was set in stone.

After returning to Grandma's house that night, I believed my mission was accomplished and I would remain at Grandma's house. I was such a brat, and I knew this woman would want nothing to do with me. A week later, Dad came back, packed my stuff, and moved me back into the house on Washington Boulevard with him, Debbie, and her 6-month-old son, Craig. My plan back-fired big time.

CHAPTER 12

Elementary School

I was not a popular girl at school. I didn't talk to anyone. I was always afraid of everyone and everything. I kept my head down and didn't make eye contact. I tried to never make trouble, just do what I was told, and not be noticed. I didn't have any friends because my Dad wouldn't allow me to leave the house. Our neighborhood on Washington Boulevard was a rough one and most of our neighbors were black. Dad was ridiculously racist, and I was not allowed to play with or even talk to the black children we had as neighbors. We didn't live close to any of our family anymore, so it was just me and the TV.

In second grade now and in a new school that required me to take 3 MTA buses to and from school each day, I was "assigned" a friend. Peggy Sue was one of those popular, but really nice girls and the teacher thought it would be a good idea to pair her up with me. I'm sure she wasn't pleased. She was spending time with me in classes and at lunch, but I didn't know if it was because she was told to or if she liked me. I didn't care. I thought she was so cool.

Everybody loved her. She was an artist. She would just sit and draw sketches of people and they looked perfect. She could sing like no one I had ever heard. And she was so pretty. All the popular girls hung out with her. There were the two Dawns, Patty and LeAnne. I was so not part of that crowd. Although there was a part deep inside that wanted to be accepted by them. I followed Peggy Sue like a lost puppy. The other girls were nice, but the red-headed Dawn was as mean as she could be. She didn't like me at all. But honestly, she didn't like anyone, except herself. She was a bully with a beautiful face.

I really didn't know how to make friends, but I wanted Peggy Sue to like me. I don't think she really cared whether or not we were friends at first because she had so many. I was a nuisance. The other girls made fun of me and, at first, Peggy Sue laughed along with them. I think I sort of "grew" on her. My love for Donny Osmond grew because she loved Donny Osmond. I found myself loving everything she loved and before I knew it, we had everything in common. I went to her house one day and we ordered pizza. She got bright-eyed and asked me if I liked mushrooms on my pizza—of course, I did! I loved mushrooms, even though I had never tasted them. That then became "our" thing. We would often get pizzas and open small cans of mushrooms and empty them all over the top of the pizzas. I still love mushrooms on my pizzas today!

Peggy Sue became my best friend, and I was one of her best friends. That was good enough for me. We did everything together through elementary school and then went onto junior high school together. The junior high school was closer to her house and all her neighborhood friends would go to school with us too. I was trying to make friends all over again and had that awful feeling that I still wasn't cool enough. In addition to the stress of trying to fit in, the "mean" Dawn had become an even bigger bully and I seemed to be her focus because I wouldn't fight back.

She would pick and make fun of me and I would cower and cry. One day in the cafeteria as I sat with my head down eating my lunch and hoping no one would talk to me, I saw Dawn's corduroy Levi's brush past me, and she sat right beside me. I held my breath. Before Dawn could open her mouth, Peggy Sue glared at her from across the table and said, "Don't". Dawn was stunned, as were the rest of us. She quietly sat down and then Peggy Sue gave me her cupcake. She was officially my hero. She was the most incredible person in the world to me. I could breathe again even with the evil redhead beside me.

I learned that Peggy Sue was the kind of person who accepted you no matter what. There was nothing about me that frightened her away from me. There were so many times when it would have been much easier for her to walk away than to stand by my side. But she never left my side. I spent the night at her house a few times and she didn't even get upset when I wet the bed. She kept my secret, and we were inseparable. Whenever I was allowed, I took the bus and was at her house for as long as they would let me. Peggy Sue would be an important part of my life for the rest of my life.

CHAPTER 13

The Most Evil Stepmother

I should have known the day Dad and Debbie picked me up and brought me back to the house that things were going to change. I was introduced to Debbie's 6-month-old son, Craig. When we arrived at our old home, I found that Debbie and Craig had already moved in. Debbie put Craig in his highchair and she and Dad went upstairs. I was told to keep an eye on him. I didn't know what to do with a 6-month-old! He would not stop crying and screaming. I tried and tried to make him stop and I was so angry that they left me there like that. I had a new role: babysitter.

Dad wanted me to stay in school in South Baltimore, so he came up with a plan. He couldn't take me to school and pick me up each day because he was a taxicab driver and he had to earn a living. Debbie didn't have a job or a car. Each morning, I had to walk to the bus stop, which was 4 blocks away. I took the bus to a certain point in downtown Baltimore, transferred to another bus, and then to another bus in order to make the full trip—twice a day. I was in the fourth grade. Did I mention that we lived in a high crime area? Yeah.

Debbie didn't like me and didn't pretend to. I was now her servant. Whenever she was out of Kool cigarettes or Pepsi bosses, it was my job to do the grocery shopping with the food stamps she gave me. She always gave me a list and rarely did I have enough money to cover everything on the list. I eventually got over the embarrassment of having the check-out girl yell to the managers, "I've got an over-ring, and its food stamps". Somehow when I got home each time, it was my fault that I didn't choose the right items to delete so I would have enough money. I would then make a second trip to the grocery store for the rest of the items.

On one occasion, I was jumped by a group of boys on my way home from the grocery store. They beat me up and busted the bags in my hands when they found that I had no money. When I got home, I was crying and bleeding. Debbie's brother, Tommy was there. He was furious and grabbed a shotgun out of Dad's gun cabinet and went running down the street to shoot them! Luckily, he didn't find them and came home without firing a shot.

My other duties included bathing Craig, feeding Craig, changing Craig's diapers, and helping her clean every Saturday. I was also in charge of doing the dishes every day. These duties were subject to additions at Debbie's whim. Meanwhile, Debbie would lie on the sofa with her Kool's and her Pepsi and watch TV. The only thing she did was cook. We didn't have money, so sometimes she would have to get creative. We usually had soup and sandwiches at least once a week, and sometimes we would splurge and get pizza burgers from Murrays. Dinner was always on the table at 5 pm...always. The entire family was required to be there for every meal. Dad scheduled his day to be sure he was there on time every single day.

CHAPTER 14

Charles Street

When Debbie decided the neighborhood was too dangerous for her to take walks with Craig, we moved back to South Baltimore. I wasn't too upset about that because I then got to see Peggy Sue more often. We moved to a row house on Charles Street and we had a terrible roach, and mice problem. There was so much wallpaper on the walls that you could see the mice moving underneath it. It was so gross! To make matters worse, I was chronically getting head lice again and again. Each time, Debbie got madder at me.

The bed-wetting was a huge issue for her. She decided that if I "chose" to wet the bed, then I could wash my sheets and blankets by hand each time. Have you ever tried to hand wash a blanket? It's impossible. The washing part is fine, but it's impossible to wring it out. As you wring out one end and start wringing through the middle section, the first end fills with water again. It took forever and she would not let me use the washer or dryer. This was my punishment for being too lazy to get up to go to the bathroom during the night. She firmly believed I chose to wake up in puddles each morning. To this day, when I see a home with a utility sink next to the washer and dryer, it gives me chills up my back.

The house on Charles Street had one bathroom and you had to walk through my bedroom to get to it. I hated the fact that this meant that Dad would walk into my room at any point in the night. Sometimes he would just pretend to be going to the bathroom and he would close my door once he entered my room. I had no TV to watch to help me disappear. I just pretended to be asleep. It didn't matter to him.

Debbie was different than Dad's other women. She didn't take any crap from him and I think that sometimes he was afraid of her. I guess he had so much pent up frustration that he had to hit someone and since he wasn't hitting her, that someone became me. Debbie didn't seem to mind that.

Dad got home for dinner each night at 5 pm and they would talk about their days to each other. I sat quietly and ate my dinner. If I stayed quiet, I could stay out of trouble. At least until Debbie got to the part of her day where she shared how I had annoyed or disappointed her in some way. Most of the time, I would be in trouble for not "offering" to help her. I already took care of her child, did the dishes every day, and helped her clean on Saturdays, aside from doing the grocery shopping and picking up her cigarettes and sodas whenever she needed them, but clearly, she required more help.

If I spoke up to defend myself, I would get hit. If I had an upset look on my face, I would get hit. Dad didn't hit like parents are supposed to. I didn't get spanked or slapped. His favorite form of discipline with me was to grab me by the back of my hair and slam my face into the wall or the floor. Usually, the corner of the walls or the corner of the wall and the floor were his first choice. That way it hurt on both sides of my face at the same time. I guess that was his plan. And if he was really mad, he would throw me on the hardwood floor and stomp on my head with his platform shoes on.

Needless to say, I did my best to walk a fine line. I found that the only way I seemed to please him, during the daytime hours anyway, was to get good grades at school. So, I got good grades in the hopes that I would get into less trouble.

Debbie got pregnant and was due to have another baby in August. I was happy about having a baby in the house. I was never close to Craig. He was just a screaming brat. I was hoping this new baby would be different. This new baby would be a happy distraction and maybe I wouldn't have to be afraid anymore.

One Saturday morning in early August, Dad was going to work. I walked out to the front steps to watch him leave because I knew she would find some chore for me to do right away. As I watched his taxicab drive up Charles Street, I noticed dirt falling from the end of the block of row homes. That last house was a corner store. It was Mr. Sam's store. I kept watching and then rocks started falling. This didn't seem right to me, so I ran to the store and tried to get Mr. Sam's attention. He kept telling me to wait because he was taking care of a customer. I finally screamed, "Mr. Sam, I think the store is falling down! Please come outside to see!" That got his attention.

He ran outside and saw what I saw and then ran back in to get all the customers out. He grabbed his dog and ran out behind the last customer. We barely made it to the middle of the street before the whole building crumbled! After it crumbled, the next house started falling too! And then it occurred to me that our house was only 4 houses away. I had to tell Debbie! I ran to the house through the thick dust and dirt. I could barely find my way. I ran inside screaming for Debbie to get Craig and get out because the houses were falling. We ran outside together and then she decided to run back into the house to get her parrot. I was so worried about her baby, but she had to save the parrot. She handed Craig to me and ran back in. Half of the next house fell, and more dust and dirt and

I didn't know if Debbie got out. Finally, she found us, and she had the birdcage in her hands. It was pure pandemonium, and everyone was running around screaming. No more houses fell. We were now next door to a half-standing row home.

I was interviewed by the local TV station because Mr. Sam called me a hero. I remember thinking I would be famous now. I was just grateful that no one was hurt.

CHAPTER 15

Light Street

After the houses fell, we almost immediately moved out of the house on Charles Street. We moved just a few blocks away to the 1800 block of Light Street, a block of row homes just before the slaughterhouse. This block was filled with kids my age. Barbara was the only girl, but there were lots of boys. The one that really caught my eye was Jamesy. He lived just up the block a bit about 5 doors away from us.

He was so cute. He had beautiful curly blonde hair, the biggest blue eyes, the most contagious laugh and he was just adorable! I thought he might have liked me too, but he liked all the girls. Even the popular girls wanted his attention. That redhead Devil Dawn was one of them. I didn't have a shot, but I did my best to get noticed. So began my obsession with boys, or as my family called it, my "boy craziness."

Back at school, there always seemed to be a reason that Dawn wanted to beat me up, but Peggy Sue wouldn't allow it. Each time Dawn would pick at me, Peggy Sue would stop her. However, she expected me to step up and learn how to defend myself. She knew I was afraid, and she knew I couldn't fight, but she knew she couldn't always be there to protect me.

One day I was at my Cousin Doris' house and she told me I needed to start wearing a bra. She gave me one and I wore it to school the next day. It made my boobs look much bigger.

Dawn noticed, and she taunted me all day long. She was telling everyone I stuffed my bra, and I was humiliated. By the time we got to the cafeteria for lunch, I had enough. Peggy Sue watched me to see what I would do next. I couldn't confront Dawn because of my fears, so instead, I made my point my own way. I stood up from my table at lunch, reached up the back of my shirt, unhooked the bra, and pulled it off through the sleeve of my top. I threw the bra onto the lunch table right in front of Dawn and I walked out. Peggy Sue was so proud of me! I had defended myself without getting hurt for the very first time and without saying a word!

Dawn was angry. I had embarrassed her and now she was going to get me back. The next day, she was sitting next to me in the cafeteria and Peggy Sue was directly across from me. I took a French apple pie from its wrapper and was taking a nice big bite when Dawn slapped it into my face. When I looked up through the pie hanging off my face, I saw Peggy Sue glaring at me. She was willing me to handle the situation. I knew that look meant that I had to take care of this myself. I wiped the pie from my face and while Dawn was laughing at the spectacle she created, I wiped my handful of French apple pie down the back of her long, beautiful red hair! I couldn't believe I had done it! I looked across the table to see Peggy Sue's face light up. Dawn was livid and jumped out of her seat! I was so proud of myself and then Dawn was demanding that I meet her outside to fight! I had been brave enough to handle these last 2 situations with her, but I wasn't prepared to fight.

I talked my way out of the beating with Dawn, with the help of Peggy Sue and Karen, the toughest girl at school. I had the right people on my side. Dawn never really bothered me again after that. I was clearly not on her list of best friends, but our altercations ended.

At the end of each school day, I actually looked forward to going home because I got to go outside and hang out with my neighborhood friends. Barbara was a wild child. She liked doing crazy things like making prank phone calls and ordering pizzas for strangers. She had a dad who, whenever he got mad at her, would bite his own knuckles so he didn't hit her. It was funny watching him chase her up the street while biting his knuckles and her laughing at him.

In the summertime, we would stay outside until late, late at night. I was always required to stay "within hearing distance" as Debbie called it. That meant that if she were to scream my name out the front door, I had better be close enough to hear it and run back to the house. This was Debbie's way of letting me know when I needed to bathe her son or pick up his toys or do some other errand or household activity for her. I stayed with my friends until the scream came and then I was back to being Cinderella.

There was one evening when I heard the scream and found upon my return that Debbie wanted me to carry Craig's tricycle and toys down the basement stairs. I didn't understand why they couldn't wait for me to come home for the night instead of making me stop having fun with my friends. But it wasn't up to me. Jamesy had been there that night and I didn't want to leave.

Debbie was sitting around doing nothing and she didn't care if she interfered with my fun. I was really annoyed. As I carried the tricycle to the basement stairs, I mumbled under my breath that I hated her. She heard me. Somehow, she mustered the strength to get off the sofa, run across the room and kick me in my back so that both I and the tricycle went tumbling down the basement stairs onto the concrete basement floor. And that wasn't enough for her. I was also punished for a week.

CHAPTER 16

Jamesy

The beautiful boy with curly blonde hair and big blue eyes was my dream boat—besides Donny Osmond, of course. He went to Catholic school, so we didn't go to school together. He played sports and had lots of groups of friends. Our neighborhood friends were just one of his many options. For that reason, many times we were out playing, and I kept looking at Jamesy's door to see if he was coming out. He often was not there with us because he was with others instead.

When I did get to see him, I made the most of it. I was so enamored, and my parents knew it. Debbie once saw me run for the door when I saw that blonde hair outside and she stopped me. "What's the hurry?" I said I saw Jamesy and wanted to say hi. She laughed and told me that I would never be good enough for him. My heart sunk, but I wasn't ready to give up.

Jamesy was fun, his laughter was contagious, but he had a mean streak with his humor at times. He loved to make fun of people and with me; he called me "Scarface." That hurt me so much because I tried everything to cover up that scar on my forehead that Alice had given me. I would swoop my hair over my forehead and use a barrette to hold it in place, but it didn't really cover it. The scar took up my entire forehead as a child. We were kids and kids can be mean. I tried to pretend that it didn't bother me while they all laughed.

Most of the time I wasn't allowed to leave my front steps even if my friends were out. There didn't have to be a reason. Debbie just wanted me at her beck and call. Whenever I needed an escape, I would just sit on the front steps and watch everyone. My friends would try to get me to play, but I had to say no. I wasn't allowed. They would wander over now and then to include me in their conversations, but if Dad was home, no one came near our house. They were all terrified of him.

Sometimes I would sit on the front steps and no one was outside. I just watched the other neighbors, and the cars drive by. Often, Jamesy would come home from whatever adventures he was having, and he would see me on my steps. He would come down to sit with me. I would run into the house and grab a comb so I could sit behind him and comb his hair. He loved it when I did that. I loved that I could be that close to him.

Since we didn't go to school together, I personalized my notebook with my own version of graffiti. On the inside I wrote "Bunny and Jamesy" and I even wrote "Bunny Whittington" to see how it would look. He never knew this. Of course, he knew I had a crush on him, but every girl did. I was just one of many and we weren't even old enough to date yet.

Any day I could sneak a peek at Jamesy was a good day.

CHAPTER 17

Billy – 1977

Shortly after we moved to Light Street, Debbie finally gave birth to the new baby. Billy was beautiful. I often pretended he was mine. I used to imagine how different my life would be when I had children of my own. Their lives would be so much happier than mine and I would never hit them. The home we would live in would be filled with love. Billy would be my "practice" child. I loved taking care of him and when he got into things and got into trouble, I didn't get annoyed. I thought he was so funny and so cute.

One evening after dinner, Debbie and Dad went upstairs and told me to take care of the boys and clean up the dishes. I was 13, but that was still a lot to do all at one time when it came to a baby and a 3-year-old. Craig was a downright monster, especially when he was left with me. In retrospect that was probably because he sensed that I didn't like him much. Billy was just a baby, so I put him in his playpen and put Craig in front of the TV so I could clean up the dishes.

As I carried the dishes into the kitchen, I called my friend Barbara.

There were no cordless phones in those days, so this call kept me in the kitchen. I would peek out now and then and saw that both boys were fine. Craig was still watching TV and Billy was playing with something in his playpen. Then I heard Craig yelling, "Ewwwwww!" I looked in to see what was happening and saw Craig pointing at Billy's playpen. Billy had pooped in his diaper, pulled the diaper off, smeared the poop all over the playpen and the wallpaper behind the playpen and he was eating it! He was covered in poop! It was so disgusting, and I was going to be in so much trouble! I had to work fast because if Debbie and Dad saw this, I would be punished for a month!

I quickly worked to clean up the mess, starting with cleaning Billy and setting him on the sofa next to Craig. I asked Craig to keep him still and out of trouble so I could clean the playpen and wall. As I was cleaning, Debbie came downstairs. I was punished for a week.

One Saturday afternoon, I was outside with my friends. Debbie went to the front door screaming my name, as always. I could tell from her tone that I was in trouble. What had I done now? Her eyes were huge, and she was shaking because she was so angry. As I walked in the door, I made sure to stay out of her reach. She shoved my opened diary in my face. She had found my diary and she had read it.

And now I was in trouble? She didn't appreciate my innermost thoughts, specifically the fact that I had written that I hated Craig. None of my real secrets were written down, I was smarter than that. But she was furious that I would write such a thing about her sweet, innocent boy. She sent me to my room and said she would let my father deal with me when he got home. I lay in the top bunk of the bunk beds that I shared with Craig and waited for Dad to get home. Was I really in trouble for this?

Yeah, I was.

Apparently, when Dad came in, Debbie shared the story, complete with lots of melodrama. He came running up the stairs and started yelling at me. He, too, couldn't believe I would write such things. I made the mistake of saying that I couldn't believe she would read my diary. With that, he grabbed my hair (as always) and pulled me off the top bunk of the bed onto the floor. He then dragged me down the stairs, still by my hair, headfirst. I was screaming the whole time and Debbie was standing at the bottom of the stairs with her arms crossed and a smirk on her face. She was pure evil. She wasn't going to stop him. Once at the bottom of the stairs, my journey continued as he dragged me through the dining room, through the kitchen and then he threw me head-first onto the cold concrete back yard. Everything hurt, especially my head. I was afraid to try to come back into the house, so I curled up next to the back of the house trying to keep myself warm. I didn't have a plan this time. I was completely terrified to move. It got dark outside, and it became so cold. I had nothing to cover me. Finally, Dad came outside and told me to get in the house. I was then punished for 2 weeks.

During my punishments, I would play with Billy and I would imagine life without this family. Somehow, I knew my life was going to be better when I got away. I knew I didn't belong here. I knew that I was learning from watching my friends, my friends' parents, my teachers, and even TV. I was becoming a chameleon. I was learning how people should behave, how beautiful women carried themselves with class, how people handled disagreements without violence. I became a "people watcher" everywhere I went. If I wanted out of this life, I would have to learn how to be like people outside of this family. I realize today that I was living a life of intention and didn't even know it yet.

As Billy got older, I taught him how to walk. My friends would come over sometimes and we would have him walk back and forth to us. He was so cute! One day I would have a little boy just like him.

CHAPTER 18

Michelle and ReeRee

I got my first "job" babysitting for a family across the street. They had 4 children and the 2 oldest were beautiful little girls—Michelle and ReeRee. The parents enjoyed a weekly date night, and I would babysit for them. I played with them, gave them their baths, read to them, and put them to bed. I wasn't allowed to have friends over, so I watched TV. I remember watching "Roots" while I was babysitting one night. I wasn't allowed to watch it at home because Dad hated black people so much.

After the kids would go to bed, I wanted a snack. At first, the snacks were easy to find. They were either in the cabinets or on top of the refrigerator. Then they weren't out in the open, so I had to search for them. I always found them, and I always ate them. It didn't occur to me that they were hiding the snacks from me. They never said anything. I'm embarrassed now.

I don't know if it was my snacking or something else, but they eventually told me they didn't need me anymore. That was fine with me. I kept missing chances to see Jamesy while I was there.

The houses on Light Street were small, just like Charles Street. Upstairs, there was a master bedroom in the front of the house, the stairs led up to an open bedroom in the middle, which I shared with Craig in the bunk bed, and the only bathroom was in the back. Billy slept in a crib in Debbie and Dad's room.

One night, very late at night, I heard Dad scream, "FIRE!" I jumped and fell out of the top bunk and then ran into their room. Michelle and ReeRee's house was burning. Flames were so big and they were reaching across the street. I was sure our house was going to catch fire too. Fire trucks arrived and firemen were running into the burning house. All the neighbors were outside watching, horrified. I saw across the street that Jamesy and a couple of the other boys were trying to help the children get out through the windows. Dad wouldn't let me go outside so all I could do was watch in horror. When it was all over, Michelle and one of the babies had died. I was devastated.

A couple of weeks later we learned that the family was not coming back. To this day, all of the neighborhood kids talk about that horrible night.

CHAPTER 19

Vacations

My family's idea of a vacation was either a day at Kings Dominion, going to the shore house, or camping in Patapsco State Park. I had bad memories of all of them, so I decided "real" vacations were going to be the memories I would create with my boys. Every single year from the time Joe and I split up until they were moved in, we had vacations. In the beginning, those vacations were for a week in Ocean City, MD.

Each year we went to the same hotel and stayed in the same room, which had an ocean view and a nice little kitchenette. We would arrive at the hotel, unpack and then go grocery shopping so we had staples there for us. We would spend our days at the beach and our evenings at the boardwalk or at the amusement parks. Sometimes we would take their friends with us too. It was awesome each and every time.

As my income increased, we started taking better vacations. I took them to Disney World, and we brought their half-sister Kristen too, a Disney cruise and we even went on a 10-day Mediterranean cruise. The Mediterranean trip was my dream, and this was the most expensive trip I had ever planned. I can tell you that I never went into debt for a vacation. I made sure to save money each year just for the purpose of these trips.

Needless to say, memories were made, and I gave both of the boys the travel bug. One checkmark on my column for creating something special for us.

CHAPTER 20

Alice & Little Paul – 1975

As with most surprises in my childhood, it began with a knock at the door. Alice had stopped by to talk to Dad and Debbie about Little Paul's health. She said he had a brain tumor and needed emergency surgery. Since Alice was a compulsive liar, Dad guessed she wasn't telling the truth. She just wanted money. Dad told her to bring Little Paul over so he could see him for himself. They argued a bit and finally, she agreed to bring Little Paul to the house. When she did, he was acting really odd. He wouldn't talk to me and he always talked to me. He wouldn't even look at me.

They didn't stay long, and Dad was convinced it was a big lie. He told her he needed to hear this from a doctor and of course, he never heard another word about it. I felt so bad for Little Paul that his mother made him pretend to have a brain tumor so she could get money. In retrospect, I'm sure Dad wasn't paying child support, but to put your child through that was just ugly. I guess people do what they think they have to do.

I didn't see Little Paul again for ten years.

CHAPTER 21

Don't Say A Word

That was the mantra in our home. Nothing was shared outside of our home regarding what went on inside our home. I had never said a word to anyone about the abuse. In my mind, Dad was all I had, and I didn't know what would happen to me if he was taken away. I was afraid of foster care and I knew in my heart that in time, I would get out.

Meanwhile, it seemed that my daily life was in segments. There was my time at school with my school friends when I was trying to get good grades and trying to become more accepted. There was my time at home, which was filled with anxiety as to what was going to happen next. And then there was my time outside with the neighborhood friends. I acted differently in every situation. I remember watching the movie "Sybil" and I wondered if I had multiple personalities like her. I felt like I did, but I had control over them. I chose which personality to use when I needed it. It was an interesting game for me. It started because I knew I had to hide the family secrets that went on inside our home, especially the big secret.

Who Says You Can't Go Home?

It had been a while since Dad had "bothered" me. He couldn't climb into my bed anymore in the middle of the night because Craig was on the bottom bunk. He was also rarely alone with me. Whenever he had the chance, he took advantage of it. The end was near.

One evening Debbie took the boys to visit her mother. I hurried outside to be with my friends so I could avoid being alone with Dad. He caught me before I was out of sight and made me come back. Why didn't I just go with Debbie and the boys? I did as I was told. It was just like all the times before, until he stopped and looked at me with disgust. I was shocked and then I noticed he was horrified by the fact that I had begun to grow pubic hair. He pushed me away and told me to go to my room. I was thrilled. It was over. I was free from him doing those things to me. I would learn that since he didn't have that option with me any longer, his temper would grow.

Dad was a maniac about keeping secrets. If anything, that went on in the house was repeated back to him by anyone, there was hell to pay. In conversation, sometimes I let simple things slip but nothing important. Things like we got a new TV or Dad took a taxi fare to New York City. He hated anyone knowing anything about our family business.

One evening, he found out that I told someone something. I don't remember what it was, but it was nothing important at all. I had gotten used to the beatings and I even expected them.

But this time, he was wearing those platform shoes. After he grabbed my hair and bounced my head off the wall a couple of times, he threw me to the floor and repeatedly stomped on the side of my head. I didn't always scream because that seemed to please him.

This time I screamed for sure.

The next morning, I was leaving for school. As I walked across the street, Miss Doris, who lived directly across from us and was the mom of my friends Brian, Johnny, and Stevie, stepped outside her front door to talk to me. She gently touched my arm and told me that she was calling Social Services. She said she heard me screaming last night and she had heard me many other times too. She wanted to do something to help me and she wanted me to know what to expect when I got home from school that day. I looked her straight in the eye and told her that she was mistaken. We must have had the TV up too loud. I was sorry she was worried, but there was nothing to worry about. And I walked to school. I left her standing there stunned. She did not call Social Services and I had once again saved my Dad. I didn't understand why I needed so desperately to protect him, especially since he didn't protect me. He hurt me often. But my instincts were to protect him, and I longed for him to love me like other dads loved their daughters, but I was never good enough.

CHAPTER 22

The Shore House

Debbie's family had a shore house somewhere in Maryland. There are a lot of shore areas in Maryland, so I don't know exactly where it was. Since we were always broke, we would take our vacations by going to the shore house. It was an oversized garage with no heat and an outhouse behind it. There were no rooms, just old furniture arranged to make it a living area and a kitchen area with just a table. There were no appliances either. We would pack food in coolers and grill outside each night. We brought blankets and pillows and slept on the floor.

We loved it there! Oftentimes, Debbie's brothers would join us, especially David. David spent a lot of time with us and I really liked having him around. It took the pressure off me to always having to look after the boys and he was really nice to me. I was never allowed to bring friends with me to the shore, no matter how much I begged. I would get bored after a while and then I started asking if I could bring one of my cousins instead. They agreed to let one of my cousins join us. I won't list her name in an effort to protect her. I put her in a position that weekend that I never knew would end up as it did.

Debbie would bring me and the boys to the shore house for the week and Dad would join us for the weekends. My cousin just wanted to come down for the weekend so she waited until Dad could bring her. He picked her up on Friday night and then headed to the shore. It got really late and they hadn't arrived yet. We were worried and had no way of reaching them. I fell asleep before they finally got there. I saw my cousin in the morning and was so happy to see her. She didn't seem like herself, but I thought it was because she was so tired because of getting there so late. We didn't do anything special that weekend, just swam and layout in the sun. It was a pretty uneventful weekend, but I was so glad that she was there.

A couple of weeks later, my cousin's mom called the house, and she was furious. I couldn't hear the conversation and I didn't understand what was happening. Dad kept telling me to go outside, but I was worried! He demanded that I go outside, or I would be punished. So, I went out and waited. My cousin had shared with her mom that my Dad had found out that she was smoking cigarettes during the ride to the shore house. Dad offered her a cigarette in exchange for a favor. The favor was oral sex.

My aunt was hysterical and shocked that her brother would betray her like that. She was calling the police and she was calling Social Services and she was going to make him pay. In his frenzy to keep her from reporting him, he reached out to his other family members and told them that my cousin was lying, and my aunt was out of control for no reason. One of the family members asked me if it was true. I lied for him ... again.

I was embarrassed, humiliated, and felt so guilty that I didn't protect my cousin instead of him. I had been hiding the secrets, but I didn't know that he was hurting other children too. This was my fault for not telling the truth. But I was terrified of telling the truth. I didn't know what would happen to me. Covering for him had become a habit and my instinctive answer was always to deny. I couldn't face her anymore.

Somehow the whole situation blew over and no one spoke of it again. I never forgot and my guilt never dissipated.

CHAPTER 23

Erdman Avenue – 1977

We moved again, and for the first time, I was very upset about it. We were moving too far away! I was leaving Peggy Sue and Jamesy and Tommy and Brian and Stevie and Barbara. I didn't want to go. Dad and Debbie didn't care. We were going whether I liked it or not.

It was midway through 8th grade and I was going to have to take buses again to finish the school year and then I would have to change schools for the 9th grade. I had never had to change schools, but this new house was very far away. After I cried my eyes out, I thought this might be a chance for me to really reinvent myself. I could meet new people and I could use my chameleon talents to be whoever I wanted to be. This could turn out to be ok. I could take the buses and still see Peggy Sue and Jamesy and they could visit me too. It would be fine.

The bus rides to South Baltimore to see them were 2 long rides on 2 different buses. Our house was on a busy road and there were lots of kids my age there. I felt outside my element for some reason. Maybe knowing I was no longer in South Baltimore?

I felt like I didn't belong (again!) even more than I usually did. So, I kept to myself. I coiled back up into my shyness and was afraid to step out. I tried to keep in contact with my friends in South Baltimore, but the distance was too much. Dad wouldn't give me money for the bus, and no one wanted to come to my house.

Peggy Sue, LeAnn, and Patty came to visit once. That was great! But it was just one time.

Another time, I took the buses with my new friend, Rose, to see Jamesy. He grabbed his friend, Joe and they waited for us to arrive. We spent the day with them, but Jamesy was different around me. He kept his distance and was not warm like I remembered. When they walked us back to the bus stop at the end of the day, I knew I wouldn't be making the trip again. It just wasn't the same anymore.

CHAPTER 24

Rose

The bus ride to and from school each day led me to meet my new friend, Rose. She and her little sister, Crystal went to a Catholic school downtown and I would sit with them whenever we caught the same bus. Rose reminded me of Barbara. She was fun, and she laughed loudly. She did love being the center of attention and I admired that, especially since I was such a wallflower at the time. We became friends, but the friendship rarely left the bus when we got off. Rose was one of the cool kids. I was not.

Slowly one neighborhood kid or another would say hi to me. That would lead to a short conversation and then there was familiarity growing. I was the new person everyone wanted to learn about. The boys paid more attention to me than the girls. The girls thought I was a snob because I didn't initiate conversations and kept to myself. I didn't wear make-up and I definitely didn't have the cool clothes, but neither did they.

Slowly, I was welcomed into the groove. My new friends in this neighborhood had fun in very different ways than we did in South Baltimore. We lived next to a golf course, so in the summer evenings, we would run through the sprinklers that automatically went off each night. It was so much fun! We would hang out at each other's houses too, but no one wanted to come into my house. Again, they were all afraid of Dad.

Our house was right next to the corner store. When I sat on the front steps, I always had someone to talk to. Everyone that walked in and out of that store would get a smile from me. I couldn't say hello unless they said hello first. I definitely got over that. The downside to living next door to the corner store was that I was constantly buying Debbie's Kool's and Pepsi's. Even with it being right next door, she still would not buy them herself.

Sometimes the neighborhood kids would see me sitting on the steps and they would congregate around me...until Dad came out and yelled at them to get away from his house. How humiliating.

Everyone hated him.

Meanwhile, nothing really changed between Debbie and me. Most of the time, she would try to find something to punish me for, so I stayed clear of her as much as I could. But sometimes that didn't work.

One evening after dinner, Debbie and Dad wanted to play the new board game they had gotten me for Christmas. The 3 of us sat at the kitchen table. Debbie had been mad at Dad and she wasn't acting normal. He kept asking her what was wrong, and she kept saying nothing. He eventually looked at me and said, "Isn't she acting weird?" and I stupidly responded, "Yes". At that point, her anger was turned to me. She jumped out of her chair, grabbed my brand-new board game, and ripped it in half. Dad got up quickly and walked out of the room.

Now she was taking it all out on me. She was screaming at me and calling me names. She chased me around the kitchen like a maniac. It had to look like an episode of Tom

& Jerry. I was really scared to let her catch me because I had seen her fight with Dad, and I didn't know how to fight. I was screaming for Dad to help me, but he stayed in the living room watching TV and ignored us. As I ran around the table, she reached across the table and grabbed the front of my shirt and she ripped it right off me. I was stunned by my sudden nakedness and I stopped running.

The next thing I knew, she had me on the floor of the kitchen and she was punching me in the face and pounding my head on the floor. I tried to hit her back, but I couldn't get a shot at her. I also didn't know how to make a fist. She finally told me to mind my own business from now on and sent me to my room. This was the one and the only fistfight I have ever had in my life and I didn't even get in a good shot!

CHAPTER 25

Debbie's Good Side

This will be a very short chapter. Every now and then Debbie would actually act like a mother. She would sometimes share with me what her life experiences had been. She had never known her natural father and her stepfather hated her. She was the oldest child and she spent as much time out of her home as possible. She was born in the late '50s, so her teenage years put her in crazy times. She was a flower child in the late '60s and she'd experienced a life that I never wanted to know. She would tell me stories about the parties she went to and the drugs she took. She would get on the back of motorcycles with men she didn't know, and they would force her to have sex with them in order to take her home. She was even gang-raped during a drugged stupor one night. The one thing I can credit her with is embedding in me a fear of drugs. I would remember those stories for the rest of my life, and it kept me safe.

CHAPTER 26

My First Jobs

At 14 years old, I had already learned that clothes were everything. Debbie outright refused to buy me Levi's. She would take me to Epstein's and buy me whatever was on sale, but mostly I wore Wranglers. All the cool kids, both in South Baltimore and in the new neighborhood wore Levi's. Then designer jeans were starting to become a hit and they were even more expensive. There were cute tops and jackets, and shoes and Debbie would not buy them for me. It was time for me to get a job.

I found a place that would hire kids from low-income families. I got a job working at a summer day care center. I was so excited that I would be making my own money and I would be able to buy the cool clothes I wanted. I had to take a bus to work each day, but I was ok with that. I enjoyed working with the kids and I really enjoyed a small feeling of independence. We were paid every two weeks and I couldn't wait to get my hands on my first paycheck. I had already walked past the stores I was going to shop in, and I had already found things I just had to have!

That first paycheck was for a whole $75 for two weeks of work. It's not a lot now, but to me, it was enormous. I ran in the front door and excitedly showed Debbie my check. To my surprise, she took it from my hand and said they were going to use it to go to Atlantic City that night for the weekend. I never saw that coming. She took my first paycheck. She never saw another paycheck from me again after that.

Once the summer daycare program ended, my job ended. I had gotten a taste of making my own money and buying my things and I liked it a lot. I was too young to get another job, but once I turned 15, I could. Just a few months later, when I turned 15, I got a new job working at Gino's fast-food restaurant. I could work as many hours as I wanted and control the size of my paycheck each week. I loved that!

If I saw a new pair of designer jeans or a new pair of shoes I wanted, I just worked more hours and I got it. I hid my money so Debbie couldn't take it and instead I threw away all my hand-me-down clothes and filled my closet with everything I wanted. Somehow that closet made me feel rich.

Meanwhile, Aunt Dot and my cousin Doris were moving in with us. Aunt Dot and Uncle Lee were having problems so the two of them left him and their two boys, Lee and Billy. Doris was pregnant too. I was inspired to not let that happen to me. I would have babies when I was ready and not before.

CHAPTER 27

Hamilton Junior High School

I had to start at a brand new junior high school for just one year before heading to high school. Most of my friends in my neighborhood went to private schools or they were a couple years older or younger than me. This was not going to be fun. All the clicks would already be established. I was coming in alone and once again; I would be an outsider. I was getting used to this. I was even an outsider in my own home. I didn't belong there, and Debbie would certainly be happier if I wasn't around.

The people on this side of town behaved differently than people in South Baltimore. There weren't any fist fights, and everyone seemed to carry themselves differently. They weren't as poor as we were, so I didn't let anyone know how poor we were. There was also much less drama. I watched and took it all in. I just waited for someone to start a conversation.

My first friend at school was David. He had failed a couple of times and was much older than the rest of us. He was 18 and in the 9th grade. He even had a mustache! He was very nice to me, but he scared me. One day he showed up at my house. I didn't know he knew where I lived. Dad lost it when he saw him. I explained to David that our friendship could only be at school as my Dad wasn't going to accept me hanging out with boys, especially not one with a mustache.

Melinda was the first girl to talk to me. Then her friends, Leslie, Mary, Judy, Cricket, Mary Lou, Nancy, DeeDee, Michael, Steven and Honsu and there were many more. They took me under their wings. No one picked on me; no one made fun of me. Before long, I DID belong!

One day shortly after school started, Melinda invited me to a dance at St. Anthony's Church. I knew I had to go if I wanted to be part of this crowd. My other new friend, Mary Lou, told me that her mother would drive me home after the dance, as long as I could find a way to get there. I found a way. I took a bus!

I waited for Melinda at the front door of the church. When she got there, she brought me to the parking lot, where a car packed with teenagers was waiting for us. Everyone was laughing and having a great time. One of the guys took us to the back of the car, opened the trunk and revealed bottles of Boones Farm wine. I had never had a drink before. To not panic, I just went along with it as if I had no issues with drinking. I had to act as excited as everyone else and I had to stay cool.

We filled our McDonald's cups with wine and climbed in the back seat of the car. It tasted like Kool-Aid. I noticed it wasn't affecting me like it was everyone else. What was wrong with me? I drank more and still nothing. I kept drinking and I said nothing, but I laughed along with them and pretended something was happening. Eventually, everyone started heading toward the dance hall and I got out of the car to walk with them.

GRAVITY! Oh my! I guess sitting still wasn't the best way to determine how drunk I had become. Still trying to stay cool, I stayed quiet and composed. Others were being really silly and dancing crazy. I sat down in a chair and watched. I said my ankle hurt, which it often did, but that wasn't the reason this time. I hung in there like a trooper and no one had a clue. They thought I was cool—how about that?

Mary Lou's mother came to pick us up and drove me home. The car ride home made me so sick. I got out of her mom's car and crossed the street to my house. As soon as her mom began to drive away, I vomited all over our front steps. I didn't realize Dad wasn't home and he would soon be stepping in the vomit when he did get home. All I was concerned about was getting in the house and up the stairs to my bed. I then experienced my first bout with bed spins. Ugh! Why did people like to do this?

When I woke up the next morning, I was afraid to go downstairs. Dad must have seen or stepped in the vomit, but he didn't mention a thing. Everything was normal. I didn't get caught!

I thought about it a lot. I did enjoy the feeling the alcohol gave me, I just didn't like the vomit and bed spins. I decided to try drinking again, but without going quite as far as that night. I found it amazing when I drank because it calmed me. It took away my anxiety, my fears and gave me more confidence. When I was drinking, I could be fun and not melancholy. When I was drinking, I could forget what I had to go home to.

My drinking became a regular thing. I drank as often as I could. I drank whatever I could get my hands on. Since I didn't have much money of my own then, my selections were limited to whatever my friends had on hand. I found out I liked Southern Comfort. That took me from zero to drunk quicker than anything else. I had to be careful with it, but it was awesome. I also found that since my school friends lived so far away, I would simply make plans to go to Melinda's house and I didn't have to be "within hearing distance" anymore.

I never...ever got caught drinking. I did it a lot and it continued for quite a while.

I had so much fun with these new friends. We got together every morning at the local store before school started and we hung out, laughed and acted silly. We walked together after school; them all the way home, and me to the bus stop. We got together on weekends too.

Melinda's mom was fantastic. She was beautiful, she was smart, and she didn't need a man to take care of her.

As I got to know her more, I had never met a woman I respected more than her. She worked a full-time job, had a nice home and gave her two children the best of everything. The thing she demanded first was respect and she got it. She didn't spoil them ridiculously, but they were a happy family. I so wished she could have been my mother. But I often wished my friends' mothers could have been my mother.

If only.

Melinda became my best friend. We were the same size, but she was blonde, and I was a brunette. We wore the same size clothes, but we had different styles. I liked flashy things and she was more subdued. She was my savior from that evil house of mine like no one had been before. I was learning a whole new way of life through her and her mom. No women worked full-time in our family and not even in our neighborhood in South Baltimore. But this woman was not a victim. She was proud. And her kids were proud of her.

Even though Melinda and I were so close, I never told her our family secrets.

CHAPTER 28

Belonging

With this new part of town and new friends, my new self was, for the first time in my life, starting to feel like I belonged. No one knew what my life at home was like, not even Melinda. I was able to have fun with these new friends and I was not the brunt of their jokes. I didn't have head lice anymore and no one knew that I ever did. No one knew that I was a bed wetter either. I was included in their plans and invited to all their parties. I was one of them. This was amazing, but there were so many secrets that I had to keep to myself.

In retrospect, I look back at these days and I realize that the person I am today was formed by so many different people in my life. This would continue to happen throughout my teenage years and even into my adult life. I learned to carry myself and dress with the grace of Anne, Dad's old girlfriend. Peggy Sue taught me to stand up for myself and I was less afraid to speak my mind. Melinda reinforced the grace of Anne, but added a sense of calm, pride and honesty. You could always count on her to do the right thing and when she made a promise, she meant it. She didn't even lie to her mother...ever.

She and several others had been caught that night after the St. Anthony's dance. When it came to the parents' attention that our whole group was drunk, punishments were going down all over town. Then it was mentioned that there was a new girl in the crowd and the parents wanted to know who it was. Melinda would not give them my name. Meanwhile, Melinda's mother told her that if she ever drank again, she would not get her driver's license when she turned 16. Melinda never drank a drop for the rest of that year. Honestly, she never even tried to sneak one in. She was truly that honest.

Pretty soon, the buzz was going around about where everyone would be going to high school. I had never considered this to be a big deal, but my new friends did. I had just become a real part of the crowd and now the crowd was dividing. I had good grades, so I pretty much had a choice of which school I wanted, but I didn't know what I wanted.

No women in my family had worked and I didn't have a clue what I wanted to do. I didn't have the confidence that I could do anything. I think I just expected to finish school, get married and have kids. That's all I knew. That's all I ever wanted–my own "real" family, but first things, first. I had to choose a school. My zoned school was Lake Clifton and that was a very rough school. Not an option for me. Melinda, Mary and I applied to Western High School which is the oldest all girl public school in the country and one of the top schools in Baltimore.

All three of us were accepted.

The rest of the school year was a bit sad because so many were heading in so many different directions. We had fun while we still could and promised that we would keep in touch. Unfortunately, that doesn't usually happen.

I had lost touch for some time with Peggy Sue, so I decided to call her to tell her about my acceptance at Western. She had applied and was accepted too. I couldn't believe that we would be going to school together again. I had such big plans for how much fun we would have, and I couldn't wait for Peggy Sue to meet Melinda.

CHAPTER 29

Western High School

While I knew I could get good grades, I feared the expectation that I would have to keep an 85 average in all my classes to stay in this school. It wasn't just a local school; it was a college prep school. I had never been pushed to do anything except household responsibilities and Dad and Debbie's demands, but they never suggested that I do anything to better myself. My life revolved around how whatever I did benefited them. This was my first step in learning to do things for myself and my future.

I needed to develop a work ethic that would help me as an adult once I got out of this awful situation at home. I had to learn to believe in me and trust my instincts. My first step was walking into that door and finding my place among the smartest young women in Baltimore.

Western is an all-girl school, and it is shaped like an "L" with the Baltimore Polytechnic School attached as another "L", creating a big square. Poly was a school mostly for boys, so we had the benefit of being in classes without boys but being able to hang out with them before and after school and at lunchtime. The "Quad" was the area between the two schools where we hung out and flirted with the boys before and after our classes.

Peggy Sue and Melinda both took college prep courses. I knew I wasn't able to go to college, so I took the business courses instead. That meant I didn't have any classes with either of them. We would see each other in the hallways and at lunchtime, but it wasn't the way it used to be. Peggy Sue and Melinda didn't seem to like each other much. It was very tense trying to spend time with them together and it rarely happened.

I felt very different now. I wasn't the poor little girl that needed Peggy Sue to take care of her anymore. I had developed new friendships and I was popular. I think it left Peggy Sue feeling uncomfortable and I didn't know what to do to fix it. We also lived so far away from each other.

Meanwhile, Melinda and I went to and from school together and were together all the time in the quad. Peggy Sue certainly found other friends and it probably wasn't that big of a deal to her, but I was uncomfortable with not being able to be the way we used to be.

For me to ride the bus with Melinda and Mary, I had to catch 2 buses. I walked 3 blocks to a bus stop each morning to catch the first bus, then I would get a transfer and take the second bus that my friends were on. They had already been picked up by that second bus by then, oftentimes the bus was too full and the driver would not open the front door to let anyone else on. During those times, our guy friends, who knew I was there at that bus stop waiting for them, would pop out the back window of the bus. I would hand them my books and they would pull me up and in through that window.

It was always fun on the bus ride to school. There was usually a radio playing and we would sing and laugh. Sometimes the guys would bring alcohol on the bus with them.

Melinda wouldn't drink it, so out of respect for her, I wouldn't drink it either, but I wanted to. Whenever Melinda wasn't there, I would join them, but I never did it in front of her. There were times that I arrived at school at 8:00 in the morning and I was totally trashed.

Whenever I drank, I felt so fearless. It was the perfect escape for me. I didn't have to pretend not to live the life I lived at home. I just forgot that was my life. I felt so free. I was in the 10th grade.

After school, we would run across the quad and jump on the Poly buses so we could ride home with the boys. I think the school security guards caught onto us because the bus schedules changed so that the Poly buses would leave before the Western classes were over. That didn't stop us.

Melinda and I would often cut our last period class and hide in the bathroom on the first level until just the right time and then we would run across the quad as fast as we could so we didn't get caught. I was never much of a runner. My legs don't go back and forth as much as they do side to side. I didn't move forward as fast as my legs went and it looked pretty funny too. Melinda had to run in front of me, so she didn't laugh and lose her momentum. On top of that, I would often fall. I was so clumsy, and it was always a good joke once we made it onto the bus. It was never a surprise to anyone when I showed up with grass and mud on my pants.

There was always so much going on at school. There were so many guys at Poly. I learned to be quite the flirt and I was like a kid in a candy store. There were the potheads who hung out on the stage area in the quad, the book worms who sat in the grassy areas and studied, and the quiet girls who stayed on Western's side of the quad and then there were us. The flirty girls from Western who hung out on Poly's wall; that's where you would find us each morning before school and throughout our lunch breaks.

Our high school mascot was a dove, so all our students were considered "doves." Our Class of 1982 mascot was Snoopy. I love that doves represent Jesus and peace and I have doves all over my home. They make me feel warm inside because they represent so much to me.

During class was another story. It was all work. I was really glad that I had taken the business courses because I enjoyed the work I was learning. I learned to type and when I graduated, I was typing 120 words per minute. I learned shorthand, which helped me in the future with my secretarial jobs. I learned accounting which helped me for the rest of my life. I learned many business administration principles and that led to my success in business as an adult. I am forever grateful for Western High School for preparing me for my life.

CHAPTER 30

Debbie A.

In homeroom class we sat alphabetically. My last name started with an A and the girl beside me was also an A. Her name was Debbie, and she was beautiful, vivacious and strong minded. She was different from anyone I had known. She was like a wild stallion. She carried this attitude that she was the center of the world. She knew who she was, and she didn't care if you liked her or not. She lived by her own rules and was as free as a bird. She came and went as she pleased and didn't apologize to anyone for anything.

It seemed to me that she had everything, and I immediately resented her. I watched her and I paid attention to everything she did. In the classroom, she didn't offer answers and she always seemed to be annoyed to be there. It was almost as if she expected the teachers to be grateful that she gave them her time. At least that was my perception.

One day at lunch, I decided to go chat with the cute guys that hung out on the stage. Debbie was there and was getting all the attention. She really knew how to flirt, and I was still learning—now I was learning from her. I was much coyer, but she was overtly flirty. I hadn't had any competition for attention yet at this school and I wasn't particularly happy about this. After several attempts to start conversations and being ignored because Debbie had them listening to her, I needed to take action. I was never a mean girl, but I could be if I needed to. This seemed to be a time that I needed to. As I watched her perform, I noticed her wet armpits and I loudly said, "Debbie, what are those two big wet spots under your armpits?" A couple of the guys laughed, but Debbie was unimpressed with my feeble attempt to embarrass her. She didn't lose a step. I gave up and walked away thinking, "I'm about to get my ass kicked!"

I deserved it, but it didn't happen. The whole thing didn't even register to her. She was still the center of attention. I was now embarrassed that I had behaved like Dawn, my nemesis from elementary and middle school.

The next day in class I fully expected to be punished by Debbie for my actions. Instead, for the first time, she turned around in her chair and started a conversation with me like we were old friends. To my surprise she was quite delightful. No wonder the guys liked her. I now wanted to be her friend. I wanted to see what made this girl tick. That was the beginning of one of the longest friendships of my life. Debbie would teach me so much about life, expectations and acceptance and she was to be a force in my life for all of my days.

CHAPTER 31

Hampden

Western High School is located in an area of town called "Hampden." Debbie lived right up the street from the school. As our new friendship grew, I spent more and more time in Hampden too. Debbie's mother did not like me at all. This was new for me because all my friends' mothers loved me, but not this one. She didn't even try to pretend. She made it crystal clear. Debbie told me not to worry about it, so I didn't. It became a game to me after a while. I got a kick out of seeing her get annoyed with me for no reason.

Debbie had a driver's license and a car. That was a big deal to me. Our family vehicle was a taxicab, so there was no hope for me driving anytime soon. Our weekends were spent putting on make-up, low cut blouses and jeans that were way too tight and driving around Hampden as fast as she could. We went up and down all the small streets, just to see what was going on and who was out. Sometimes we would drink, but most of the time we didn't. Debbie had lots of guys interested in her. Everyone played second fiddle when it came to the attention of the male species. I just got used to it. As an observer, it was quite a show. I was learning more and more every day.

I was noticing that I was becoming a chameleon. There were parts of me influenced by each of my close friends. With this friend, it was a fun spirit and a sense of authenticity that I would take on. I was becoming a person who was not an imitation of another person, but a conglomerate of other people, to become the person I wanted to be.

That first summer after school ended, Debbie invited me on a trip with a bunch of friends to Ocean City, MD. I had never vacationed anywhere other than camping and I was so excited to see the ocean. I had saved money from working at Gino's restaurant and I was definitely in. I fell in love for the very first time in my life with the beautiful ocean, and when I was away from the city, I was truly free. I was able to leave all the drama and all the problems at home and I was completely free in this new exciting world, even if it was just for a day or two.

CHAPTER 32

High School Boys

There were many, many boys at school. There were so many to choose from and I had a lot to learn. One thing I didn't know was that I was prettier than I thought. I always saw myself as cute because of my personality, but when I looked in the mirror, all I saw was insecurity, a big scar on my forehead and super skinny arms that made me look like Olive Oyl.

Since I was getting more attention from the plethora of boys at Poly, I was coming out of my shell a bit. I loved flirting, but I knew I was terrified to be alone with a boy. I liked to kiss, but I didn't want their hands on me ever. I learned that few high school boys were okay with that. I eventually got the nickname of "PT", which stood for prick teaser. I hated the nickname, but I wasn't interested in changing my behavior at all. I didn't care when they got annoyed and I didn't care when they got mad. I had control over these situations, and I wasn't giving in. I had no interest and no desire to do more than kiss. This was my first exercise in realizing my power.

In the fall of my first year at high school, we had a school dance. Some of the male friends I had made at Hamilton Jr. High were now at Poly. I had a crush on one of them, but he always had a girlfriend. Just before the school dance, he and his current girlfriend broke up, so I took a chance and asked him to be my date for our dance. He said yes and I was excited and scared. This was my first date ever. I didn't want my parents to know so I told him I would meet him at school that night. I was totally in my glory. We danced, we laughed, and we had a blast!

We even started kissing on the dance floor. He was kissing my neck too and I liked it a lot. He was very sweet and didn't make any moves that made me uncomfortable. If anything, he made me want to spend more time with him because he didn't push my boundaries. I hoped for many more dates with him.

The next day, however, my Dad flipped out when he saw a big hickey on my neck. I had no idea and was mortified. How did Michael leave a mark without me knowing it? I was busted and I was punished, and I was called every name I could imagine. Somehow Dad took that hickey and made it into a full night of debauchery. No matter what I said, he didn't believe me. I didn't care because I had beautiful memories from my evening, and I know what I did and didn't do. Another punishment for doing nothing wrong didn't affect me either. I was only looking forward.

After telling Michael what had happened at home, I guess it scared him away from me. He was off with another girlfriend and I was left with my memories.

There were many girls at school that the boys would turn to to heal their wounds. One of them even made it known to everyone that she was free with sex because she had been sexually abused at home. Everyone felt sorry for her. I detested her. How dare she share such personal information and use it as an excuse to demean herself. Didn't she want better...like I did? I could have said so much to her and about her, but I kept my mouth shut and stayed clear of her drama. She could have my leftovers if she wanted them.

As the school years went by, I dated several boys from Poly. That first spring, another guy named Michael was showing some interest in me. He was a junior and I was a sophomore. He asked me to his prom. His friend, Jay, then asked Melinda to the same prom. We were so excited. We were brand new at the school and we were going to proms already, and on a double date.

Melinda and I were thrilled to shop together for our prom gowns and her mom took us. I had saved a little bit of money from Gino's and I found a dress for just $20.00. I was thrilled!

My parents had no idea any of this was happening. They had concluded that if it didn't cost them money, they didn't care. I must, however, give them plenty of notice before making plans so they didn't make plans for me to babysit. That's all they cared about.

I planned to get ready at Melinda's house for the prom. Her brother was driving us to the prom because Melinda wasn't allowed in boys' cars at all. We were all dressed up and looking cute and couldn't wait for all the fun.

Only there was no fun. Our dates were boring. I was drawn to Jay, Melinda's date, because he was funny. It turned out that Melinda was drawn to Michael because she knew him from her neighborhood, and she was more comfortable with him.

We went to the ladies' room and decided that we needed to switch somehow. We were laughing hysterically about it, but we knew there was no way we could manage that effort. It was the most fun part of the night though. To our surprise, the boys had the same thought. We learned the following week that they had the same discussion and the next thing you know; I was dating Jay.

Jay was an absolute sweetheart. I nicknamed him "Teddy Bear" because he was just so snuggly! He always had me laughing and he was so sweet to me. He made me feel safe and cherished and I wanted to spend every minute with him. This was my first experience like this but the future with him scared me to death. As I got closer, I knew he would want more. I couldn't. I just couldn't go there. I decided to take it one day at a time, knowing full well that it would end at some point.

Meanwhile, I was very focused on getting good grades at school and I was working at Gino's. Debbie made me help her clean every Saturday and I had to keep a watchful eye for whenever she might want me to "offer" my help. There didn't seem to be enough hours in the day to get it all done. I was getting up for school at 6:30 in the morning, then coming home and walking to Gino's to work until 11pm. I would then walk home, with mace in my hand, and once I arrived home at midnight, I had to do my homework. I wasn't getting enough sleep. One of my friends at Gino's told me about diet pills. I didn't need to diet, but I needed something to keep me awake. I felt that diet pills would be okay because they weren't illegal, and they really did work. I was afraid I might get addicted to them, but I took my chances, and that problem was solved.

CHAPTER 33

Belair Road Friends

Back at home, the chameleon I was becoming was looking to grow some more. My friends in the neighborhood weren't very adventurous. I was bored. Other kids hung out a few blocks away. They hung out with my friend Rose, from the bus. Now and then I would wander down to Rose's house and spend some time with her and her friends. They were completely different people.

Rose lived with her mom, stepdad and her sister, Crystal. Her mom was a great lady that everyone loved. She was known in the neighborhood as someone who always wanted to help. There were sometimes runaways that took refuge at their home and Rose's mom helped them for as long as they needed.

Rose was a pistol! She had no fear and no boundaries. She would sneak her boyfriend in through her bedroom window at night and when she would come downstairs in the morning, she had hickies all over her. I don't know how she got away with it. She would say and do things that I would never have the nerve to do or say. I felt like I was always in a state of awe when it came to her. I just sat back and watched it all happen.

Rose's friends were very different from the friends by my house. They did drugs in the alley behind her house. They smoked pot and popped pills. I was afraid of pills, so I tried to smoke pot, but all I did was cough. They laughed, but they accepted me. Since I couldn't comfortably smoke with them, they offered me alcohol instead. That I liked.

As I drank, I got more attention from the guys there, but I stayed clear. They were much more advanced than me and I was completely uncomfortable with the thought of being too close to any of them.

One evening as we were in that alley, Rose's Dad came outside yelling at us for the noise. He said he was going to call the police and one of the guys said something smart to him. He then came out of his backyard and was coming toward us. Everyone started running in different directions. I was never a runner, but I tried. He caught me by my arm. I was speechless and didn't know what to do. Then one of the guys turned and saw what was happening and he ran back, pushed Rose's Dad off me and picked me up and ran. I was rescued. It was so exciting and exhilarating and we drank and laughed the rest of the night.

When I got home, Debbie's brother David was sitting on the sofa. I came in drunk and sat right down on the sofa because I was afraid to even try to walk. David looked at me and laughed. I put my finger to my mouth and said, "Shhhh."

He said, "You're gonna be in so much trouble."

I "Shhh'd" him again.

Then I noticed the yelling upstairs. I asked him if they were fighting and he said yes. I remember laughing and knowing I was next. Sure enough, Debbie came running down the stairs and she saw me. She gritted her teeth and yelled, "This is all your fault!" I didn't know how it was my fault, but I just sat there and watched her come toward me.

She stalked across the floor, grabbed a handful of my hair and yanked it toward the floor. My drunken, limber body just folded over and before I knew it, I tumbled upside down and was sitting on the floor with Debbie still holding my hair. It didn't even hurt. I looked up at David and started laughing hysterically. David was laughing too, and Debbie was stunned. She just turned and stomped into the kitchen. Once again, I did not get caught drinking.

CHAPTER 34

Time to Go

My stepmother, Debbie, was having some issues with how busy I had become. She didn't have me around all the time to bathe her children and fetch her cigarettes and sodas. She was picking fights with me constantly. I just tried to keep myself busy and work as many hours as I possibly could at Gino's. She was furious that I wasn't there to eat dinner with the family every night and she was even more furious that I wasn't around to do the dishes either.

I was getting more and more used to eating fast food instead of the meals that she cooked because I was spending my dinner hours at work instead of at home.

On the weekends, I often opened the store at 6am and prepared the salad bar and I would work until 2pm. I would usually eat my lunch late and then there would be arguing at home because I wasn't hungry when dinner was ready at 5pm. I never understood this argument. Finally, one Saturday afternoon, the mood was just right for an argument of ridiculous proportions. I was sent to my room and punished for a week because I wasn't hungry at dinnertime.

I was so fed up with this.

Later that week, between school and work, I stopped at Rose's house. I asked her if I could talk to her mother about possibly staying there for a little while. Rose took me inside and I sat down with her mom, Bearl. Bearl had previously been a single mom for quite some time, raising two daughters on her own because she had left her abusive husband. She had been stricken with polio at the age of three and fought her entire life to be treated just like everyone else. A year or so before this day, she had been involved in a car accident. That accident took away the use of her legs. Bearl was relegated to a wheelchair for the rest of her life but she was now happily married to a wonderful man.

I explained to Rose and her mom that I had problems at home, but that I had a job, and I would pay rent if she would let me stay there. I had a lot of trouble trying to tell her anything because I had NEVER told anyone what that home was like. I did manage to tell her that I was regularly beaten and that I was punished for not being hungry. Her husband, Bob, was the man who caught me drinking in the alley behind their home. He was a little unsure of me, but he respected his wife's decision.

She told me yes.

As I walked to work that night, I felt a ray of hope, but it was surrounded by intense fear. How could I possibly accomplish this? I put it out of my head and just did my job. I would know when it was the right time.

Close to a week later, on Friday, I didn't have to work. I hadn't spoken to anyone in the family since I had been punished and it was making Debbie madder by the minute.

She kept yelling at me to talk to her and I refused. Then I finally glared at her with contempt and said, "Don't worry. I have a plan and I'll speak to my father about it when he gets home."

Wow, that was the wrong move on my part! She immediately smacked me across the face. I ran upstairs to my room. She ran behind me and was right at my heels. I got to my room and slammed the door before she could get there. I was trying to lock it and she was pushing the door from the outside. Finally, she kicked the door with her black boots and knocked it off its hinges! I ran to my bed and kept yelling for her to stop. Her face was so twisted with fury! She was angrier than I had ever seen her, and I had seen her angry on many occasions!

I pushed myself back on my bed as far away as I could, and she walked around the side of my bed with her teeth clenched. She was cussing and telling me that she didn't know who I thought I was and yah-de-dah. I wasn't paying attention because I couldn't imagine what she was about to do.

She moved right beside me and punched me in the face! I jumped off the bed and fell into my dresser. She came at me again and swung her fist to punch me again. This time I moved to the left and her hand went right through my dresser mirror. Blood squirted everywhere! She was screaming and still clenching her teeth as I grabbed her arm and kept telling her to let me put it under water. She just stood there bleeding, staring at the blood, clenching her teeth. Instead, she pushed me down onto my bed and wiped the blood across my face. It was so creepy, like something you would see in a bad horror movie. I finally dragged her into the bathroom and put her arm under the running water in the sink. I didn't know if she needed stitches or not, I just wanted to stop the bleeding. I helped her wrap it, but we didn't say another word to each other. She went downstairs, and I went back to my room.

What just happened?

How creepy was that? I knew she would twist this to make me the bad guy. I knew that when Dad got home, I was in big trouble. I knew the time was right for my big move.

In preparation for the inevitable, I took a small box that was filled with my shoes and dumped the shoes out. I packed a couple of days' worth of clothes into the box and the little bit of make-up that I wore, along with my toothbrush. I had never been so terrified as I waited for Dad to get home. The minutes felt like hours. My future was completely unknown. How was I going to get out the front door? How badly was he going to beat me this time? I was going to turn my back on him for the first time in my life and he was NOT a fan of being dismissed.

There were so many emotions going on: betrayal, fear, anxiety but at the same time, there was finally a light at the end of the tunnel, if I could just follow that light. I had a place to go. For the first time, I was choosing where I would live rather than being put there. I was strong enough! I was 16 years old and I was going to move out and pay rent! That part didn't scare me at all. Getting out that front door was all I had to focus on.

I heard Dad walk into the house. I took a deep breath, grabbed my little box and walked to the stairs. I went halfway down the stairs and stopped. Debbie was giving him the rundown on the events of the day—her version anyway. She actually told him that I made her cut her arm. Well, if moving out of the way of a punch made her cut her arm, I guess I was guilty as charged. I just stood there saying nothing. I watched his face get redder and redder and he kept looking from her to me. Then he noticed the box in my arms.

He strode across the floor to the bottom of the stairs and demanded to know what was in the box. I stood up straight and tried to pretend not to be scared. I told him I was leaving.

He laughed.

I said nothing.

He was pacing across the floor, clenching his fists. Debbie was standing near the front door with a smirk on her face. God, I hated that woman. He asked me where I was going. I told him I had spoken to a friend's parents and they said I could stay there. He demanded that I call them so he could talk to them. I did. He yelled and screamed into the phone and then slammed it back down on the receiver. Meanwhile I ran back from the phone and back up the stairs to my box. It was now a showdown. There was only one way out of the house, and he was standing in front of that door.

As I stood my ground on the stairs, I waited for my opportunity to run. But again, I'm not much of a runner. I was terrified of what he would do if I got within his reach. He had beaten me so many times, but this was my ultimate betrayal of him. I had no idea how badly he would beat me. It had all been set in motion and I couldn't give up now. It was time for me to go.

It seemed to go on forever—his pacing and taunting me about how I was planning to get past him and my trying to hide my intense fear. Now during this time, there were no cordless phones. We had two phones in the house: one in their bedroom and one on the dining room wall. The phone on the wall had a very short cord because I wasn't allowed to stay on the phone for more than 10 minutes. They made sure the cord was too short for me to sit down and talk too long. Debbie walked into the kitchen and, as luck would have it, the phone rang. Dad walked into the dining room to answer the phone and I had a clear path.

I took it! I ran as fast as my little legs could carry me, with my box of three outfits and I got out that front door before he could catch me. I kept running because I was afraid that he would run after me. I should have remembered that he didn't do anything in public. He wouldn't have chased me onto the public streets because then people might see him for who he really was.

I ran without looking where I was going. I didn't look forward and I didn't look back. I just watched my feet! After two blocks, I was losing my breath and I slowed down. I looked up and there was Rose's dad, Bob. He was walking toward me. He was coming to get me! At that moment, he was my Prince Charming.

CHAPTER 35

What Had I Done?

After leaving the house with my one box of clothes and being rescued by Bob, I was numb. Bob took the box from my hands and put his arm around me as he led me down the street to my new home. I knew I was now safe, but my head was swimming. When we walked in the front door, Bearl was waiting for me with a big, warm hug. I was a total zombie. I couldn't talk. I couldn't even explain what had happened.

I sat on the sofa and stared straight ahead for what seemed like an eternity. I knew I was finally free, but there was a big part of me that wanted to run back home and beg my dad for forgiveness for walking out on him. I had always been so loyal, but now I was with a new set of strangers, and this time, he would be coming back for me. There was so much to process.

They gave me Crystal's bedroom that night, and she slept with Rose. My mind would not stop. Did I do the right thing? Was Dad mad at me? What would happen now? Could I really be doing this? The one thing I knew was that I could finally sleep without being afraid that he would climb into my bed.

CHAPTER 36

My New Family

The big move had happened in mid-September. I had to go to school on Monday and explain to my teachers and my counselor that I didn't live at home anymore. No one seemed to be shocked. They were very understanding and told me that if I needed anyone to talk to, I could come to them. I knew I would never do that.

My biggest problem was that Dad and Debbie refused to give me the rest of my things. I had taken three outfits with me and they weren't letting me come back for the rest. They did, however, leave my book bag on the front steps for me. I went to Gino's and asked for more hours. I needed to give Bearl money each week, as I promised, and I needed to buy new clothes. Bearl didn't charge me a certain amount of rent, she just told me to pay whatever I could. I was determined that I would pay my way and I would not take advantage of her kindness. I worked more hours, I went to school every day, did homework every night, took more diet pills and I tried to blend in with my new family.

They were honestly wonderful to me. Bearl was so understanding and she was so warm. The only person I could compare her to was Lula Bell. I was comfortable in her presence. I had not been that close of a friend with Rose, but our friendship would grow too.

Bob was an odd man at times, but he loved his family. He was truly a good man. Crystal was funny, she had a love/hate relationship with the family cats, and I had never been around cats before. They were quite entertaining. Crystal would simply walk into a room and the cat named Spice would wake up and attack her for absolutely no reason. He never hurt her, but she would freak out! Those cats made me laugh more than I ever remember laughing at anything else.

Bearl became my Mom in every way that mattered. Bob became my Dad too. Mom would sit with me at the kitchen table or on the living room sofa and we would talk for hours and hours. She wanted to know what life was like for me. I didn't tell her everything. I couldn't. I was afraid she would judge me. I shared as much as I could muster up the strength to share and that was bad enough. She listened, and she cried with me. She also shared with me what life had been like for her. She was a survivor, and she was a comforter. She would single-handedly change my life.

Meanwhile, Jay was still my boyfriend and he was so worried about me. Mom and Dad told me I could invite him over so they could meet him. They adored him, of course. Life just seemed to have taken a detour, but most of my life stayed the same. I just wasn't living in the same house anymore. I wasn't being beaten anymore, and I didn't hate going home from school anymore. It felt nice.

I did miss my little brother, Billy, though. I sort of missed Craig too, but I really missed Billy. I would call the house now and then. Dad would never talk to me and Debbie was just nasty. She wouldn't let me talk to them or see them. Sometimes I would sit around the corner and wait for them to come outside to play. Craig was six and Billy was four and since they lived just a block from the golf course, they would sometimes play at the end of it. I would hide behind cars and sneak up close to them. Billy was always so happy to see me. Craig would get panicky and worry that he would get into trouble for talking to me. I told them I missed them, and they shared their worries about me. I gave them a little bit of money to buy candy at the corner store, hugged them hard, and went back home. I didn't worry about them too much because they were Debbie's kids and she didn't treat them like she treated me. She wasn't afraid of Paul so she wouldn't let him be mean to them either. But Debbie was pregnant again and now she didn't have me to lean on. This would be interesting.

CHAPTER 37

The Ring Dance

I went about my life daily with blinders on. I didn't even realize it back then, but it had become a way of life for me. Push back the things that upset me and move forward. The problem was I never dealt with the things that bothered me. I just pushed past them only to find them haunting me for a very, very long time.

Life with Mom and Dad, as they preferred to be called, was good. There was peace in their home. There were normal arguments between the parents and their kids, but I didn't get in trouble. I walked the line. I knew that even though I was being treated as a member of the family, I was not blood and I had to keep both feet inside that door. Besides, this house was easy to live in. Everything I did was so appreciated. When I vacuumed the floor, I was complimented on doing a good job. When I got a report done for school and got a good grade, I was not only praised, but it was framed and hung on the wall. I was so happy to be away from the drama.

I still wet the bed every night though. That was something I couldn't understand. I truly believed that by leaving that house, it would stop, but it didn't. Mom was disappointed, of course, but she accepted that it was a problem for me and never once made me feel bad about it.

I went to school each day and went to work from there. I worked as many hours as I could. Aside from giving Mom money to help with my living expenses, I had things to buy, including my class ring and my senior portraits, which were going to add up to be quite a chunk of cash.

Mom and Dad bought my class ring for me. I worked, I saved, and I paid for my senior pictures by myself. I was so proud of myself, probably for the first time in my life.

The days went by, the weeks went by, and then the months. I secretly waited for my Dad to call me. I don't know what I wanted him to say, but I just wanted to hear that he missed me. I knew I couldn't go back, but I wanted him to ask me to come back. I wanted to mend fences. But no calls came. It ate me alive whenever I let myself think about it.

November arrived and our Junior Ring Dance was coming up. It was scheduled to happen on the night of my 17th birthday. Even though I was no longer involved in the politics of being Class Vice President, I still wanted to participate whenever my schedule would allow it. I made arrangements at Gino's and took up the job of being in charge of decorating the gym for the dance. I spent the entire day in that gym, working to make it a beautiful dance hall. We hung streamers and blew up balloons and rearranged furniture and set up tables and everything else it took to transform that room into a dream ballroom. By the time we were done, it was gorgeous.

I had just enough time to finish up, catch the two buses it took me to get home, get showered, and ready for the dance. Mary and Dave were picking up Jay and me so we could ride with them since neither of us drove. I spoke to Mary while I was working in the gym and we made our plans. I confessed to her that I hoped my Dad would at least call me on my birthday. She said she knew he would.

But he didn't. I tried so hard to be excited about all the work I had done all day and to be happy to be going to the Ring Dance with Jay. All I wanted to do was cry. I had been gone for 2 months and he hadn't spoken to me at all. Now it was my birthday and still no call. I tried to shrug it off, but I wasn't doing well at it this time. When Mary, Dave, and Jay picked me up, I kissed my new Mom and Dad and jumped into the car.

Dave was coaching a baseball team at the time and he had a substitute standing in for him that night. He asked if we minded stopping by just for a minute to see how his team was doing. Mary and I were fine with that. As we drove to the field where the game was being played, Dave and Jay got out of the car to check out the game. Mary handed me my birthday present. It was a fifth of Southern Comfort...my favorite, and just what I needed at that moment. As we sat in the car waiting for the boys to come back and take us to the dance, Mary and I drank the entire fifth of Southern Comfort by ourselves straight from the bottle.

I have no memory of the rest of the evening. The following is a recap based on what was shared with me by others.

My 98 lb. body could not handle that amount of alcohol on an empty stomach. Did I forget to say that I didn't eat all day while I was decorating the gym? Yeah, that. I don't even remember Dave and Jay getting back into the car. When we arrived at the school, Dave and Jay both took an arm and carried me into the school. When we got to the stairs, my legs were like wet noodles and they were having trouble getting me downstairs to the gym. As they struggled, the Vice Principal of the school, Mr. Wasserman, was walking up the stairs. I slid out of Dave and Jay's arms and fell down the stairs into Mr. Wasserman.

After the fall, to add insult to injury, I vomited on him. Security officers then rushed me into a classroom and discussed calling 911 to rush me to the hospital to have my stomach pumped. My friends explained that there were no drugs involved, it was just alcohol, but the school staff was having trouble finding my heartbeat. They then decided to call my parents, but they weren't sure where I was living. After checking with my friends, they called Bearl and Bob.

Needless to say, they weren't happy with me. Bob got right into his car and drove to the school, which was about 40 minutes away. When he arrived at the school, I was still unconscious and my whole body had been wrapped in a tablecloth so my dress wouldn't come up and expose my behind as he carried me to his car.

I am told that once I was in the car, I objected to leaving the dance. I kicked and screamed and threw my body around while he was driving, causing my left foot to get stuck in the steering wheel and we spun in the middle of a major intersection. He got my foot out of the steering wheel and continued the drive home. Once home, he had to carry me into the house. I again fought him and punched him in the face, breaking his glasses. He carried me upstairs and put me in my bed.

To this day, I don't remember any of it. What I do remember is waking up the next day. I had been drunk on many occasions, but I had never experienced a hangover. Until that day. When I awoke, I found myself lying upside down on my bed with a kitchen pot next to me. I still had my dress and my shoes on. I started to sit up and realized I couldn't lift my head. It felt like I was lifting a ton of bricks on top of it, so I laid there and panicked as thoughts ran through my head.

What had happened? I had been a virgin up until that night. Was I still? How did I get here? What happened to Jay and my friends? Ugh, what kind of trouble would I be in with Bearl and Bob? I couldn't bear the thought of what I was going to face when I finally did get out of that bed.

I couldn't go back to sleep because I couldn't stop my mind from wandering. I tried and tried but couldn't remember a thing. Then I saw Crystal walk past my door. I tried to yell her name, but I had no voice. I was even more terrified. I figured she had to have gone to the bathroom, so I waited for her to walk by again. Finally, she did, and she peeked in. I frantically waved her into the room. She walked in like I had some contagious disease. I whispered when she got close enough to hear, "What did I do?"

Crystal was always full of drama, but at that moment, I wasn't sure if her drama was taking over or if it was real. All she said was, "Oh Bunny. You're in sooooo much trouble!"

Great.

Just what I wanted to hear. I asked her why I had a kitchen pot next to me and she told me that I threw up all night long and then I had dry heaves, which explained the loss of my voice. I asked where Mom was, and she said she was sitting at the dining room table and had been writing me a letter for a long time. She told me about getting my foot stuck in the steering wheel and breaking Dad's glasses.

I had blown it.

I just knew they were going to kick me out. They had enough going on in their own lives and they didn't need me bringing them more trouble. It was time to face the music and accept that this was all my fault.

I got to my feet and Crystal helped me get to the stairs, but she wouldn't go down the stairs with me. She didn't want any part of it. As I walked down the steps, I saw Mom, still writing at the dining room table with a scowl on her face. I pulled up a chair beside her and waited.

She let me have it!

She yelled she growled, she cursed at me through clenched teeth and she let loose. I just kept nodding my head in agreement. I had no excuse, and I knew it. She didn't deserve what I had done and neither had Dad. After she shared her feelings, she demanded to know what had gotten into me. I confessed how I had been feeling about my dad and my birthday. She didn't understand. Why would I hold feelings for this abusive monster? I couldn't answer that. It didn't make sense to me either.

In the end, she didn't kick me out. I apologized to both of them from the bottom of my heart. I vowed to make it up to them. Somehow. Of course, I was punished, but not beaten. I couldn't go out at all, but she told me that I needed to call Jay because he was worried sick about me. That was a call I wanted to make in private because I had to know EXACTLY what I had done the night before.

I went into the living room and called Jay. His mother answered. She already didn't like me much and now I could tell I definitely was not on her good list. He got on the phone and was frantic. He was so sweet. I asked him what I had done, and he told me the whole gruesome story. Jay was too much of a gentleman to take advantage of that situation and I was ashamed of myself for thinking it. He was a really good guy. A good guy that I wouldn't be allowed to see for two weeks except at school.

On Monday morning, as soon as I arrived in homeroom class, I was told that Mr. Wasserman wanted to see me. I had been expecting that. I knew I was in trouble, but I didn't expect to hear what I heard when I sat down in front of his desk.

After discussing the events of the dance, he said, "You do not exemplify the standards of a Western lady and you are therefore expelled from this school."

What?

I was shocked and horrified! I couldn't be expelled! This was the only stability I had in my life! If I left here, I would have to go to Lake Clifton, and I was pretty much guaranteed no future with that school. I had to talk and talk fast, and I did. I begged and pleaded and promised. I told him about my life at home and explained to him that I was trying so hard to start a new life for myself. I just couldn't walk away from my education at Western. I promised I would do anything just to stay there. He sat there quietly and listened. I was still frantic, pacing the room, and continually pleading. He finally asked me if I would agree to go to every member of the school faculty who had witnessed the events of that night and apologize to them sincerely.

I agreed.

He told me to do it now and come back to him with what had transpired. He then gave me a list of every teacher, office staff member, and security guard who witnessed my transgression. I proceeded to hunt down each one of them and gave them my most sincere apologies. Some of them just nodded but were still disenchanted with me. Some hugged me and gave me advice on not drinking like that again. Some warned me that I could have died and to my surprise, some of them chuckled. They were just glad to see that I was ok.

I went back to Mr. Wasserman and told him everything. He was surprised at how quickly and efficiently I had covered the list. He then told me that he would put me on probation. He would allow me to stay at Western, but if I had one more slip-up, even cutting a class, I would be expelled, and he would not give me another chance. I almost jumped over his desk to hug him. I was so grateful, and I had to prove to him and to everyone else that I WAS a true Western lady. I would earn my diploma from Western and I would not mess up again.

I have to admit now that I did cut classes now and then but was never caught. Other than that, I never messed up again at Western High School.

CHAPTER 38

February 17, 1981

How many people remember the exact date they lost their virginity? I do.

Why?

Because I was so very, very afraid. Also, because I was the last of my friends to cross the line and I refused to be left behind. And because I had no idea about any of it. My fears were so extreme because I suffered from flashbacks of the abuse from my dad. I was afraid I would freak out and cause a scene. I never paid attention when he "bothered me" as I called it. I zoned out and left my body. I was now 17 years old and I needed to own my own body, but could I?

Jay and I planned it. On this particular day, school was closed for "Energy Conservation Week." His mother didn't live at home with her teenage boys. They were mostly taking care of themselves except for paying the rent. She would stop in now and then though. His dad was not a part of his life at all, so he and his brother stepped up and took care of everything. He told his brother to find something to do that day and I told Mom Bearl that I was going to hang out with him for the day. She didn't know his mom didn't live there.

I got on the bus to go to his house and I was a nervous wreck. While I don't remember any of the details, I do remember thinking, "What's all the excitement about?" It hurt! It was not fun, and I didn't care if I never did it again. Jay didn't seem to be excited about it either and it wasn't his first time. Maybe I did something wrong? I had no idea, but things were about to get interesting because of all days, his mom showed up!

He ran downstairs when he heard the door and I waited in his room. I then heard his mom yelling. He had told her I was there. Now she was angry, and I was afraid to go down the steps. I had hoped she would leave the room so I could leave without an altercation, but that didn't happen. She waited at the bottom of the stairs with a scowl on her face and her arms crossed. She glared at me as I descended, and I ran out the door. So much for hoping his mom would like me. Now I had two strikes against me—one for the ring dance and one for this.

My friends had told me that once a guy starts having sex with his girlfriend, he expects it more regularly. Yep, that happened. I tried to like it, but it did nothing for me at all. He seemed to be enjoying himself, but I was missing something. We didn't get much alone time together because I was terrified his mom would show up again but now and then, I would give in.

One Saturday afternoon I was there to watch him play baseball. He loved it and I enjoyed watching him have fun. His team won, and he was in a really good mood. We went back to his house and he led me upstairs. Ok, it's time for this again but this time was different.

Something happened!

This time I was getting a glimpse of what all the fuss was about. When I lost my breath and squinted my eyes as tight as I could, my body was responding big time to whatever he was doing. When we were done, I asked him, "What the hell was that?" He laughed hysterically and it was then that he had realized that I finally got it. I told him if he could do that each time, I was in.

Jay was a senior at Poly, and I was a junior at Western. We had two proms to go to that spring and then the summer break would begin. Things were going to be so different for him because he would now need to find a job and start becoming an adult. I still had another year of high school and then I would be doing the same. College wasn't an option for either of us because our parents were not in the position to support those goals and guidance counselors at the time didn't spend a lot of time guiding.

Right after the proms, Jay called me one day and said his mom was taking him and his brother to Ocean City, Maryland for two weeks. She suggested that he break up with me before he left so he could explore his options and be uncommitted for that time with his family. I couldn't believe he was telling me this over the phone. He was breaking up with me for just two weeks so he could be uncommitted...and then what? He would meet other girls, with his mother's blessings, and then come back and expect me to pick up where we left off?

No!

I had given him a part of me, and I didn't deserve this! There was nothing wrong with our relationship. This was just his mother creating a problem and he allowed her to. I told him that if he broke up with me, it wasn't for two weeks, it was for good. He said Ok. And that was it.

Of course, I cried like a baby, but I stood my ground. I was not going to be treated the way Paul had treated all his women. He tossed them aside whenever someone new and shiny smiled at him. Jay wanted that same thing. When he returned from Ocean City, he called me and wanted to see me. I refused. I told him he had decided and now it was for him to live with it.

I was done.

CHAPTER 39

Summer of Fun

That summer I worked like a maniac at Gino's, getting as many hours as I could so I could make as much money as I could. I hung out with my friends and spent a lot of time with Debbie A. Debbie was certainly a force to be reckoned with and she took me under her wing and showed me how to have fun.

Debbie had a lot more experience with guys than I did. I shared things with her, and she shared her stories with me. She had no boundaries. If she wanted something or someone, she took it. She made it happen. At fifteen, she was the manager of a Royal Farm store in her neighborhood. She was proud, she was beautiful, and she was fierce. Girls in her neighborhood were afraid of her and so were many of the guys. If she didn't like what you had to say or something you had done, it was within her wheelhouse to fight you. She was the only girl I knew who had beaten up guys and she was as small as me. She took no crap, and she made no excuses for it. We drove around that neighborhood in her car, up and down streets and alleys and it was always an adventure, I spent many nights at her house, and I learned as much as I possibly could from her.

One day she told me she was going on a bus trip to Atlantic City with her mom and her friends. It was very inexpensive, and they gave you free chips to play games when you arrived. She asked me if I wanted to go and I said sure. I saved up $200 and caught the bus to get to Debbie's house to catch the bus to go to Atlantic City. We were the only people on the bus in our age group and it was a hoot. I had never gambled before and I didn't know if I would like it or not, but I was willing to try. When we arrived, they gave us chips and we went inside the first casino we saw. It was so bright and loud and crowded! I felt like I was in a circus with so many characters running all around me. I didn't know where to start! Debbie told me to try to slot machines first, so I did. I didn't like it. I wanted to go to a table and see what that was about, but I had no idea how to play any of the games. I watched the blackjack table for a bit and then decided to give it a try. It was fun, but I was losing. I watched my money disappear before my eyes and I didn't like that part at all. There was so much more I could do with $200 than just throw it on a table for strangers to take from me. After I lost $50, I left the table, went to the gift shop, bought a paperback book. I went back to the bus we came in on. I sat on that bus for 4 hours reading the book and waiting for everyone to return so we could go home. I still had $150 in my pocket and I was proud of myself. Clearly, gambling was not for me!

Another day, Debbie took me to a pool party at a local rec center in her area. I met so many of her friends that day and it was hard to remember all their names. Then I spotted this dark-haired guy walking toward us. I couldn't stop staring at him. He was beautiful. I asked Debbie who he was, and she said his name was Jimmy R. He wasn't part of her social circle, but she knew a bit about him, and she introduced me. I didn't know what to say to him to create conversation and it was very awkward. We smiled at each other and had a very short conversation. He had to get back to his friends.

I then knew that I needed Debbie to teach me how to flirt. I watched him laughing with his friends, but I couldn't figure out how to make myself part of his fun that day. Then it was time to go and I didn't get to say goodbye.

The summer months went by quickly and then it was time for our senior year at Western. I was thrilled yet terrified. I didn't know what I wanted to do for a living when I graduated. The family expectation was to get married and pregnant and just be a good housewife. I didn't want that for myself. I wanted to make my own money, be my own person, and reach my own goals. I just didn't know what they were yet.

CHAPTER 40

Senior Year

Western High School certainly knew how to celebrate their seniors. We had a senior assembly where Oprah Winfrey was our key-note speaker. This was way before the Oprah show, but she was a local newscaster in Baltimore, and we were quite excited to hear from her. With Western's all-girl school status, seniors wore all white for every event. There was a sea of white on the day of the assembly and afterwards a bunch of us drove to Little Italy to share lunch. As we walked along the promenade of the Inner Harbor, we got lots of attention.

Another special event happened early in my senior year too. One morning in October of 1981, I walked out into the quad to join my friends for our morning routine of hanging out before school started. As I walked to the wall on Poly's side of the quad, I spotted the dark-haired guy from the pool with Debbie A. that previous summer. Jimmy R. went to Poly? I had no idea! I walked up to him and said, "What are you doing here?"

He was just as shocked as me and we were both quite happy to see each other. We quickly exchanged numbers before we left for class and I was too excited! He was even cuter than I remembered him, and he had the very best smile and laugh.

Our conversations on the phone began and love was in the air. I knew he had been dating someone, but I didn't know who and he somehow made himself available very quickly. As Forest Gump would say, we were like peas and carrots. We were together every morning, every day at lunch, after school and on the phone every night. He was adorable, he was funny, and he was the same size as me. Since I was just 5", I found that to be the cutest part—we even wore the same sized designer jeans.

I had only been intimate with Jay and I wasn't in a big hurry to start being intimate with anyone else. I needed to wait a minute and get a solid grounding with Jimmy R. before I took that step. When we finally did, oh my God it was amazing every single time! I couldn't get enough!

He would giggle at me constantly because I held him off for a while and then I was all over him. He had certainly flipped a switch in me!

We were both graduating in May. We were both fine with our grades and meeting graduation requirements would not be difficult. We decided we could miss a day of school here and there and hang out. There were often school-time parties for those that chose not to go to school and we would join them sometimes and play quarters. Jimmy R. was not living with his parents, but instead was living with a couple named Brad and Sue. He had the basement as his room and since they both worked during the day, we could slip into their home and spend alone time together. In retrospect, I can't remember doing a thing without him for that entire school year.

Everyone loved Jimmy R., and everyone thought we were the best couple. We got along beautifully, and every day was amazing. As time went on, of course, we began having disagreements. Most of my issues with him were based on his drinking. He wasn't the same person when he was drinking, and I wanted him to work on it. He didn't want to work on it. It became an issue between us, but nothing earth-shattering. As the New Year approached and all the pomp and circumstance of proms and graduations started, we were in a whirlwind. Our first un-official outing was Senior Cut Day.

I knew I was planning to cut that day and spend the day with Jimmy R. and my friends. After my episode a year and a half previously at the Ring Dance, I decided I should share my plans with Mom. I told her it was Senior Cut Day and that most of the Seniors would not be in school that day. She knew my grades were fine and she permitted me to cut school. I felt so much better about that, because I did not want to get in trouble again.

Our friend, Mary, had a little Vega car that always struggled getting up hills because it didn't have much power. On Senior Cut Day, those of us that attended squeezed into different cars and we drove to different parks and areas around town and drank like crazy. There were no drunken driving laws at that time and most police officers would just stop you and tell you to go right home. If that were to happen, we would do just that...go right home. But on this particular day, we weren't given that option.

I remember having a lot of laughs and I remember lots of cars following each other from one location to the other. I remember Jimmy R. drinking too much and I remember trying to get him to cut back. I remember we started arguing over it and I was desperately trying not to create a scene. I don't know if people knew we were arguing or not. I was drinking way too much myself and it was all very fuzzy to me.

We got into Mary's car again to go to the next location. As we hit the hill at Northern Parkway, her car started puttering, as usually. This puttering annoyed and embarrassed her and since she had squeezed 6 people into her little Vega, she knew weight was the issue. She floored it. I was sitting on Jimmy R's lap in the center of the back seat. He and I weren't speaking to each other and I was trying to hide my tears. I wasn't looking forward when we crested the top of the hill. I didn't see the parked car broken down in the fast lane on Northern Parkway right over the top of that hill. Mary didn't have time to react. She had floored it and as we crested, we picked up speed and smashed into that broken down car.

It happened so fast. I don't remember flying through the center of the two front seats and smashing my face into the windshield. I just remember that I had a bloody nose and didn't know how it happened. Everyone was climbing out of the smashed car and Jimmy R. was complaining that his legs hurt. I climbed out of the car as I was holding my bloody nose with my jacket to stop the bleeding. I watched as Jimmy R. hobbled over to the sidewalk and leaned against a fence writhing in pain. I sat on the sidewalk watching others attend to him to make sure nothing was broken. Someone yelled over to me that they didn't think anything was broken. That made me feel better.

As I watched from my seated position on the sidewalk, I started to feel light-headed, so I decided to lie down on the sidewalk. This was not rational, but I was clearly not in a rational state. I would never just lie down on a sidewalk.

My next memory was being in an ambulance hooked up to equipment and having an EMT trying to wake me up. She kept shaking me and telling me to stay awake. I kept whispering that I was so tired, and I just needed to sleep. In her frustration, she finally yelled that if I didn't wake up, I might not EVER wake up. I forced my eyes open in terror.

What had happened? Where was I? Where was Jimmy R.? The ambulance pulled up to a hospital and they hurriedly pulled me out on the stretcher. They had me covered with white blankets and they had a big white ice pack on my face. I could see a bit under the ice pack, and I saw Michael running over to me. He was frantic and trying to make sure I was ok. As he was yelling at the nurses about my condition, I realized, I couldn't talk or move. I couldn't just sit up and tell him I was ok. My body wasn't cooperating at all. He thought I was dead, and he was freaking out and I couldn't console him. Jimmy R. was nowhere to be found.

The hospital wanted my personal contact information. One of my friends gave them my phone number but they didn't give them Mom and Dad's number, they gave them Dad and Debbie's number. When I woke up later that day in a room, Dad and Debbie were there in my room. I didn't know where Mom and Dad were, and my head hurt too much to ask questions. I don't remember much conversation, but Dad was crying and telling me he thought he had lost me for good. We hadn't spoken in almost two years, so I was very surprised by his reaction. I was grateful. I had to pee, but the nurse said I couldn't get out of bed. I had to pee in a bed pan, so Dad left the room and Debbie did her best to help me use the bed pan.

As I tried to lift myself from the bed and place the pan beneath me, I saw my reflection in a mirror behind Debbie. I started screaming right away! My face was horrible! My nose was moved to the left side of my face, there were cuts all over my face and dried blood everywhere! I looked like a monster! The nurse ran back in and helped Debbie with me. She kept trying to calm me down and told me that I had smashed my nose, not just broken it, but smashed it in little pieces! The blood would clear up, the windshield glass cuts would heal, and I would need surgery for my nose. She assured me that it would be fine in the end and I should be grateful all 6 of us were alive.

After a few days in the hospital, Dad and Debbie took me home to their house. I didn't know what to do about Mom and Dad and they said they were going to handle it. Dad insisted that I stay there so they could get me to and from doctor appointments and my surgery. Since Mom (Bearl) was in a wheelchair and Dad (Bob) was away at work often, I thought it would be easier for them to not have to worry about my transportation issues. I let Dad and Debbie handle the details.

A few days after that, Mary and her mother came to visit. When Mary saw me as she walked into the front door, she sobbed and kept apologizing. I felt so bad for her and told her it wasn't her fault. We all went into it by making bad decisions. What I didn't know at the time was that Mary was arrested after the accident. She spent time in jail, but I don't know if it was a night or a couple of days, but she had been through the wringer already. She shared with me that no one else in the car was hurt—just me. It figured! But I was glad she didn't have to go through this with other people too.

Since we had no health insurance, and since I would have a mountain of bills coming up, we had no choice but to file a claim against Mary's car insurance. Someone had to pay the bills. When that was decided, I called Mom (Bearl) and talked to her about everything. I asked her if we could go through her attorney, Mr. Gladstone, and she said yes. I had met him earlier that year through Mom and Dad.

I had shared with them that I thought I wanted to be a legal secretary so they suggested that I spend a couple of days in Mr. Gladstone's office so I could see what a legal secretary really did. I loved it! He was a great man and I had decided after spending those days in his office that I would pursue a job as a legal secretary after I graduated. But for now, I just needed his services.

While I stayed at Dad and Debbie's house, I got to spend more time with Craig and Billy, and my new baby sister, Melissa. I had the surgery on my nose, and it didn't work. They told me I would need to do it again. I asked if they could wait until after graduation and they said yes.

Before all this started, I had been in conversations with Debbie A.'s sister, Kathy. Kathy was renting a townhouse near my school and she wanted a roommate to help her with expenses. I decided to move in with her right after graduation. I decided to stay at Dad and Debbie's until then, rather than move back to Mom and Dad's and then out again a couple weeks later.

CHAPTER 41

My Prom

Neither Jimmy R. nor I drove, but he was friendly with Debbie A. and her boyfriend, Marty. We decided that we would ride to the prom with them. As the date got closer, Debbie A. and I would chat about our preparations for the prom, but like most teenage girls, we didn't pay attention to what the other one was saying.

That became painfully clear when she and Marty picked up Jimmy R. and brought him to my house. I noticed right away that Jimmy R. and Marty had on the exact same tux. Then Debbie walked into my house and she and I had the same gown on. The only difference was her dress was all white with a purple sash. Mine was all white. We were going to walk into the prom looking like twins, but she and Marty were blonds, and Jimmy R. and I were brunettes.

After the initial shock of it all, we laughed and left for the prom. It was an amazing night, and we had an absolute blast! After the evening ended, the 4 of us went to Denny's for a midnight snack and we laughed hysterically as Marty cleared all of our plates because he was so hungry. It was the best night!

After the four of us grew older and moved on to new relationships, we had this amazing memory to make us smile. Within a couple of years, Marty would pass away from a terrible car accident. Ten years or so later, Jimmy R. would be killed by an unknown assailant, while he was intoxicated. All Debbie A. and I have now are memories and photos.

CHAPTER 42

Independence

I was back at Dad and Debbie's when I was released from the hospital. I was busy preparing for my move to Kathy's place and buying clothes that would be appropriate for working at a law office. Again, I got some pointers from Sharon. I had mentioned to Debbie A. that when Jimmy R. returned from Ocean City, I was breaking up with him. She agreed with my thought process. Since they lived in the same neighborhood, she saw him before I heard from him. She asked if I had broken up with him yet? He was quite surprised and especially angry. He called me right away and demanded to know what that was all about. I tried to be delicate, but I had to be stern. I wanted more from life than to have a man who swore he loved me but made choices like partying while I was having surgery. My mind was made up and that was it.

After the screaming match that ensued, I hung up the phone and cried like a baby. Yes, I made the decision, but I knew I would miss him. I had high expectations for myself and others. I needed to be very careful because I had watched Paul trick women into believing his love and commitment for many years. I wouldn't accept that way of life.

Jimmy R. would make another appearance in my life much later. After Joe and I split up, I drove through Hampden one day and saw him unloading a Pepsi truck at a grocery store. I stopped to say hello. It had been so many years since we saw each other. He was divorced with 2 boys too. We exchanged numbers. One evening we met up with his twin sister, Kim, and her husband. Kim was excited to see me again and hoped we would be able to see each other more often. I had been through so much over the years and all I could see was that Jimmy R. still had a big drinking problem. I saw him a couple of times, but the last time I saw him he was in bad shape with the alcohol. I told him I was too old for this. I never saw him alive again.

A couple of years later, as I was doing a one-on-one PartyLite training at my home, Debbie A. called me and gently shared that Jimmy R. had been murdered. I couldn't believe it. I made a bunch of calls to verify and it was true. We went to his funeral and all I could do was stare at his body in the coffin. I hugged his mom, met his ex-wife and his children. His sister was inconsolable, and I left rather than bother her. It still hurts my heart to think of that day. But Jimmy R. was finally no longer tortured by his demons.

CHAPTER 43

Vice President of my Class of '82

It was now our senior year at Western and Melinda, Mary, and I were hanging out together all the time at school. We were like the 3 musketeers. We went to dances together with our boyfriends. Melinda was with Warren; Mary was with Dave and I was with Jay. One night while sharing a bottle of Southern Comfort, Mary had the grand idea that she would run for President of our class. That was kind of out of the blue, but it sounded like a great idea. We then decided it would be fun if I ran for Vice President and we could rule together. So, it was decided. We would start our campaigns.

It turned out to merely be a popularity contest. We made posters and shook hands with everyone. It was quite funny, and I didn't take it seriously at all.

The election came and the winners were chosen. Mary was not elected President, but I was elected Vice President. I had such mixed emotions. I was so excited, but I was sad for Mary. This had been her idea after all. I couldn't believe I was actually popular enough to be voted Vice President of the class. Mary was disappointed, of course, but she handled it like a trooper. She was so happy for me and I was so grateful.

But now what? There was a job to do. There were meetings to attend and decisions to be had and I was now an integral part of the process.

Back at home, I had to explain to Debbie and Dad that I had run in the election without telling them. I didn't expect to win, so I didn't think it was necessary to share. In truth, I didn't want to hear any crap about it. At dinner, I told them I had exciting news. I shared and no one said a word. They just kept eating. Finally, Dad asked if I was getting extra credit for it. I said no. He grunted and asked, "Then what's the point?" I said, "Nothing," and continued to eat my dinner in silence.

For the next few weeks after the election, I had to stay after school to attend meetings at least once or twice a week. Dad was not happy. I didn't understand why he even cared. I was still home in time for dinner and I had worked out my work schedule so it wouldn't conflict.

However, Debbie was complaining that she wasn't getting any help and my new responsibilities at school were interfering with my household duties. That's actually what he told me. He then told me that since I wasn't getting any extra credit for this, I was going to have to quit and he forbade me to stay after school anymore. I tried to argue the point until I saw him get angry. I couldn't believe I was going to have to quit as Vice President of my class just so Debbie didn't have to take care of her own children.

Humiliated, I went to school the next day and went to see the Vice Principal, Mr. Wasserman. I explained the situation to him, and he was as upset as I was. He told me he would call my dad and talk to him for me. I said okay. He called and Dad just got even angrier. He yelled at Mr. Wasserman and told him to mind his own business. There was an assembly that week where the entire Class of '82 would meet, and I was now told to give a speech announcing my resignation.

My first actual job as the Vice President was to resign. This was the most humiliating thing I'd ever had to do. As I looked out amongst my peers, I looked for my Dad's support, but he didn't bother to show up. He said I had gotten into this without his permission and I was now to get myself out. So, I did. He would never understand how big this was to me. I was stepping out beyond myself and I was doing something big. I was the Vice President of my class, but he held me back, just as he had done all my life.

My excuses for my Dad's behavior ended that day.

CHAPTER 44

Graduation and Job Search

During my recovery time, the school was sending work home with my friends and I was trying to stay current with everything from home. I also decided to use the time to begin searching for a job. Not only was I interested in a legal secretary position because of Mom and Dad's lawyer, but also because of my friend, Sharon. I use the word "friend" here, but truly, she was more of an acquaintance at that time. She was 5 years older than me and she worked at a law firm. She lived next door to Dad and Debbie in the upstairs apartment above the corner store, with her husband, Tony.

Each day I saw Sharon wait for the bus to pick her up in front of the house and I saw her get off the bus at the end of the day. She was stunning! I loved the way she dressed, I loved the way she carried herself and she was always so nice to me.

First, I had to finish school and solidify that diploma. All good! I walked across that stage and was so proud of the woman I was becoming. As Dad and Debbie and other family members congratulated me, I could think of nothing more than my next steps.

I went through the newspaper and checked all the listings for legal secretary jobs. Western had taught me typing, shorthand, business administration, accounting, and a plethora of other skills that would help me. I tried to sift through the ads to be sure they weren't employment agencies because I had heard bad things about them. I saw one big ad that said, "No Experience Necessary! Starting at $140-$170 a week." I only made $.35 an hour at Gino's so that sounded like a lot of money to me!

I began making calls to line up interviews and I realized that I had nothing to wear. I didn't own a dress, other than a holiday dress and all I wore to school were jeans. I did, however, make a yellow skirt in my home economics class that year. It was decided, I would wear that yellow skirt and a white blouse, and I would be fine.

With each phone call to attempt an interview, I was getting more and more disappointed. Most of the job offers wanted work experience and the article that said, "No experience necessary," was an employment agency. Finally, I found one and was able to speak to the attorney. We set up an interview for that week and I got to chat with Sharon about where to get off the bus downtown. As luck would have it, my interview was in the same building as her job. She gave me pointers and I was all set.

Meanwhile, Jimmy R. called me one day and told me that since school was now over and since I was going into the hospital for a week for nose surgery, he was going to Ocean City with his friends. Sound familiar? Yeah, it struck me too! He was not going to be there with me through the surgery and recovery? He was choosing a party over me. I kept my thoughts to myself and knew the decision that had to be made. I was an adult now. I had turned 18 the previous November, I had graduated high school, I had lined up a new job with growth potential and I had a new apartment. It was time for me to focus on myself and I had no time for childish behavior anymore.

CHAPTER 45

Jimmy S. – 1982

As I sat on my front steps, a brand new pretty white Camaro pulled up in front of my house, and the driver yelled my name. It was Jimmy S., a guy who had dated a neighborhood friend a year or so previously. He was a few years older than me and he was always nice. I apologized for looking rough and explained that I had just broken up with my fiancé. He immediately asked me out. He wanted to take me to dinner at his parents' house not far away. I was stunned, but decided, why not? I told him I needed to shower, and we made plans for him to pick me up in a few hours.

This was so odd, but I was suddenly happy again. As much as I loved Jimmy R., I was beginning to finally love myself more. I ran inside and told Debbie that I had a date. She was surprised to see that I walked onto the porch in tears and walked back in with a date.

Jimmy S. picked me up a few hours later and he didn't seem to notice the efforts I had taken to look nice for our date. I was surprised only because I looked horrible when he saw me earlier that day. When we arrived at his parents' house, he scooted me past his family and into the first-floor powder room, where he asked me to wash my face and "get all that crap off" my face. I was stunned for a minute and wondered if I should do it or leave. I decided to just do it and see what would come of the evening. Bad decision—I didn't show him who I really was at that point. Instead, I gave in to a request that I should have stood up for.

I felt degraded, but it was my own fault.

When I walked out of the bathroom with a clean face of no make-up, he introduced me to his mom, dad, uncle, and brother. I immediately knew they were an amazing family. By the time I left their house that night, I was in love with every one of them. THIS was the kind of family I wanted to be a part of.

We began dating and he helped me move into Kathy's place. He supported my independence and was excited about my new job. In retrospect, I see now just how much God was working in my life.

Moving into the townhouse with Kathy just two weeks after graduation wasn't even scary to me. Knowing that I was now solely responsible for myself was exciting. I somehow knew everything was going to be ok.

Kathy was completely intrigued by my family story. I still hadn't shared with ANYONE the details of living with Paul. I didn't know if those words would ever come off my lips. I couldn't change what had happened, but I could change my future. As Kathy asked me questions, the answers caused even more confusion. She wanted to dig in and solve the mysteries.

One day I got off the bus from work and she was waiting for me. She proudly announced that she had found my mother's side of the family. She had the name, address, and phone number of my mother's ex-husband and had verified that my two brothers lived there. It was almost Labor Day and she insisted that Jimmy S. drive me to Worcester, MA to meet them. He was on board and so we went.

CHAPTER 46

Knock, Knock – 1982

I guess it was my immaturity at that point that caused me to not announce my trip to my mother's ex-husband. I thought it might be a nice surprise to meet me. Jimmy S. and I drove all the way to Worcester and got there just before sundown that Friday night of Labor Day weekend. Kathy had mapped it all out for us and we found the house very easily. I went up to the door and knocked a few times. A woman answered the door and I assumed it was my brothers' stepmother. I spoke immediately and said, "My name is Bunny and ..." and she cut me off.

She said, "I know EXACTLY who you are. You look just like your mother. I knew this day would come."

We walked in and she asked us to have a seat in her kitchen. I explained to her that my roommate had been super curious about my background and she had located them so I could meet them. Her name was Mona. Mona told me that my oldest brother, Dale, was in Japan in the army. She had his picture on the wall and I was so happy to see that I looked like him. She then told me my other brother, David, would be walking in at any moment and I could meet him. She called into the next room and her husband, my brothers' Dad, walked in. He saw me, said a quick hello, and bolted out of the room. It was clear that my appearance made him uncomfortable.

As we sat at the table, Mona asked me question after question about my life. It was very friendly, and I felt safe there. Then David walked in. I was to learn very quickly that not only did David NOT know that Mona wasn't his biological mother and he did NOT know that he had a mother who had died when he was 3 and he did NOT know that he had a sister, but he did know that his life was being turned upside down at that very moment.

I felt terrible about this! His reaction was horrible! He stormed out of the room, he paced, he yelled, and he refused to talk to me. He took off out the door and drove away. I looked at Mona stunned. She told me that he was probably going to blow off steam at the bowling alley, but I could wait until he came back.

The questions ensued and I had plenty of questions too. No one had ever given me any solid information about my mother. I knew absolutely NOTHING about my mother's family. Mona wasn't going to help me with that either. She said my mom's family were all horrible alcoholics, and they were mean, and she wouldn't allow the boys anywhere near them. She was not going to give me the information either. I explained to Mona that for years I had written to Worcester, MA to get my birth certificate and they kept returning my money and telling me that they had no record of me. I explained that while I was there, I was hoping to get to the Records Department for the City and pick it up from them directly. She asked me what my last name was. I told her and I could tell she knew something I didn't know. She went into the other room to chat with her husband for a minute and came back telling me that he would take me to the Records Department the next morning and we would get my birth certificate. I was a little scared of that man, but I agreed, as long as Jimmy S. went with me.

Finally, David came back in and was not happy to see that I was still there. She made him sit at the kitchen table with me, but she couldn't make him look at me or talk to me. It was so disappointing. I had such high hopes for a happy reunion and to find a place where I belonged. It was obviously not here either.

Mona kept me in conversation and David sat across from me with his arms crossed. I noticed that he reached down to untie his shoes and when he removed his shoe, I saw that he had a strange foot, just like me. I said, "Wow! My feet look like that!" He looked me straight in the eye for the first time and said, "What?" I repeated myself and decided to take off my shoes and show him.

Now he was ready to talk. He asked me if I knew that I had Muscular Dystrophy.

"No, I don't," I said. "I just have funky feet."

He got up, walked across the room, and grabbed an encyclopedia, which was earmarked for a certain section. He opened it in front of me and showed me pictures of feet just like mine and a caption of "Charcot-Marie-Tooth", a neurological disorder that is classified as Muscular Dystrophy. It didn't scare me because I was obviously fine, but then he wanted to talk. He told me about the numerous surgeries he had and the prognosis for him. His was much worse than mine, but now he believed me.

This disease is hereditary, and he could never figure out where it came from. I explained that our mother had it and his face was full of shock, awe, and anger all at once.

We then talked about our clumsiness and I realized I had more issues with my legs and feet than I thought. I did fall often. I always had skinned up knees and I often dealt with leg cramps, aside from having hammertoes, which interfered with certain styles of shoes. His interest in learning about me was growing but I knew this family had to have conversations about this event and I should head to the hotel to give them time to do that. I explained where we were staying, and Mona told me what time to come by the next morning to go to the Records Department.

CHAPTER 47

Not My Daughter!

Jimmy S. and I arrived at Mona's place at the designated time, and we got into Big Dale's car for the drive to the City. We got to the Records Department, and I asked for my birth certificate and gave them all my information. They checked everything and came back to tell me that there was no record of me. Damn it! I was right there! I was born there, and I needed my birth certificate. They asked if I could have a different last name. I didn't think so, but I had them try my mother's maiden name.

Nothing.

They asked for another option. I looked at Big Dale and gave them his last name. This time they came back and asked what my father's name was. At this point, I wasn't sure I knew any answers anymore. I was clearly not born with Paul's last name since that was the first name I gave them. I had no idea who my father was now, so I told them I didn't know. They came back with my birth certificate with no father on it and Big Dale's last name.

Jimmy S., Big Dale, and I all stood there staring at it with our mouths open. Suddenly, Big Dale erupted with, "You are NOT my daughter! I don't know why she did this!" And he kept yelling. I held up my hand to signal "stop" and said, "I don't care! I needed my birth certificate and now I have it. I'll have questions for my Dad when I get back to Baltimore."

I think Big Dale was relieved that I didn't jump on him for answers. I wanted to drop it and get back to spend more time with my brother and that's what we did.

When we got back to their house, Mona asked to see the birth certificate. I showed it to her, and she and Big Dale left the room to have a conversation. David, Jimmy S., and I walked around outside and chatted and got to know each other a bit more. We started taking pictures and I was playing with his little sisters and brothers. It ended really, really well.

By Monday morning, when we were ready to leave, David told me he didn't want me to go. What a big difference this weekend made. He started with denying our relationship and ended with him wanting to hold onto it. We promised to stay in touch, and Mona promised too. I had a big tearful goodbye with David, and we headed back to Baltimore.

Was Big Dale my real dad?

How would I ever really know? My mother was the only person who could tell me for sure, and she certainly wasn't able to do that. I had to talk to Paul and find out the rest of this story.

When I got back to Baltimore and went to see Paul, he wasn't talking. He didn't want to talk about the past. How convenient for him.

CHAPTER 48

My First "Real" Job

Getting off the bus in downtown Baltimore was like being in the "That Girl" TV series! I caught myself looking up at the tall buildings the way Marlo Thomas did back in the day. I looked as nice as I could with my yellow skirt and white blouse with reasonable heels.

The office building was small, and I had to meet the attorney, Art, in his office on the 5th floor. I didn't know what to expect, but Mr. Gladstone's office was huge, and I was surprised that Art's office was much smaller. It was much more laid back too, and much more my style. Art was a nice man, but I was very nervous. I knew I was going to have to explain to him that I had another nose surgery scheduled and wouldn't be able to start work until after that recovery. First, I had to make him believe I could do a good job for him.

He was impressed with the fact that I was graduating from Western from the Business Program. He asked me questions about myself and I tried to be vague because I didn't want to give him too much information about my dysfunctional life. He asked me how much money I wanted, and I proudly stated, "$140 - $170 a week."

He said, "I could start you at $140, but I have more interviews, so I'll have to get back to you." He asked for my phone number, and then, I told him about the surgery. He told me he would be deciding at the end of the following week. I told him I would still be in the hospital. We decided that I would call him to get his response rather than him trying to catch me between nurses and doctors coming in and out of my room.

What I would learn many years later is that Art knew from the sadly made yellow skirt that I wore that day that I really needed that job and a chance at a better life. His decision was made, but he wanted to be sure. That following Friday, after my second nose surgery, I called Art and learned that I had a job!

CHAPTER 49

5 Light Street

I was officially "That Girl!"

Every day I got on the bus first thing in the morning, walked a few blocks and stepped into our little office building. The small lobby had one small area with a reception desk. 2 small rickety elevators struggled to make it to the 5th floor. This building had 11 or 12 floors, so I was glad I was able to get to our floor so quickly.

Art was a great boss! He had a lot of appreciation for everything I did. I was very organized, and I never left things undone. He did mostly guardianship work and he had to teach me everything, but I was a quick learner.

He taught me how to use an index system, how to pay the clients' bills, the daily procedures with the court and other attorneys, etc. It was just the two of us, sharing space with another attorney and his secretary, who was an older woman named Anne. Anne and I shared the reception area and we got along great, even though there was such a huge age difference.

As the "honeymoon period" passed in my working relationship with Art, we became friends. We laughed a lot and enjoyed each other's personalities. Sometimes I would go to work and just not feel like working. When he came in, I would tell him, and he would let me sit in the client chair in his office and help him straighten up or just listen to him make calls so I could learn how to handle those things for him. I was always very neat and clean. It was something my stepmother Debbie had beat into me.

One day I carried a pile of client folders into Art's office and couldn't find a place to put them. Everything was a mess in there. He insisted that he knew where everything was, and it was not a mess. I challenged him and pointed to current piles quizzing him about what was there. After a few shots, he started to get annoyed. I didn't want to make him angry, so I just said, "I'm going to straighten up just so I can find a place to put these files, ok?"

He said, "Fine, but don't move anything!" There was a table to the right of his desk that I could see the possibility of straightening for space for these folders, so I headed that way. He immediately reminded me NOT to move anything! I told him I was just straightening; I was not moving anything! He then said, "Don't move that pile at all! I just put that there!" It was too late though. I had already lifted the folders as we both looked over and saw a rotten banana behind the pile! Obviously, he hadn't JUST put that pile there! I cannot explain to you just how hard we both laughed, but I will tell you we BOTH had tears running down our faces!

To this day, this is one of my favorite memories of my first real job!

There were so many more memories over those few years, and I cherish them all. Like, I said, it was a great "first" job. I realized pretty quickly that I was outrageously underpaid. I had no one to blame but myself. I told him how much I wanted to make based on that newspaper ad. He was just being as frugal as he possibly could get away with.

Two years later, I found a new job working for an accounting firm. I chose a salary demand that was just a bit higher than the one Art had refused, and they agreed without question. I now had to learn a whole new business.

CHAPTER 50

Divorce Number One

Within the first year of marriage, Jimmy S. and I bought our first home together. It was a sweet townhouse near Mom and Dad. Because of the car accident I had been in, I received a settlement from the insurance company. We both had good jobs and my settlement helped with closing costs and setting up our new home. It was very exciting to be a 19-year-old homeowner.

We had lived with his parents after getting married and stayed there until we were able to move into our new home. I adored his mom and Uncle Lew and I loved living with them. Even though I was excited about our new home, I hated moving out.

Once we moved, things weren't the same between Jimmy S. and me. We argued and bickered over everything. One night we had plans to visit my friends to watch their wedding video. He was being an ass and said "we" weren't going. Well, I was going with or without him. That didn't sit well with his controlling nature, but I was standing up for myself. I went...alone.

When I came back later that night, Jimmy S. was gone and so were his clothes and our dog. Our phone wouldn't work for some reason and to this day I believe he cut our phone lines. I was crying because I never saw this coming. It was close to midnight and I walked the neighborhood trying to find a pay phone. When I found one, I knew not to call his mom that late, so I called his sister. She said he wasn't there. I knew he was.

I hung up and walked a few more blocks. I was still crying when I knocked on Rose's door. She was married at this point and had a baby girl. I stayed there that night, but I didn't sleep.

I went home the next day to find Jimmy S. back with his clothes and our dog. I had so many questions, but he didn't want to talk about it yet. He just wanted to teach me a lesson. A lesson? I had a lesson for him. I went back to Rose's place and filed for divorce.

CHAPTER 51

1987

All I ever wanted was to be married, have babies, love them, raise them and be everything in the world to them. It was December of 1987. I was more than 2 weeks past my delivery date with my first child. I had just turned 24 and Joe, my 2nd husband was 31. I had married my first husband when I was 19 and that lasted just over one year. Nothing traumatic, it just wasn't meant to be. I learned quickly that I was in love with his family and not with him. But with Joe, this was real! He was beautiful, charming, he loved me, and I loved him. Finally, I would have a real family of my own. We would live happily ever after, right?

Our life together was so much more than I ever expected for myself. We sold his home, and we were having a home of our own built in a new development. While the house was being built, we lived with his parents. It was challenging to me as a new wife and expectant first-time mother, to live with his family because once again, I didn't feel like I belonged. It was temporary though and after just a few months, I would be in a brand-new home and it was the home of my dreams.

5 months later, at 8 months pregnant, we were moving into our new home. I would never have to move again! I could finally have a solid footing and a real home that no one could take from me. I felt like I was in heaven.

On December 3rd, Ryan was born. When I laid eyes on my newborn son, I saw true love for the very first time. Nothing could ever prepare me for this. My entire world changed that day and I was filled with love like I had never known. Ryan would prove to be my greatest gift. He would also prove to be my greatest challenge. I would learn that a mother's love will be tested to limits beyond your grasp and then rewarded to the pinnacle of emotion and back again, and again, and again. Just like me, just like his Dad, Ryan had his own personality, his own strengths, his own struggles, his own perceptions and a heart and capacity for love like no one I had ever met.

Childbirth was tough for me. I've always been petite, and this baby was not particularly large, but one I couldn't deliver on my own. After being induced and spending 12 hours in labor, the baby's heart rate was dropping. They put me in a birthing chair to get gravity to help. I was sitting in a big hard plastic chair with a big empty space in the bottom. The doctor pulled his little rolling chair between my legs while the chair lifted me up so he could catch the baby after I pushed him out. Did I mention that I was completely naked at this point? Yeah. The anesthesiologist was behind me, my husband was there, nurses were there, and everyone's focus was on my whoooha!

When that didn't work and the baby's heart rate was dropping farther, it was time for an emergency c-section. I was not happy. To top it off, I had to be moved to another room for the procedure and the baby had already crowned so I couldn't walk on my own. With the anesthesiologist holding me on one side (in a sitting position with my legs spread) by my back and leg with the doctor on the other side doing the same, a nurse opened the door to take me to the next room (again, while I'm completely naked with my legs spread) and as the door opened, there stood my father-in-law! My panic over the situation was then combined with the ultimate humiliation of what was just exposed, and I burst into tears! We never spoke of this!

In the end, of course, it was all worth it. After a smiley faced cut in my abdomen, the most beautiful baby I ever saw emerged from my body and my whole world changed. The most amazing miracle of life was undoubtedly the happiest day of my life. Every woman should be able to experience this complete joy. I can't imagine how this joy could be tainted, unless your baby is doomed to have an absentee father, like Tessie had to deal with.

CHAPTER 52

1990

Joe had been married previously, just as I had been. His marriage lasted a bit longer than mine and they had a child together. Kristen was just 3 years old when I met her, and she was gorgeous. Joe and I had met on my 21st birthday at a nightclub, but we had known each other from our jobs—mine as a legal secretary and his as the UPS man.

We had flirted but didn't even know each other's names until we ran into each other that night. I fell hard and quick! I was happy to hear that he was such a great dad to Kristen, and I didn't want to interfere with that relationship. I was so afraid I would become one of the many faces of women that would come in and out of her life, like I had grown up with. I avoided spending time with him when he had visitation with her, and he eventually called me out on it. I took the leap and fell totally in love with her too!

When we moved in together, she was like my living Barbie doll when she spent the weekends with us. I loved buying her the cutest little clothes and dressing her up and fixing her beautiful long blonde hair! I would dress us alike sometimes too. She was 5 years old when we had Ryan and 2 ½ years later, we added another baby boy to the family.

I had to convince Joe to have another baby. He already had a boy and a girl, but I wanted another baby. Our marriage wasn't very strong at that point, but like Tessie, I thought a baby would help fix it. In all honesty, even if it didn't fix it, I wanted 2 children from the same father. I always dreamed of having 2 children that would be close in age, grow up together and who had the same parents.

Cameron was the easiest baby ever; from the day he was born. No delivery drama, they just skipped the whole labor thing and just cut me open without any issues. I even got to choose which day he would be born on—within a reasonable time frame, of course. His due date was September 25th.

That COULD NOT happen.

That date happened to be Paul's birthday and I would not let my child share that monster's birthday, if I could help it. The doctor agreed to do the c section on September 18th instead. I was thrilled.

Cameron was a sleeper! He never cried or fussed, he just ate and slept. Ryan was such a busy two-year-old that I was very grateful, yet amazed. Ryan was a sweet big brother, and he was always so protective of me. He wanted to help me with everything, including taking care of the new baby. Of course, as they grew, their relationship would morph into many different types of relationships—both good and bad. It wasn't completely as I had hoped for them, but these two would be my lessons in accepting what I can control and what I can't.

After Cameron was born, I had to back to my full-time legal secretary job. It was so difficult. First there was the day care situation. When Ryan was born, daycare was an easy choice. The woman who had taken me into her home when I was a 15-year-old runaway, Bearl, was thrilled to have a baby in her home each day, helping me to raise him, while I went to work. I dropped him off each morning on my way to work and picked him up each evening on my way home. Meanwhile, I got to see her daily and I loved her so much. I enjoyed sharing as much time with her and her husband, Bob, as I could.

When Ryan turned 2, I wanted him to have more interaction with other children. I found a daycare home with a lady highly recommended who could provide the social and educational skills I wanted for him. Right about that time, Bearl was diagnosed with cancer and she would go through hell and back for the next 3 years.

Being the over-protective parent that I was, I met with the new daycare mom and I amended her contract that stated that she was not, under any circumstances, to put my son in a car without previous permission from me. I had been in a couple of car accidents and I knew that I would never be able to forgive anyone who had caused my child harm.

Everything went great until I was almost due to deliver Cameron. I arrived to pick up Ryan from daycare one day and all the children were in the backyard playing. The daycare mom and one of her friends were sitting at the picnic table supervising the playtime. As we chatted and while I gathered Ryan's things, the friend shared with me that they had taken all the children to get ice cream. I turned to the daycare mom and asked why I wasn't called. She said it was no big deal. I asked how she got all those car seats into the car. She responded that it was such a short drive, they just used seatbelts. Ryan never went back to that daycare again.

After Cameron was born and when I went back to work, I needed daycare from someone I trusted to take care of both of my boys. Bearl couldn't do it because her cancer treatments were all consuming. I tried a home daycare in my neighborhood for a few weeks, until Ryan advised me that the daycare mom left Cameron alone sleeping in a playpen while she left to pick up the other kids from school. They never went back there again.

I was sharing this information one day with Darlene, Paul's 5th and latest wife. She offered to step in. Darlene was a nice woman and she was full of love for my boys. She wasn't educated and she smoked cigarettes constantly. After talking to Joe, we decided to make her an offer that would require specific demands from her. It would also require me to somehow address my history with Paul by confronting him for the first time in my life. I chose to do that confrontation in the form of a very long letter, wherein I explained that this offer was for Darlene alone and he was not permitted in our home without our presence. I told him that while I had never addressed my childhood with him, I had never forgotten a thing, and I refused to allow him access to my children so he could never hurt them the way he had hurt me. I had never pressed charges, but I would put him through hell if he even considered harming my boys. There was no response requested and there was never another mention of it again – until our final encounter in years to come.

CHAPTER 53

Chasing the Money

I spent just 3 months with the accounting firm. There was a personality clash between the office manager and me. We agreed on only one thing; our extreme dislike for each other.

She would find some way to dig at me every chance she had. Oddly, I had become quite confident in my work and my work ethic. Her issues had nothing to do with my work, so I dismissed her attitude. Of course, that didn't help matters at all. Finally, we had a huge blow-out argument where I screamed that I quit and ran into the ladies' room to compose myself. She followed me and insisted that I couldn't quit because she was firing me! This chic was a total "right-fighter!"

We were in each other's faces and I wanted so badly to just punch her in the face! Deep down I knew that I couldn't make a fist and even if I managed to make one, I was gonna get my ass beat. I decided against physical violence and instead used my "city girl foul mouth" to frighten her. I think we were both scared and irate at the same time. I left that day and never looked back!

My next job was at another law firm. This was a personal injury/bankruptcy firm. It had 4 attorneys, a law clerk, and 1 other secretary. Our firm was in the Belvedere Hotel and it was quite nice. It was there that I met Debbie S. She was the other secretary and quickly became another BFF! Since we were both young, I was 20 and she was 23, and since we were both broke, we often went upstairs to the 13th floor of the hotel and had free happy hour food for dinner on Friday evenings.

We would take turns loading our plates from the buffet in the hopes that we weren't spotted and kicked out. Jimmy S. and I had just ended our marriage and Debbie and I began hanging out together nearly every weekend.

It was at this job that both Debbie and I noticed our hot UPS man! We both flirted with him and he flirted right back. We didn't know his name, but we waited for him every day.

Debbie stopped flirting after I ran into him at the club and started dating him. It was Joe, the father of my future children.

A couple of years later, when my annual raise was ignored, it was time to move on again. My next job was with a very large firm with lots of attorneys and lots of staff. My job was working for the managing partner with corporate law. I had lots more to learn. It was at this job that I finally got to use the shorthand I had learned in high school. I enjoyed working with my boss, Sandy, but the monotonous nature of corporate law would not last for long.

Joe and I were married while I worked there, and Ryan was born during that time too. After Ryan was born, I cut back to 4 days a week at work to try to balance life better. It turned out that I needed extra income even more than I needed more time.

Onto the next.

I began working at a medium sized law firm—this time specializing in insurance defense. I now had to learn the opposite side of the law from personal injury. At this job, again, I worked for the managing partner. I loved my job there and I adored my boss. Len was a super caring, super involved boss and he took me under his wing as if I was one of his children, even though I don't believe he was old enough. He was a great man and he helped my confidence grow in leaps and bounds.

One day I announced that I was pregnant with our second child. Len wasn't happy about it. He knew too much about my home life and thought I was making a mistake. I wasn't. This was all planned by me. One way or the other, I would be thrilled to welcome another baby in my life, whether my marriage worked or not. I was afraid for Ryan to be an only child. I wanted him to have someone he completely belonged to. You can only understand that philosophy if you were a lonely single child. My job was to create a wonderful life for my children, and I was willing to do whatever I had to.

Len was very intuitive also. I always thought I did a good job of hiding my issues, but he could see through it. Every time he noticed something, he would call me into his office, sit me down and talk through it with me. There were many issues at home, but I loved my husband and I thought that we could work through anything. Of course, that turned out to be untrue. With Len's support and direction, I eventually went to the courthouse to file for an ex parte order against Joe.

Our firm had recently broken away from the mid-sized firm we had been part of and now we were a bit smaller and new people were joining us. One of Len's new partners was Ron. When it came time for me to go to court to extend the ex parte, Len was busy, so he had Ron take me to court. I barely knew Ron at this point, and I was super uncomfortable that he would now know about this ugly part of my life. Ron was very sweet and very helpful. He knew I didn't want to get Joe into trouble, but I needed him to acknowledge that his behaviors were not acceptable. At that hearing, he was ordered to start therapy and it was suggested that I go to therapy on my own as well. We both did and our separation went on for a couple of months.

I moved out of the house with the boys and we moved into Paul's house with his new wife, Darlene. It was very cramped with us there and I'm sure it was quite an imposition. The boys and I lived in 1 small bedroom, we got up early each day for me to drive them back to our neighborhood to go to daycare and then I had to backtrack to get to work. It was a lot and I was exhausted and on top of that, flashbacks galore.

It was not a healthy environment for me. It wasn't healthy for the boys either as they had to watch brutal fights between Paul and Craig and Billy, and finally, the roaches. I opened the silverware drawer one morning to make breakfast for the boys and roaches were climbing all over the silverware! I screamed and jumped! Darlene disgustedly got up from her chair, grabbed a spoon, put it under running water and abruptly held it out to me. She said, "Stop being a baby. It's no big deal." Oh, but it was! I swore my children wouldn't live this way!

On a side note, Ron and I had become dangerously close. He was there at work each morning when I arrived, and he was more than happy to hug me each day. One morning as he approached me, I put up my hand and said, "Please don't." He stopped and I explained that I was under so much stress and my silly self was growing to like his hugs too much. He giggled and came in for one anyway. That hug ended with a kiss. That kiss led to an illicit relationship. I was separated, but my husband wanted me back. I didn't believe I could trust him, so I didn't know if I would ever take him back. Ron was a married man, and I knew his 2 young daughters. This was wrong on every level. Ron and I discussed it many times, but he had a power over me that I couldn't resist. It was dangerously fun at first, but then it got scary. I didn't want to lose my job and based on all the soap operas I had ever watched; this type of thing always comes out.

Joe was still calling every day and making promises I knew he couldn't keep. Finally, I made a decision. I ended things with Ron and moved the boys and I back to our home. We would give it another try.

Back at work, Ron wasn't happy to have been dumped. He came out to my desk and put his credit card in front of me and then returned to his office. That had previously been my clue to make a hotel reservation. I picked up the card, went into his office and said, "No" as I put the card on his desk. I went back to my desk. It was now war. He picked and picked and picked at me. He was constantly questioning my work and assuming I was on personal calls. Being the person I am, I get personal with regular clients and other attorneys. I would have to hand him the phone to prove it wasn't my family or friends. The stress was worse than ever, and I wasn't convinced that I had done the right thing, but this was not going to continue. Everything and everyone were getting on my nerves and I blew up one afternoon and quit!

After I left the firm, Ron told Debbie A. that I was trash talking about her to him and sharing her secrets. She called me and blew her mind! I tried to calm her down to explain what happened. She didn't want to hear it. This led to us not speaking for two years.

The next job was with a one-man law firm specializing in taxicab defense. This would be an easy transition. I stepped in and made it mine right away. It was the best job. I took on the title of "paralegal" as I met with clients, prepared petitions and other pleadings, worked with attorneys and did all the filings. Morty was a sweet older man who let me run with it.

3 months later, my left arm died as I typed, and my career was over. I was devastated. After I trained another employee to take over for me, Morty called me into his office to tell me what a pleasure I was to work with and suggested I get into sales. Sales? I didn't know the first thing about sales, except for watching Joe struggle with his many sales jobs over

the years. I thanked him for his help and told him I would figure out something.

As I walked out that door on that day, I just knew that life as I had known it was over. I was still miserable in my marriage, Joe didn't make enough money on his own to take care of us, and now I was damaged goods and couldn't help. I was completely despondent and sunk into another depression. It was the first deep depression since the boys were born and I knew that my thoughts of the bridge were not an option. I didn't think of asking God for help because I didn't believe strongly anymore. I believed this had to come from me. I had some serious work to do.

CHAPTER 54

1992

This would be a year to change nearly everything in my life. The fairy tale had been short lived. My marriage was simply miserable, and I was trapped. Joe and I had split up and gotten back together, but the wounds would never heal. Daily life was a chore and stress were the only thing we had in common. One day in late July, while I was at work at a law firm, typing a legal document, my left arm dropped. It just fell from the keyboard and wouldn't move. I couldn't lift it, I couldn't move it, and I couldn't even move my fingers. I was frantic!

I ran into my boss' office and tried my best to not be hysterical. As he tried to manipulate my arm and fingers and everything was completely numb, my mind was racing for answers. This must be the Muscular Dystrophy that I had been diagnosed with at 18. It was finally taking hold of me. I knew I would have to go back to Johns Hopkins Hospital to see the neurologists again. That was the only answer I could come up with.

As if things weren't already bad enough...now this? My boss was at a loss and told me to go home, call the doctor and keep him posted. I had such a huge workload and felt so guilty for having to bail on him like that. He was truly a sweet soul and assured me that they would work things out and he would be waiting for me to come back as soon as possible.

Calling the doctor at Hopkins was something I never wanted to do again. I had gone to them in 1982 when I found out that my mother's family had a disease called Charcot-Marie-Tooth, which fell into the category of Muscular Dystrophy illnesses. I had to be tested at that time to see if I carried it too. Of course, I did. I learned during that first appointment that I had it and that my future children would have a 50/50 chance of having it as well. They had to do nerve conduction tests on me to see the severity of the nerve damage. Nerve conduction tests are basically where they put electrodes on parts of your body and run electricity through you.

They turn up the electricity until they get a reaction from the part of your body that they are testing. For me and this disease, that would include my elbows to my fingers and my knees to my toes. This was the most horrible, painful, brutal test I could have ever imagined. And it went on for what seemed like hours of torture. In the end, I was told that I did in fact, have it, that I would carry it on to my children, and that there was no telling how bad it would get or what my prognosis would be. Nice, right? I went home and felt that was a wasted exercise in torture and that I was fine. I would never do that test again!

But God laughs when we think we have control. When I went back to Hopkins this time, 10 years after that first visit, I learned that I was putting too much stress on my body and that I would no longer be able to do my job; the only thing I knew how to do. I was told that the numbness would end at some point and that I would regain the use of my arm, hand and fingers. The doctor said that this would happen again if I didn't follow his advice.

My faith in God was not very strong at that time in my life. I felt that I had learned throughout my life that the only person I could count on was me. I had to have the answers and

I had to control my destiny. I now had a miserable marriage, 2 children under the age of 5, a mortgage and bills that required my income along with Joe's, and my life was passing before my eyes. I couldn't handle it all. The only answer I could come up with was driving off the bridge on my way home. I had thoughts about that bridge often.

I was now a complete failure. We would lose everything, and it would be my fault. My children would live in poverty, despite everything I had tried to do. My marriage would end, we would lose our home and my children would suffer. I was despondent. I've never cried so hard in my life. I finally put on my soldier hat and went through the motions to make it as tolerable as possible until a new idea came along.

Meanwhile, Joe had been putting together a wooden swing set in our backyard for the kids. When I got home from the hospital, we sat and discussed it all. We had no answers. I had no disability insurance, so my boss laid me off so I could collect unemployment for a couple of months. It made me feel like a cheater, but I knew it was the only way to get by. I became a stay-at-home mom with my left arm in a sling and I managed to get by the best I could with one working arm, while raising the boys, making meals, and keeping our home clean.

I became a robot. I had no feelings, and I couldn't share my fears with anyone. I felt dead inside, and the bridge was still calling my name. The sling stayed on my arm for 3 months. The financial struggles were devastating. I was filled with resentment on top of everything else because my Mom had passed this on to me and wasn't there to help me through it. I now carried this disease and had to worry that my children would suffer with it too.

Deep depression took me over. I could no longer even tolerate my husband. My only source of energy was for my boys. I believed that as long as I was breathing, I would be the best mom I could. I would NOT bail on them the way my mom had bailed on me. I would NOT let them suffer because of my issues. I would protect them no matter what. I would make sure I broke the cycle of violence and despair so my children's childhoods would have zero resemblance to mine.

CHAPTER 55

August 1992

I was so used to working a full-time job and I was bored to death with the walls of my home closing in on me each day. I would get up each morning, make breakfast and Joe's lunch, get the kids together and walk Ryan to school. I'd then come home, figure out the cheapest way to make dinner, clean, do laundry, play with Cameron, and then head back to school to pick Ryan up. I was, for the first time, finally able to go on field trips and that made me very happy.

When the neighborhood kids came home from school, the boys would play in the court beside our home and I would sit on the curb with the neighbors watching them play. What a huge difference from my life of being a legal secretary in downtown Baltimore. I had gotten up to dress each day and when I walked around downtown, I would look up at the tall buildings and think I was like Marlo Thomas in "That Girl", another TV show that I grew up watching.

I had loved being a professional and living that life. I felt accomplished, I felt like I was good at something and I was proud. That life was gone and now I was sporting an arm in a sling and talking nonsense to neighbors while keeping the kids occupied.

One day after school, we decided it was such a beautiful day that we would spend some time on the new swing set Joe had put together. All the neighborhood kids were excited to join us, and they were having a blast! The swings and the fort at the top with the sliding board were overtaken by kids from the whole neighborhood. I was so happy to see my boys having so much fun!

Cameron wasn't yet 2 years old, so he couldn't play unattended. The stairs to the fort were pretty steep and challenging for his little legs. I taught him how to pull himself up one rung at a time while the other kids were playing. He was so cute. He eventually demanded that I step away and let him do it himself, so I did. I stood back and watched his feet hit each rung securely.

Our next-door neighbor's mom came outside and walked over to the fence to chat with me. Her grandkids were among the kids in our yard at the time. I continued watching Cameron as he climbed and then just as he reached the top of the steps, a piece of wood that I thought was secured at the very top of the fort came dislodged. Just as Cameron's little hand rested on the platform of the fort, the wood came down and chopped his finger off!

The screams from him, from the other children and me, had to be deafening. I went completely brain dead and had no idea what to do next! I grabbed Cameron with my one working arm—his finger dangling by a piece of skin and blood squirting all over us, and I ran out into the middle of our street screaming for someone to help me. As luck would have it, our neighbor across the street, Tom, had just come home from work. I ran to his door and pounded like a maniac! He came out, saw us and all the blood, grabbed Cameron from my arm and ran back into his house. I followed him as he put the finger in place, wrapped it tightly and then got Ryan, Cameron and me into his truck to rush us to the hospital.

I'll never forget trying to console Ryan as he cried thinking his little brother was going to die. We arrived at the emergency room and while I registered, Tom called Joe at his job to tell him what had happened. Joe was on his way. Tom waited with me until he got there. While I was registering, I learned that since I had lost my job just weeks before and had therefore also lost our health insurance, we were going to have to wait to be seen as an uninsured patient.

We sat in that waiting room for 5 long hours with Cameron screaming in pain. I was embarrassed and humiliated that we were in this situation and that this hospital treated us so badly. This baby was suffering because I had lost my job. I made a terrible scene as the clock ticked by and when we were finally seen and his little finger was sewn back on, we were told that it had been off for too long and probably wouldn't take. That was unacceptable!

The next morning, I was on the phone. From working with attorneys, I knew that Union Memorial Hospital in Baltimore City had a hand clinic. I called them and explained this whole situation. Cameron was seen within an hour, the bandages were removed, and the finger repair was redone and rewrapped. His finger survived! This amazing doctor who stepped in for us never even sent us a bill.

Lesson learned. Never give up! You just have to ask for what you need.

CHAPTER 56

September 1992

The miserable daily routine continued. My arm was still in a sling, but feeling was starting to come back. The problem was that the feeling was excruciating pain! I had shooting nerve pain from my elbow to my pinkie and ring finger. I had decided I would not go back to the doctor. I would just deal with it.

One afternoon as Cameron and I waited outside Ryan's kindergarten class for him to be dismissed, one of the moms, a woman named Laura, approached me. I had never spoken to any of them before, so I was surprised. She told me she was having a home party of some kind that night at her house and would love if I came. I knew where she lived because we would see her leave her house on our walks to school.

Her house wasn't like the rest of the cookie cutter homes in our community. It was different and I was always interested in seeing the inside. I told her I would check with my husband and would try to come. When Joe got home, I promised that if he let me go, I wouldn't spend more than $20 and that I really needed a night out. It was just around the corner. He agreed and I called a friend from one of my previous jobs so she would go with me.

I thought Laura told me that she was having a jewelry party. While she had a small bit of jewelry on display from one company, the party was a candle party. I never burned candles and I felt the urge to leave. I think I had become so used to not socializing that being there made me uncomfortable. I looked around at her beautiful home and was glad I got to see it, but I also noticed that only 1 other person was attending this party. I couldn't leave. That would just be rude. So, we stayed.

The consultant's name was Barbara. I was surprised that she had so much to say about candles. It wasn't just candles, it was accessories and home decorating ideas. I was watching with new eyes—eyes that were thinking outside the box. I liked this. Could I do this with just one working arm? She said she earned an average of $100 per party. I could do this at least until the end of the holidays to make money for Christmas for the boys. Then she started talking about earning a free trip to Hawaii. I had been to Hawaii before with my friend who was with me that night. This was very interesting. I paid attention to everything she said and everything she did with a focus on whether or not I could see myself in her shoes.

I could. At the end of the party, I went up to Barbara and told her I wanted to do what she did and asked her to sign me up. I fulfilled my promise to Joe and only bought 1 dozen votive candles, which cost me less than $15. But I had bought into so much more. My entire life was about to change for the better!

CHAPTER 57

January 1993

PartyLite is the name of the direct sales company that sells candles and became my vehicle for changing my life. My business started when I held a starter party of my own in late October 1992. I was told to schedule 6 parties within 2 weeks. I'm a rule follower so I did. I was determined to make the most of this venture and give my boys a fabulous Christmas! After working for lawyers for 10 years, I was suspicious of all the perks of this business and its no commitment policy. I planned to get what I could while I figured out my next plan for income.

Those first 6 parties were fun. I made money! This was pretty easy. The best part was that I was still a stay-at-home mom, but now I got to have a social life while I was getting paid! My goal was to make money for Christmas—which I certainly did, and then I was planning to quit. But I couldn't quit yet because I had 17 parties booked for January. So, I figured I would keep doing this until the parties stopped. In early January, my leader Barbara invited me to her home in Columbia, Maryland for a workshop/training. Her leader, Lynn from New Jersey, was planning to join us.

Lynn was magnetically passionate about this business. She explained the leadership and lineage structure to me and told me that she needed just one more leader so she could become a Regional Vice President. She told me that my numbers submitted proved that I was the best person for that job. This lit off all kinds of lightbulbs in my head. I hadn't felt that confidence about doing a great job since I lost my legal secretary job. Could this be my next adventure?

I hated working with women in offices because they were always complaining and making excuses. I didn't want to be out there recruiting new people and then having to be their leader. Lynn and Barbara laughed and explained that it's very different in this business and they would help me with everything. I felt honored to be asked to fill this position and I didn't want to let Lynn down. If I did this and she got her promotion, I could always quit afterwards. I agreed to give it a shot.

I went to New Jersey the very next weekend for a multi-regional kick-off and I was hooked. The Kool aid was now running through my veins!

From mid-January through March 31st, I had sponsored 7 new consultants in just 6 weeks! I was so enthusiastic that people couldn't tell me no. I put out the expectation that everyone started the same way I did; 6 parties in 2 weeks. On March 1st, I was a new Unit Leader of the Camry Accents unit. My unit was built to accent the lives of Cameron and Ryan! Lynn was the brand-new Regional Vice President of the Solid Gold region!

On top of that, I had officially earned 2 all-inclusive trips to Hawaii that I had heard about that first night at my friend Laura's house. And if that wasn't enough, I was recognized for being #1 in personal sponsoring for the entire company for sponsoring those 7 new consultants in 6 weeks.

I now knew for sure that this was my future and that all the bad things that had happened the year before were meant to bring me to this point. I would never be an employee of someone else again. I was a successful entrepreneur, and the sky was the limit. Boy did I have a lot to learn!

Joe and I went on the all-inclusive trip to Hawaii that I had earned, and it was incredible.

Joe was a huge hit too. He was such a flirt and all the girls loved him. He was also enough of a guy's guy that all the men loved him too. Everyone thought we were a great couple. We were good at hiding our issues from other people. We both played the roles we had to, and we enjoyed the trip. I knew there would be many more in my future, but I didn't realize this would be the last one with him.

CHAPTER 58

July 1993

My new business with PartyLite was going great. While I thought I would just promote to Unit Leader to help Lynn get promoted to Regional Vice President (RVP), I learned quickly that the position of Unit Leader (UL) would require me to continue sponsoring new consultants until I found the people that WANTED to grow. Out of my first 6, only 2 held on past the first couple of months and by July, I had sponsored 10 more.

My friend, Debbie S. had joined with me and the two of us decided to go to PartyLite's National Conference in July in Boston. It was so exciting to do a "business trip" for the first time in our lives. We joined the rest of Lynn's new region and we learned so much. We had a blast and we were energized by the time we left.

On the plane ride home, I told Debbie that I wanted to go for Regional Vice President too. To make the dream solid, I needed to choose a region name, but I wanted something different—something with flare—something that would stand out among the rest.

Debbie and I bounced ideas back and forth on the plane. Some ideas were hysterical, and some were just not a good fit.

Finally, I said I wanted something Italian because I believed all my life, I was Italian. I don't remember which of us came up with it, but when I heard the word "Bravissimo", which means "a job well done", that was it! I WOULD become the Regional Vice President of the Bravissimo region, and it would start now!

Once we got home, I shared the dream with our entire unit, and they were all on board. There were no other consultants in Maryland now because after I promoted to Unit Leader in March, my sponsor, Barbara quit PartyLite. We had a wide area to grow and I was determined to build the business to replace my legal secretary income. I loved the fact that I could stay home with my boys and still earn a good living. I was even more in love with the idea that I could eventually earn a 6-figure income with this company. That was a dream I never allowed myself to dream until now. I had learned throughout my life that if I want something, I couldn't wait for it to fall in my lap. I had to make it happen. I continued sponsoring and soon Debbie A. Joined too. She would prove to be another huge success. We were growing like wildfire.

My biggest issue was Joe. He worked in sales and he had zero respect for time and schedule. He would come home when it suited him, and I could not rely on him to be there when I needed to leave for a candle party or a candle meeting. Rather than argue about it repeatedly, I started interviewing neighborhood teenage girls and found Kristy, who lived just 2 doors away in the court beside our home. Kristy was still in school and she could come over to watch the kids until Joe finally got home. It was an extra expense, but it forced me to be more creative with my efforts in selling to make up for the expense. Kristy eventually became my assistant as well. After the boys went to bed, she would do paperwork or me. It was a win/win situation for both of us. Besides, she was the sweetest person and the boys loved her.

Everything was falling in place to make my dream come true.

CHAPTER 59

The Grave – 1993

Peggy Sue was the second person I sponsored into PartyLite. She was a natural choice to join me and she was excited to see if it could be as successful for her as it had been so far for me. We had moved on with our lives and didn't spend a lot of time together. She was in a relationship and had a beautiful daughter, to whom she gave my middle name. Peggy Sue still lived in the city and I now lived in East Baltimore County. While this doesn't sound far, people that live in the city just aren't comfortable leaving it. So, when Peggy agreed to start this business with me, I was out of this world stoked. I would get to spend time with her again.

God brings people into your life for a season, a reason or a lifetime. I believe this with all my heart. Peggy Sue is one of the rare people in my life who is a season, a reason AND a lifetime!

A phone call came in early spring of 1993. Peggy Sue was crying hysterically. Her ex-boyfriend, the father of her daughter, was dead. He had been found hanging in his mother's basement from an apparent suicide. I couldn't catch my breath. I didn't know what to do, but I knew I needed to do something. I listened as she cried, and I offered my help in any way. I knew there were things to do, but I had never buried anyone before so I couldn't be specific. His family had dumped the whole thing in her lap. After much talking and crying with her, I told her I would be there the next morning to spend the day with her doing whatever she needed to be done. There was no way I was going to let her do that alone.

We took his suit to the drycleaners, we went to the funeral home to make arrangements, we went to the florist to choose flowers and we went to the cemetery to choose his plot. That was something I never wanted to do. I had never been to a cemetery in my life and I had planned on continuing that path. I just didn't understand the need for people to deliver flowers to a patch of dirt and it made me cringe to think that while you're walking to a certain site, you are walking on top of other people. It totally creeped me out, but Peggy needed me, and I was not going to let her down.

She had chosen the cemetery that his mom was buried in. While we were in the office, she explained to the salesman that she wanted him near his mom. They had two spots that were available and asked if she wanted to see them. Of course, she did. I would now be walking on top of dead people.

It wasn't a quick choice. I couldn't imagine what she was feeling, and I certainly wasn't going to rush her. While I tried everything, I could not to vomit, I nervously struck up a conversation with the salesman while she made her decision. I told him that I had never been in a cemetery, to which he asked if I had never lost anyone. I said I had lost my mom at a young age, but I had no idea where she was buried. He asked me what her name was. While I thought that was a strange question, I figured cemetery people must be strange people. I told him her name and thought nothing of it.

Peggy finally made her choice and we went back into the office for her to complete the contract. While she filled it out, the salesman was busy with paperwork or so I thought.

When he found what he was looking for, he came over to me and handed me an index card ... with my mother's name on it. Of all the cemeteries between Baltimore City and Worcester, Massachusetts, I had somehow been led to the very cemetery she was buried in.

I was speechless and frozen. I looked over at Peggy and she was too. Emotions were flying all over the place. First of all, fear (I didn't want to do this EVER), anger (he's making this about me and I'm here for her), hate (what do I care? She left me when I was a baby), empathy (Peggy is now crying again), responsibility (what do I do now?) and then my mind stopped, and God spoke to me. Not a voice, nothing crazy, just a thought process that could not have come from within me.

I realized that I had spent the better part of the last 24 hours feeling so desperately sorry for this young man with a young daughter who was so unhappy in his life that he felt his only answer was to take his own life. And yet I had spent my entire 29 years hating my mother for doing the same thing. I felt the hate lift from me. I stared at the index card. She had just turned 21 when she died. She was nearly a child herself. I had hated her for a desperate decision. She did not deserve that hate.

The salesman asked me if I wanted to see the grave. I quickly and loudly said no. Both he and Peggy were surprised. I looked at Peggy for help and she could see that I was freaking out. She simply said, "Yes, we will." I nodded and waited, not knowing what would happen next.

After she completed the contract, we walked on the path between a couple of sections of gravestones. The salesman was carrying the index card and when we got to a specific section, he was counting headstones. It took him a minute of walking back and forth and I was confused as to why he was finding it difficult to locate her grave. While I continued standing on the path, he looked over at me and waved to me to join him. I was walking on dead people again. I was so distracted by that thought that when he pointed down, I thought I must have missed something. I was between 2 graves. I looked up at him and said, "Where?" He said you're right in front of it. There was no marker. There was no name plate. She was in an unmarked grave.

This made me so sad. It was as if she never existed. Dad, his family, her family from Massachusetts...no one? I stared at the patch of dirt and didn't know what I was supposed to be feeling. I didn't know her. I had no point of reference for feeling. I didn't love her; I didn't miss her. I didn't know anything about her, and she didn't know anything about me. It was so awkward. I felt like Peggy and the salesman were expecting me to say or do something and I had nothing. I finally said, "Hi. I didn't know you were here, and I just found you by accident. I don't know what to say right now, except that when I can afford it, I will put a marker on your grave. I've gotta go now." I walked away as Peggy and the salesman followed me.

CHAPTER 60

November 1993

It was my 30th birthday. Oddly, I had felt for many years that I wouldn't make it that far. My mom was 21 when she passed, and I figured I would die early too. There were times when the dark depression came over me. I wanted to go, but I knew I could never purposely leave my boys.

Joe had decided to make a big effort to celebrate my birthday; the grandest gesture during our time together, but it would prove to have been too late.

On the Friday before my birthday, his parents took the kids, and he took me to New York City to have a nice dinner. We then saw "Phantom of the Opera" on Broadway and spent the night at a nice hotel. It was awesome. I wanted so much to love him as I had before. That love was crushed by the lack of respect that had grown in me towards him. How can you have love without respect? I couldn't. I went through the motions and thanked him, but I felt nothing.

We drove home on Saturday evening, and when we arrived at the house, my friends Debbie S. and Peggy Sue had gathered friends and family to surprise me with a party in my own home. I knew I had left the house a mess when I left on

Friday and I was so embarrassed that they had to clean my home too, but they knew that meant I would be surprised. As the door opened, no one turned on the lights for a minute and all I heard was Ryan yell out "Happy Birthday Momma!" The lights then came on and it was an incredible gift! I had never had anything like this before!

Yet, I was empty.

When I woke up on Sunday, my actual birthday, I walked into the bathroom and looked at myself in the mirror. I had accomplished quite a bit in my life. Legal secretary for 10 years, 2 beautiful boys, had started my own business, was surrounded by friends that loved me, had overcome a bad episode with Muscular Dystrophy and had handled more than my share of traumatic situations in my 30 years. But at the center of it all was my marriage. I cried at my reflection as I realized that I could not grow old like this. I had to find a way out of this marriage.

CHAPTER 61

Bearl

When I ran away from home at the age of 16, I moved in with the family of a neighborhood friend. They were instrumental in changing my perspective of the world. They loved me like I was their own. Bearl and Bob (who wanted to be called Mom and Dad) had 2 girls at home, Rose and Crystal. For 2 years, they were my family.

Mom (Bearl) had gone in and out of hospitals a lot and it seemed that no one was able to help her. I wouldn't accept that. I was sure she would make it through. I was wrong.

At one point, she was in Johns Hopkins Hospital. I would stop there several days a week on my way home from work to visit her. As time went by, those visits were more and more disturbing. She was failing and she was suffering terribly. I brought the boys in to see her one evening and she was happy to see that Cameron was walking. She told me she had been worried because he was taking his good old time with it. Not very long after, I got the call that she was not going to make it through the night. I rushed to the hospital to be by her side. I wanted her to know how much I loved her and that I was there. It was the worst thing ever—to watch her struggle to breathe and gurgle to catch her breath.

Dad and their friends, Greg and Nancy, were there too. Rose and Crystal chose not to be there and didn't understand how I could watch this. I just felt like it was the right thing for me to do. Her breathing struggled more and more until finally, she took her last breath. We sobbed uncontrollably, while Dad held her lifeless body and cried. I was numb all over.

Joe put the boys in the car and came to get me because I could not drive. I tried to hold myself together as we drove home quietly so I wouldn't cause the boys to get upset. I tried to calmly explain that Nanny was now in heaven with God. Cameron was only a year old, so he didn't understand. Ryan was asking questions and I was trying to answer. He asked if he could see her. I told him she was now a star in the sky and when he looked up at the nighttime sky, he could send her his love. He cried a little, but not much.

When we pulled into the driveway and got them out of the car, Ryan stood there, looked up at the sky, and said, "Mommy, which one is she?" I told him she was the brightest star he could see. He found the brightest one and said, "I love you, Nanny.

Good night."

CHAPTER 62

Divorce Number Two - April 1994

After only 17 months since starting my own business, I had reached the second leadership level with PartyLite. I was booking, selling, and recruiting enough to get national recognition from the company and had placed in the top 3 for several categories. I was feeling like a Rockstar. The money was coming in. I was still able to be a stay-at-home mom for my boys. I had a sense of myself again, and I was the best mom I knew how to be.

One day, when Joe came home from work, he found me sitting at our desk with the calculator and bills. He asked me what I was doing. I told him I was making a budget.

He said, "We have a budget."

I said, “This one doesn’t include you. You can go now.”

He'd had enough too. He simply got up, went upstairs to pack his bags, and left.

It had come to that. As a reader, please understand that my children are my highest priority. They are my world.

When I decided to write this story, I chose to omit any information that could cause them pain and any information that could hurt relationships within the family. This part of my story will not come with details, and it will not be a he-said, she-said drama. Our marriage was magical until it wasn’t. I learned so much, and I believe he did too. We were the best parents we could be, and we still are. I had many more lessons to learn, and I wouldn't be who I am today had I not decided to marry him or to divorce him.

So…that was it.

I was now venturing into a new role—a single mother running a business. I learned within the first few months it might have been a good idea to wait another year. Finances were not what I had expected, divorce wasn't easy, and having my boys leave me to visit their dad so often was heart-breaking, especially on holidays.

I would think back to those days when I would hide in the TV shows. I believed that my life would mirror those shows one day. I would have a happy family in a beautiful home, and there would be no violence, and everyone would be happy. I knew that was childish thinking, but I also believed deep down that life shouldn't be that hard. Life should be pleasurable, not leaving you feeling miserable day after day. I should not think the boys would be better off if I wasn't there anymore—that was what my mother did, and I would never, ever do that to them.

I can tell you without hesitation that those boys kept me alive. My mother's choice kept me alive. I cried until I could cry no more, and then I decided that since I had made this decision, it was my responsibility to create the life I expected. It wasn't going to come to me; I had to go get it. I would learn that dark times would become part of my life, but I knew I was strong enough to conquer it.

My marriage to Joe taught me a lot about myself. I adored him, but in the end, I had lost respect for him. Respect is an enormous part of relationships. I can't respect the person, I can't be happy. He taught me what I liked about myself and what I didn't. One thing I learned is that I was too young and immature when I married him. I thought I was all grown, but in reality, I had no idea who I was. Instead of growing personally, I became whatever he wanted me to be…until I didn't. My biggest lesson was to appreciate our time together, appreciate the family we created and move on to find what was right for me. I had a lot more mistakes to make.

CHAPTER 63

What I Believe

I believe that everyone comes into your life for a season, a reason, or a lifetime. I believe life is about lessons and if we do not learn the lesson the first time, we are going to have the situation pop up again and again until we finally learn the lesson. My beliefs are as a result of my experiences and as a result of those that have affected my life. I am a Christian and The Lord is my Savior. I also believe in reincarnation. I believe that as a baby spirit, we know the lessons in our next life that we need to learn so we can move onto the next level. We choose our parents, and we choose the overall situations we will be going through. The goal is to do our very best in those situations and eventually, the final move will be to rejoice with the Lord for eternity. I believe that each lifetime is a form of purgatory and that's why life is not easy.

I have at times throughout my adult life gone to a spiritual advisor or psychic, not because I completely believe in what they say, but because of my own curiosity. I look at it not differently than reading my horoscope. How close can they be and is there a real science to it? Over the years several of those people have given me comfort and made me feel better about my life.

CHAPTER 64

Setting Goals

With PartyLite, I was trained on so many strategies for setting goals and I soaked it all in. Goals were really helpful for me. Having a destination would motivate me to get there. I learned that I really had a mind for business, and I had the dedication to my goals, especially when I could find a way to make it about my boys.

My first goal had been to narrow down our household to the 3 of us...done. But it could have been done better. Now we were broke. I was working as much as I could, but I had to pay babysitters in order to do my candle parties and attend my meetings, which were in New Jersey...2.5 hours each way.

Joe moved to the Eastern Shore and he was 1.5 hours away, so he couldn't babysit for me. I had no family, so it was all on me. All my bills were late, and I was beginning to panic. I couldn't possibly share this information with Joe because that would be admitting defeat. I booked more parties and double booked on the weekends the boys were with Joe. Having Kristy do my paperwork freed up my time to do money-making activities and it increased my productivity. I was hiding my car

3 blocks away, so it didn't get repossessed and I was begging the mortgage company to give me more chance.

Our neighbors started inviting us to meals at their houses or just brought meals to our door. I was embarrassed at first, but I accepted it. I put pressure on myself to learn as much as I could as fast as I could. I was reading self-help books and leadership books on a daily basis. I was determined to be a success for my children, and I was determined to give my children everything I never had.

CHAPTER 65

Church and Easter

My neighbors, Tom and Diane were making extra efforts to help us. They repeatedly encouraged me to attend church with them. I had a chip on my shoulder in that respect because the Catholic Church I belonged due had excommunicated me when I divorced Joe. The boys went to Sunday school there and I was a volunteer teaching assistant for second graders going through their First Holy Communion. The boys and I were there every week. They asked no questions and told me there were no exceptions. I was no longer welcome there.

After months of them inviting me and months of despair, I finally said yes. This was a non-denominational church and the church itself was part of an industrial business park. It had a rock band, and everyone dressed casually. I liked it! I never officially joined, and I never attended meetings or bible study classes. I just went when I wanted to. It was comfortable and it was helpful for a while.

Easter was approaching quickly, and I had to make sure the holiday was just as good for the boys as it had been when their dad was with us. I had plans to shop for their baskets and candy, but my plans got derailed. On Friday night, as usual, the boys and I were watching a Disney movie on TV. We had popcorn and candy just like in the movie theatres. Just as the movie was ending, I took one more handful of popcorn and put it in my mouth as I was cleaning up. Suddenly, I bit down, and half my tooth came out of my mouth! I was bleeding and it hurt like crazy! It was too late in the evening to get any help so I tried to sleep, knowing I would have to squeeze in a dentist appointment the next day.

Since I didn't have a regular dentist at that time, I had to make a bunch of phone calls. Finally, I found someone that could squeeze me in to remove the rest of that tooth. But now it was early afternoon and I had not been able to do the shopping. Easter was the very next morning. I couldn't find a babysitter and I would have to take the boys with me. It broke my heart as I realized what I had to do.

I took Ryan upstairs with me and we sat in his room while Cameron was watching the Cartoon Network. I didn't know how to say it or what words to use, so I stuttered a lot. Finally, I told him I needed him to help me with Cameron while I was at the dentist, and then I needed him to stay in the car with Cameron while I ran into the dollar store for a bit. This was a big no-no, and he knew it. He asked me why I would leave them in the car alone when that was against the law. He was 6. I told him there was no other way I could get this done. He wanted to know why they couldn't come in with me. This was getting harder. I sat quietly for a moment and then I told him I had a big secret that I needed him to keep from his brother. I told him that I was really the Easter Bunny. His little face showed shock as he said, "You go around and give all the little kids their Easter baskets?" I burst out laughing and held him tight. I said, "No, I just get them for you and your brother." I could still tell he was unsure of what this meant as he walked toward the door nodding. Then he turned and said to me, "Oh wait! Is there really a Santa Claus?" I simply said, "We'll discuss that at another time!"

They were amazing both at the dentist's office and while I shopped at the dollar store. I made the trip as quickly as I could, and Ryan never told his little brother the truth.

That was the first holiday I would have to split with Joe. It was awful to have to spend just the morning with them and then to give them up for the rest of the day. This would become a routine for each holiday and it never got easier.

CHAPTER 66

Freedom to Become a Better Me

I had asked for my freedom from Joe, and now I had to step up and make it all work. I had no mom to ask for advice, and all my friends were married. My PartyLite friends seemed to be afraid of me like divorce was contagious or something. I decided to take a good look at the life I had lived for 30 years and consider the strength I had inside me. I listened to the testimonials of successful PartyLite people and thought, "Why NOT me?" I had much to do, and it started with a plan. That plan would work best if I could get Kristy more involved with the kids and me.

Kristy was on board. Once a week, she would come over to see what my calendar was for the week. She brought her homework with her, and whenever I had to go out for work, she would take care of the boys and then help me with my office paperwork after they went to bed. When I got home, she only had to walk two houses over to go home. I leaned on her so much and was so grateful for all her help. We had an agreement that if a party canceled, she still got paid a portion of what she would have earned that night. It was only fair. We had a great relationship, and I am forever indebted to her.

I have to say that the most influential person in my life regarding my growth in both business and in life was Lynn Bardowski. She became my full-fledged leader when Barbara quit, and I was so blessed for my relationship with her. We became very close, and she was always, always there for me. I had never known a more appreciative person. It seemed that every time I did well in any aspect of the business, she was sending me a card or flowers or gifts. I had never known appreciation like this, but I was paying attention. I wanted to model this trait for the people that were on my team. It's been said that people don't care how much you know until they know how much you care. Lynn cared, and it made me want to do even better,

Lynn knew she could count on me. She knew that I would take any morsel of training or support and twist it a bit to suit my personality and make it work. We became an incredible team for nearly 30 years. I respected her as a person—her style, her grace, her presence, and her ability to just keep going. I respected her as a businesswoman because she taught me just about everything I know. Lynn was the most integral part of my success because she believed in me no matter what.

CHAPTER 67

Getting Social

Meanwhile, my social life needed some work. I didn't know where to start. A couple of my PartyLite friends invited me to see a band with them and I jumped at the chance. My first time there was strange. I was a mom and I felt like I didn't belong there. I knew I had to get out of my head and get on my feet instead. I loved to dance, and it had been so long. So, I danced and danced and danced. A night club named Rascals became my new hangout.

Every weekend the boys were with their dad, I could be found at Rascals...dancing! I wasn't the shy, quiet little girl anymore. I was fearless! I was empowered. I was told by a couple of guys there that I walked into the place like I owned it. I had my confidence back, bigger, and better than ever. I was proud to be making a presence instead of being a ghost.

One night while dancing with my friends, a guy with curly blonde hair and glasses told me he liked my look. That was my first compliment from a man since splitting with Joe just a month prior. He asked me to dance and I said yes. He was quite charming and very funny. He asked me out for the next night and I was speechless. My mind was spinning, and I didn't know how to respond. I forced myself to say yes and I was so excited to have my first date.

His name was Bruce.

He picked me up at my house the next evening and took me to a restaurant recommended to me by Debbie S. I had the impression that Bruce came from a much different background than I did. He seemed like a silver spoon guy with a playful attitude. I didn't think I was good enough, but I would fake it and see how the evening went. I didn't want to give him too much information about my situation for fear I would scare him away. I planned to keep quiet and enjoy the dinner and that was it.

We arrived at the restaurant and as we walked in, Bruce told the host that we would need a quiet space for a minute before we could be seated. That was odd. The host led us to a small sofa surrounded by trees and Bruce nervously told me (yes, HE was nervous) that he had something to tell me before we started our meal. He wanted me to know that if I chose to have him take me home instead of having dinner with him, he would take me home. I was completely confused. Had he already decided that I wasn't good enough and he was trying to find a way out? My face went blank and I just waited for him to tell me what he had to say.

He proceeded to explain to me that he had been arrested for being a BANKROBBER. He was awaiting his sentencing hearing. He had robbed 4 banks, had been arrested, sent to jail and his lawyer (who was also his father) convinced the judge to set the sentencing hearing for late summer. It was April as we chatted, so that gave him 4 months. He explained that he had robbed banks because of substance abuse issues. He had just gotten out of rehab.

How about that for a first date after being married and having 2 children? I would have thought he was pranking me, but I could see the stress and embarrassment on his face. He was waiting for me to respond. It felt like an hour went by as I drifted from pros to cons in my head while he waited. I took it all in. He seemed authentic. He's going to prison in 4 months. That means I can't fall in love with him. I didn't want to fall in love quickly. I could at least have dinner with him, right? I didn't have to take on his issues. I was just here to have fun. I stood up and simply said, "I'm hungry, aren't you?"

He was funny, sweet, hugely entertaining and I had a blast at dinner. There were no visible signs of danger and he didn't seem like a hardened criminal. Until we got back to my house and I realized that I had locked myself out. My bank robber date broke into my house for me. It was pretty easy as I had left the kitchen window unlocked.

Our relationship lasted just over 2 months. I nicknamed him, "Good Time Charlie" because he had so much to do before he was incarcerated. I learned that there's nothing like a man with limited time. Bruce and I went out every chance we had. He introduced me to sushi, blues music, and front-seat sex in a moving car on a highway. He was simply so much fun and oddly enough, he was just what I needed at that time.

After those 2 months, I knew I had to step aside. I didn't want to get too close and I didn't want him to expect me to wait for him. In truth, his lifestyle wouldn't work for me and I was doing him no favors by taking up the little bit of time he had left. We broke up on good terms and promised to be pen pals when he was gone. In that little bit of time, he opened me to a new world, and I was changed forever.

CHAPTER 68

Travel Bug

As a little girl obsessed with television, watching Elvis Presley movies that often took place on tropical islands to Brady Bunch episodes where the cool aunt would show up with great gifts from her travels for her grandchildren, I wanted to see the world. I never had a specific location that stood out; I just wanted to see as much of it as I possibly could.

Paul and Debbie only traveled to Atlantic City, NJ for gambling. As a family, we only traveled to campgrounds, the shore, and amusement parks. I never saw the beach until I was 18 years old when I went to Ocean City with Debbie A. and her friends. It was amazing to me and I wanted to see more!

When I married Jimmy S., my first husband, we went on a Caribbean cruise for our honeymoon. I saw Puerto Rico and the Bahamas. I wanted more. On our first anniversary, we went to Disney World in Florida. While we were there, he caught the travel bug too and we purchased a timeshare. When we got back, his mom and his Uncle Lew demanded we cancel it. They were right; we had no business making that purchase. We were living in their house rent-free, while we saved money to buy a home. We just got caught up in the excitement and then canceled within the 3-day decision period.

When I married Joe, our only travel was to Ocean City, where his parents had a mobile home. I didn't mind at all. It was still traveling to a beach.

When Ryan was a year and a half old, I was working at another law firm and I ate lunch each day with a lady named Kathy. Kathy was a quiet lady, and she was a bit eccentric. I enjoyed our chats over lunch, and we became friends.

One day she came to work and was clearly upset. Her father was missing. He was a furniture store payment collector, and he went to people's houses to collect their payments for renting furniture. He had gone to work the day before and had never come home. A day or so later, Kathy got the call that they had found her father's body. He was murdered at a home where he was collecting furniture payments and hidden in the basement of that home. I was so horrified for her. She was so close to her dad and she was broken.

Later that day, she got another call. When her mother was notified of her husband's brutal death, she had a heart attack and died too. This was insane! At the viewing, a lot of attendees were shocked to see both her parents in coffins side by side. Many had heard about her dad but didn't know about her mom until they got there.

It was truly horrific for the family.

When the estate was settled and each child was given a portion of the life insurance on both parents, Kathy decided that she could not bear the fact that Father's Day was coming up quickly. She wanted to use her inheritance to go to Hawaii and remember her parents from there. She shared her ideas with me at lunch and asked me if I would go with her. I told her I couldn't because I had my baby at home, and we had no money for that. She told me she planned to pay for my trip too because she did not want to go alone. I didn't want to turn her down for many reasons. Mostly, I didn't want her to go alone and I wanted to see Hawaii too.

I went home and discussed it with Joe. He said no. He hadn't seen Hawaii either and he wanted to be there when I saw it. No matter how much I tried, I couldn't get him to agree. I told him I may never have the chance to see Hawaii and I would never be able to go for free. He stood his ground.

I went to work the next day and told Kathy the bad news. She was very sad, and we tried to think of other people she could ask. She decided to ask another woman we worked with, Barbara. Barbara was all in. She was excited, and I was jealous, but I was happy for both of them. Their tickets were purchased, and they were chatting nearly every day about their plans. It would be a 10-day trip.

A week before their departure, Barbara had to cancel. Something had come up and she was unable to go. Kathy was distraught and begged me to talk to Joe again. So, I did. This time he said ok. It was such short notice, and she couldn't get her money back, so all she had to do was change the name on the tickets. I was elated and so grateful. Joe and his parents would figure out the details of taking care of Ryan while I was gone, and I would be forever indebted to his graciousness.

I went back to work the next day and was so excited to tell Kathy that I could go. As soon as she walked into the office, I was jumping up and down with the news. Kathy was happy to see me excited, but she had bad news for me. Barbara had changed her mind again. Ugh! So close yet so far. I understood and bowed out graciously. Later that afternoon, Kathy came to my desk and told me she had just purchased another ticket so both Barbara and I could go. I was going to Hawaii with 2 girlfriends from work!

The next week, the 3 of us boarded a plane and set off to spend 10 days on the beautiful beaches of Maui. This was an amazing trip, and I will never forget a single minute of it.

Thank you from the bottom of my heart, Kathy.

CHAPTER 69

PartyLite Trips, etc.

As luck would have it, I was destined to do a lot more traveling than I had ever thought possible. Starting a business with PartyLite meant lots of opportunities to travel and best of all for free. My worries about never being able to travel for free were nonsense.

The first trip I ever earned with PartyLite was to Hawaii again. Crazy, right? Then the little girl from South Baltimore became a traveling fool. Free trips to Puerto Rico, Bermuda, Bahamas, Aruba, Hawaii, Cancun, Cabo, Punta Cana, Jamaica, London, Switzerland, Paris, Quebec, not to mention traveling to other cities within the US for training events. Boston, Chicago, St. Louis, Houston, Minnesota, Florida, New Jersey, Las Vegas, and Reno. I did some traveling.

On all of the free trips, I earned a double trip so I could bring a friend for free. Joe went on the first trip with me, then my friend Lori, and then Laura was my trip buddy for years after Joe and I divorced.

Then came Nick...then Laura got booted because Nick was my date. Once the relationship with Nick was over, Laura was back! So many fabulous memories, so many beautiful beaches, amazing food, laughs, and fun! Who knew travel would become such a huge part of my life?

In addition to traveling with PartyLite, we had amazing parties together. Each year, I would rent a chalet in the mountains for a weekend. All of our current leaders would come up to the mountains where we would meet for lunch along the way, get to the chalet with food and drinks and games and we would hang out in our PJ's all weekend long just bonding. Sometimes we would take the pontoon boats out and spend a day on the water. Sometimes we would hike, shop, or play a murder mystery. What we always did was laugh, play games, eat, drink, and have an absolute blast.

This "Leader Retreat" idea started when our Leader Team grew so much, and I was noticing that clicks were beginning. I didn't want that. I thought this idea would help my leaders get to know each other better and therefore become a stronger team. It certainly worked and it became a stimulant for others to become leaders in time to be invited. It's one of the things I miss most about being a Senior Regional Vice President for PartyLite.

We also held a holiday party each year at my home. My friend, Jessi was usually the caterer, and everyone got dressed up and brought their significant others with them. We would have amazing food, Ryan would be the bartender serving drinks, the new product line for the next season would be in boxes for all of the leaders to open for the first time and it was a great time. It was especially great because we got to know the husbands of each of the leaders and therefore even more friendships grew outside of the business.

And then there were the Tacky Tourist Parties. This was a party I threw for everyone that had earned the trip each year. The theme was always the same; dress up as a tacky tourist. We would put out food meant to be tacky like corn dogs still in their wrappers that they needed to microwave themselves. Chips still in the bags, which were ripped open, tasty cakes still in the wrappers, and whatever else we could find. We always had 40's of beer wrapped in brown paper bags for the guys and I had boxed wine for the girls. We would decorate the house with cardboard palm trees and lots of streamers and balloons. And I spent lots of time preparing for games to keep everyone laughing.

We knew how to keep the "party" in PartyLite.

When I wasn't traveling with PartyLite, I often needed a getaway. Once for New Year's Eve, I planned a trip with Nick to Jamaica for the holiday. Later, I went to Jamaica again with Sid.

CHAPTER 70

Nicholas

So, who is this Nick, right?

While I dated Bruce, I was introduced to so many new people—all who lived on the opposite side of the Baltimore beltway. This was an affluent area, and the lifestyle was entirely foreign to me.

I really liked it.

One evening as Bruce and I were heading out, he called his friend Nicholas, who I had never met, and invited him to join us. I was feeling silly and snatched the phone from Bruce when I heard that Nicholas wasn't going to join us. It seemed to me that Bruce wanted him there, so I thought I would invite him and make him feel better about coming out. Just that brief invitation from my voice to his created something that would become an enormous part of my life.

A couple of weeks after Bruce and I ended our relationship, I was back at Rascals dancing with my friends. As I walked off the dance floor at one point during the evening, I heard someone call my name from behind me. I turned and didn't recognize anyone. Then I noticed Louis, another friend I had met there, and I said, "Hello!"

He said, "I didn't call your name."

Now I was confused because I didn't recognize anyone else around him. The guy beside him then said, "It was me". I'd never seen this guy before. He was handsome with curly dark hair and he exuded confidence as he toyed with me to figure out how he knew my name. It was Nicholas. For the next couple of hours, we sat at the club and talked. He was intense, to say the least. When I talked to him, he made eye contact and did not get distracted. He was very interested in details and completely enveloped in our conversation. This was something I had never experienced before. We talked and talked and talked. He was magnetic and mysterious, playful yet reserved, confident, and still self-conscious. He interested me, confused me, made me laugh, and made me want to learn more about him. I was putty in his hands and he knew it right away. This was the beginning of something very special.

CHAPTER 71

Still Trying to Be Good Enough

For the next year and a half after meeting Nicholas, I put myself through torture trying to get him to choose me. I was determined to prove to him that I was his best choice. I misread his intentions initially. He just wanted a friend. So, I pretended to want to be a friend too. I ran errands for him (at my insistence), and I spent endless hours on the phone with him. On more than one occasion, we talked on the phone throughout the entire night. He shared everything with me about his life, but I only let him in on parts of my life. If I was going to win him over, I couldn't tell him the ugly stuff.

While I obsessed over him, he obsessed over his on-again, off-again girlfriend, Dawn. There's that name again, but thankfully, not the Dawn from my childhood! Many of our conversations were about their relationship. I hid my tears on my side of the telephone so I could give him advice. I couldn't understand how he couldn't see that we would be perfect together. Why did he choose to continue the battles with her? Each time they broke up, I hinted at making myself available. He flirted and teased behind the safety of the phone until they got back together again. There was no better term than obsession on my part, even when after one of our late-night chats revealed that Dawn was pregnant with his child. My tearful devastation was so hard to hide. I'm almost sure he wasn't fooled. I finally believed that my feelings were completely one-sided, and I had been a ridiculous fool. There would soon be a baby, a symbol of the love he had for another woman. I was, once again, completely unworthy.

My heart was broken. It was no one's fault but mine. I remained his friend because one small piece of him was better than none at all. The pregnancy didn't stabilize their relationship, and when his daughter was born, they were as unstable as ever. I, however, had moved on. I had to. My efforts at being my very best self didn't work. I wouldn't be his choice. Not yet.

CHAPTER 72

Eddie

My married friends were always trying to fix me up. I didn't mind. They all seemed to think that being single was like an illness, and they had to cure me. I did long for someone to love me, but I didn't trust myself to choose the right person anymore. I was 32 years old with two failed marriages, two children, and an embarrassing amount of time spent chasing a man who didn't want me. It was time for me to let my friends help.

My friend Debbie A., who was my best friend since 10th grade, was still in contact with her high school boyfriend's best friend, Eddie. Eddie's mother was from Guatemala, and he was adorable and so much fun. I remembered him from the high school days, but I didn't think he would remember me. Debbie arranged for us to meet up, and sparks flew. He was familiar and safe, and I could let my guard down.

He made me laugh and feel beautiful. He moved in with me and the boys and helped us with everything from paying bills to childcare so I could work without having to pay a babysitter, to him coaching the boys on their soccer teams. My business was growing by leaps and bounds, and he loved being part of it all. The relationship was loving and fun…until it wasn't.

We ended on good terms. I still have so many fun memories, and I cherish the time we had together.

I learned from Eddie that I needed to have a place in my life for fun. I had gotten to the point where work was my first focus, after the boys, of course. Eddie brought levity to everything he touched. I just knew in the depths of my soul that my life was going to get bigger, and this relationship would not make it through the sacrifices I was going to have to make to reach the goals I had set for myself.

I needed more.

CHAPTER 73

Nicholas and PartyLite – 1996

Throughout my short relationship with Eddie, Nicholas remained my friend. He had a teenage daughter from a previous relationship and her name was Nichole. Whenever I had parties for the boys, Nichole was invited. Sometimes they would show up.

Nicholas and Dawn did not stay together after their daughter was born. But he still wasn't showing interest in me...at least not in a romantic way. Our friendship grew stronger and I went back to trying to win him over again.

Meanwhile, I was experiencing HUGE success with PartyLite. In just over three years, I had gone from a new consultant who wanted to make extra money for Christmas that year to Regional Vice President with hundreds of consultants in my downline. My dream of being an RVP was a reality, and my new region, "Bravissimo" was a hit! I had eight leaders on my team, and we worked like a well-oiled machine. We were unstoppable. I was working like crazy, and my income showed it. I was on target to earn a six-figure-income that year!

When you promote to Regional Vice President, the company wants you to have a big celebration. They send a staff big-shot to recognize your hard work and gift you with a $2,000 bonus check, a 2-carat diamond tennis bracelet, and a Barton & Reed jewelry box.

We did it up! My leaders worked secretly to host the celebration at a beautiful reception hall. I bought an amazing red dress and rented tuxes for the boys. I hired a live band to play at the event. I had dated the lead singer, so he gave me a discount. My central unit even paid for a limousine to drive us to the venue. I felt like royalty!

I was loved by these women for my energy and enthusiasm, my training, my consistency, being by their sides, and helping them reach for their dreams. I was a completely different person, now with all the drama behind me. I was outgoing and outrageous, the life of the party. I had high expectations of myself and others and took every opportunity to work and train and grow for both myself and for those that wanted it. I was a person with no gray areas. If you want it, do it and don't complain about it. I had a no-tolerance attitude and was extremely business-focused. I got comfortable with people either loving me or hating me. If they hated me, it was their loss. I had confidence like never before. I knew my stuff, and I felt like a million bucks!

But, before I could have the celebration, could I possibly convince Nicholas to be my date? Of course, I had to play down my expectations to make it doable for him. I convinced him it was just so I wasn't there alone. He agreed, but I had already learned that he was not always reliable.

This time, he was. When he walked into the venue, my heart skipped a beat. He did it. The celebration was amazing, and it was a night I'll never forget. I'll also never forget that my boys went home with a babysitter before it got too late, and Nicholas drove me home. He lay on the sofa when he got tired because it was too late to drive home. I lay next to him. All night I stayed there, and I woke up still holding him. My arms were numb, but I wouldn't move. I was cherishing this.

CHAPTER 74

Bermuda – 1997

My PartyLite business was going strong. I finished up 1996 with just over $100,000 in income. One day when Joe and Vickie came by to pick up the boys, I had left a paycheck on the kitchen table. Vickie noticed it and was shocked. She started asking me questions, and before long, she started the PartyLite business with me. I worked closely with her and helped her build her business to earn the trip to Bermuda in May of that year. She did it!

While I was happy that she and I were becoming friends, I was still struggling with my anger and disappointment with how my marriage ended and how quickly Joe moved on with her. I liked her for who she was, but I still had trouble being around him or even discussing him. I loved how good she was with my children, and I trusted her. I chose to focus on those qualities to maintain our relationship.

After all the efforts were finished and we both had earned the trip, I realized Joe was going to be in Bermuda too.

Ugh! My friendship with Nicholas was still just that, a friendship. I reached out and explained my situation, and he agreed to go to Bermuda with me. It was free after all. In the back of my mind, I thought that if I had him with me for a week with no distractions, I could win him over. The key was getting him on that plane. I was so nervous for months waiting for him to cancel, but he didn't.

We went to Bermuda, but it wasn't "beach weather." I didn't realize that Bermuda was just across from North Carolina and therefore had the same weather. No bathing suits in May. So, Nick rented a scooter, and we rode all over the island each day. I didn't feel any guilt for not hanging out with my people, but I should have. They earned the trip believing we would all hang out together. For me, I needed to stay clear of Joe, so I did.

There were two awards events, and at both events, I was called to stage as #1 in the country for personal sponsoring, unit sponsoring, and leadership development. Nicholas was blown away! He had no idea I had become such a superstar, and he was impressed. I felt like a star and floated on cloud 9. After the final banquet, I just wanted to lie down. That evening, our relationship took the next step. After three years, he was finally mine!

CHAPTER 75

Support from Church

Since Nick was half Jewish and half Greek, our conversations about faith left us both confused. He agreed to check out my church because, as he put it, he "Wanted to know how this Jesus guy was!"

This was the first time I had ever brought a man to my church. I introduced him to a few of the friends I had there, and he shared his reason for being there. They were very nice to him, and they found him to be charming. When the services were over, my friends came over to borrow me for a moment. As Nick waited on one side of the room, they circled me in prayer. The prayer was for Jesus to save my soul and release me from this heathen that I was dating.

I just shook my head and walked away from them. I took Nick's hand and never went back to that church again. It would take a miracle to get me into another church!

CHAPTER 76

Running Brook Court

The boys were in a great elementary school that was within walking distance from the home Joe & I had bought. I was really happy with the education they were getting. The middle school they were zoned for was not even remotely close to what I wanted for them. My choices were either Catholic school or move to an area with better schools. Since I was surrounded by memories of my marriage, and many of our neighbors had dismissed me after the divorce, I thought it might be fun to check out the options.

Nick and I spent weekends checking out different areas on his side of town. There was a school district in the Greenspring area that was the top school district in Baltimore County. This area was about 45 minutes from our current home, and it was a completely different scene. It was much more upscale and way out of my comfort zone. Nick had a home of his own in the neighboring area of Pikesville, so he knew his way around. Nick also hooked me up with a friend who was a mortgage broker. Based on my brand new 6 figure income, this mortgage broker pre-approved me for a house up to $450,000.

I was leaving a home valued at $90,000, so this was a huge difference. I talked to my accountant, and he said he would prefer me to stay within $300,000, but he also knew that all I needed was a good challenge and that I would make it work. That was very nice to hear. So, Nick and I started house shopping.

We found an amazing old home shaped like a castle in the Pikesville area. The house was more than 100 years old, and it was exquisite, with a turret and winding staircase to a kitchen with a back staircase to the second floor to the wallpaper that was the same as in the White House. I was so enamored by it! It was for sale at just under $400,000. We went back and visited several times, and we checked out every aspect of the home. My biggest worry was the age of the home and the fact that it still had the original furnace in the basement. Being a single mom meant that I would be the sole source of income and responsible for all home repairs. I was afraid of committing to it, so I decided to give myself some time to think it over. A couple of weeks went by, and we drove to look at it again. It was now under contract. I cried. I had to believe it happened because I was meant to find another home. I picked myself up, shook it off, and started looking again.

Nick was driving me through an area in Greenspring Valley, close to Cal Ripken, Jr's home, showing me all the beautiful homes in that area. I had shared with him that I liked the idea of building a new home so I wouldn't have the worries of taking care of an older home and fixing old stuff. On our way out of one of the beautiful developments, we noticed a "for sale" sign in a wooded area, and I thought that might be property for sale.

We drove into the court and up a long, twisting driveway to find one of the most beautiful homes I've ever seen. It was a cream-colored stucco home with a circular driveway out front, a sports court on one side, a 2.5 car garage on the other side, and a built-in swimming pool with a Jacuzzi attached in the back yard. The house was enormous. We laughed when we saw it, and I told him to keep driving. There was no way that the house was in my price range. Nick thought it might be fun to check out the inside, especially since they were holding an open house at that moment. Just for fun, I agreed to go inside.

When we walked in the front door, we walked into an enormous foyer with a dining room on the left and a formal living room on the right. The foyer was open to the second floor, where you could see a balcony area that led to the bedrooms and bathrooms. The stairs were in front of us. You had to go down the hall to the right to get to them. Once we got to the stairs, we noticed that the stairway was right in the center of the home and you could walk around them.

The family room was huge and simply amazing. It had floor to ceiling windows everywhere. There was a 2-story stacked stone fireplace in the corner, and the view with all the windows took my breath away. The property was enormous and ended in wooded areas all around the house. I could not believe my eyes. The kitchen was gigantic, and I loved every bit of it. We went upstairs and found two large bedrooms, one small bedroom with a balcony overlooking the pool area, and one massive master bedroom with a master bath that would fit the entire second floor of my current home.

There was a finished basement with a large mirrored gym in one half of it, and the other half had a walk-up stairway to the outside. My mouth must have been watering throughout our tour. I was speechless.

When we finished, I just wanted to run out the door, but the real estate agent asked me if I wanted to put in an offer. I was stuttering like a fool as I tried to explain that this house had to be way out of my range. She told me the house was listed at $700,000. After I gulped, I apologetically told her I was ONLY approved for $450,000. I was embarrassed to say that. She told me to put in a bid anyway. What could it hurt? I didn't want to insult the owners, so I kept saying, "No, no, no!" She insisted, so I did. I offered $450,000 on a $700,000 home, and I felt like a fool. I knew it would be dismissed, and no one knew who I was so my embarrassment would stay with the agent. Nick and I chuckled as we headed out the door to see other homes.

Each home had a story, and it was fun just hearing the stories. A couple of the homes were scary and one, in particular, looked like the owner had barricaded himself and didn't leave for decades. We saw more and more of what I didn't want. I realized that the home I loved had ruined me for the day. I needed a break and to clear that from my head before I could look any more.

The next day, I got a phone call from the owner of that beautiful home. He was not pleased with me. He had been the CEO of a bank in the area. He wanted to know why I would insult him with the offer I made. I explained how I didn't want to, and the agent insisted that I make an offer because she could see how much I loved it. I was apologetic and told him I meant no disrespect. He then asked me who I was and to which family I belonged. I told him I was nobody. I didn't have a family, and I was a single mom selling candles. He calmed down a bit, and I had an opportunity to tell him how much I loved his home, but I completely understood that it was not something I could afford. He was quiet for a moment and then told me that he and his wife would like to meet me. He asked me to come to the house the next day and chat with them.

I don't know what I was thinking when I agreed to it, except that maybe as a banker, he could give me some advice and help me find a home within my range. Regardless, I planned to be on my best behavior and visit that beautiful house just one more time.

When I arrived at the home, the owners were there waiting for me. They were very nice, and I was surprised at how comfortable I felt with them. We sat down, and they asked me all about myself and my family. They were so surprised that I had no family money, no college education, no husband, no alimony, no second income of any kind, 2 young sons, and yet I was trying to better the lives of my children by moving to this prestigious neighborhood. Somehow, I won them over. After a couple of hours of chatting and getting to know each other, the husband said to me, "$450,000?" with his face all scrunched up. I nodded my head gingerly and said, "That's all I can get."

After a minute of silence, he responded with, "$459,000?" I was elated and said, "OK!" and we shook hands!

Did I just do this? Did I just commit to $9K more than the $450,000 I was pre-approved for that I didn't believe I could afford anyway?

I did!

Without hesitation, I made that commitment at that moment, and both scared the crap out of myself and felt victorious that I was going to live in this big, beautiful home with my children. How in God's name was I going to make this work? I had developed faith in myself that I could make anything work if I believed enough. It had worked so far, and it must work again. The process began.

CHAPTER 77

Determination

Now that I had committed to my dream home, I had a lot of work to do. First, I had to sell my home. I called Joe and offered it to him at the cost of the mortgage only and no extra money to me. He always loved our home, and he was currently renting. He and Vickie jumped right on it. The agreement was that they would move in as soon as I moved out. I was thrilled because the boys would still have the home they were born in, and I was free to move on with my new life on Running Brook Court.

Lots of obstacles flew at me through this process. The largest of which was that since I was an independent contractor and did not get a W-2, I had to get my home loan with the no-documentation rules. Those rules required that I have 30% of the cost of the home at closing. That meant I needed to have $137,000 in cash when we got to settlement. I had only earned just over $100,000 for the entire year before this, but I was confident that I could do it.

I would work like a maniac and I would get it done. However, by the time we went to settlement, I was short by $50,000. I shared my dilemma with the sellers, and they offered to give me a no-interest loan of $20,000 for 3 months after I moved in. Nick then used his credit cards to come up with another $30,000 and it was done.

On the day before settlement, Nick and I rented a big truck and began loading it. Joe and Vickie had agreed to settle in the morning, and I would then go to settlement in the afternoon for my new home. Nick was going to be waiting with the truck so as soon as I had the keys; he would meet me at the new home. Meanwhile, Joe and Vickie had been packing as well and they were going to move in the next morning. It was a tight plan, but doable.

However, there was another obstacle to face. The settlement for my new home was scheduled for 4pm. By the time we got everything finalized, we learned that the bank had closed so I couldn't get the cashier's check that was required. My personal check was not acceptable. It would have to be a "dry" settlement and the sellers said no. I had so many things fall into my hands so easily throughout this process and I didn't know what to do. I couldn't move in yet and Joe and Vickie were waiting to move as well. We all kept our heads on. Nick and I slept on the floor at the old home that night and when I finished settlement the next morning, he brought over the first load of stuff to the new home. We were moving out, while Joe and Vickie were trying to move into the old place. There were a few glitches, but nothing earth shattering.

I was now a single mother with 2 beautiful boys and an amazing boyfriend that I had wanted for so long and we were living in this house that I could never have dreamed of. It was happening. All my dreams were coming true.

CHAPTER 78

Making the "House" our Home

Life on Running Brook Court was magical. I simply could not wrap my mind about how this had happened. While the house was quite under furnished, I wandered from room to room just taking it all in. My first plan was to paint everything. Since Joe had refused to let me paint the white walls in our home for so many years, I determined that there would not be a single white wall in this house. I was going to have fun with this.

My income was in full swing, and I nearly doubled my six-figure income in that next year. Nick had moved in, and we had decided that he would not have to pay any bills because he had loaned me the money to get in. Instead, I would keep paying his credit card bills, and between those payments and him living there, I would be reimbursing him. His oldest daughter, Nichole, lived with us too sometimes. She had her own room and the boys both had their own rooms.

To make the house look more furnished, Nick started bringing his things in from his other home. We had extremely different tastes and I wasn't really happy with the items he chose to bring. It was a lot of antiques and large art pieces. I put my foot down when it came to his African masks and taxicab art. I hated taxi cabs because it brought back childhood dramas and I hated masks of any kind. I think that was just my subconscious believing that evil lurks behind masks.

The boys settled in and made friends in the neighborhood. My friend Debbie S., who I had worked with at the law offices years prior, had become my new assistant and she was there at the house with me each day during the week. She was a huge part of my success. I did the money-making activities, and she did everything else and I mean everything. We had a really good thing going for a long time. I counted on her immensely.

As time went by, Nick and I began having troubles. We both suffered from depression. His would leave him listless and unable to function. There were times when I had to tie his shoes for him. Mine would leave me wanting to die. He was much better with my issues than I was with his. I decided that my depressions could only last 1-2 days MAX. That was it. I was not allowed to wallow in my crap for more than that. I had too much on my plate and couldn't afford it. Nick didn't have a limit, so I tried to give him limits. It didn't work. His funks were different than mine and he didn't have the demands I had. He was a hairdresser and sometimes his clients would come to the house, rather than make him drive to his shop. I didn't mind too much, as long as he cleaned up afterward.

CHAPTER 79

Ryan

Nichole went to Sudbrook Middle School. It was a magnet school with a great reputation. Both Ryan and Cameron would follow in her footsteps into that school.

Ryan's magnet was math and science, and I was of absolutely no help when it came to his homework. I never had to worry about Ryan's grades because he excelled at everything. He was athletic, he made friends easily and he kept very busy. I would say that he was more of a social butterfly than even me.

Ryan adored our home at Running Brook and was proud to show it off. He was always inviting friends over to ride the go-cart, play basketball, go swimming, or just hang out. I loved it! I loved that our home was always filled with laughter and that his friends enjoyed being there. I could never bring friends to my home as a child, so I was thrilled that he knew he could.

I always threw big birthday parties for them and I wanted all their friends to be there.

One of the best was when Ryan and his friends had a pizza party in the basement that ended in a huge food fight, with Cameron at the top of the stairs throwing oranges at everyone from a safe vantage point!

Another awesome memory was when Ryan turned 13. Since where we lived was a predominantly Jewish area, all of his friends were having Bat and Bar Mitzvahs. Ryan wanted one too and I decided why not? I rented a hall, hired a DJ, arranged the catering, and invited all of his friends. It was a fantastic 13th birthday party!

When Ryan went on to high school, he chose the local school, Owings Mills. I wish I had known more about that school before I agreed. We could have made a better choice.

He did great with his grades. He got a part-time job at 15 and was showing signs of responsibility. He bought a used car and with the help of my friend Jay, he modified it to be his dream car. Within the first week after passing his driver's test, he was hit by a drunk driver and the car was totaled. Fortunately, he was fine, but his spirit was crushed. My heart broke for him.

Meanwhile, there were issues coming to the surface, and I was in denial. A lot of kids experiment with alcohol, right?

CHAPTER 80

More on Nick

We developed this on-again, off-again relationship. There was no doubt that we loved each other. The doubt was whether or not we were compatible. I needed more from him in terms of compliments, commitment, and drive. He needed more from me in terms of respect. We weren't giving each other what we needed. But the love kept bringing us back together. There was never violence or anything horrible between us, but with each break-up, something would be broken and would never heal. Eventually, we were both too broken for each other.

We went on PartyLite trips together, he helped me with my regional meetings, and he stayed with the kids when I worked or traveled with PartyLite. He was a bit scattered at times, so I had to do a lot of reminding and checking in, but I knew his heart was in the right place. He loved my boys, and I loved his girls.

One day as I was preparing to leave for a party, he was taking a bit too long getting home. I couldn't leave until he got there because I never left the boys alone. When he arrived, I kissed him and ran out to the garage to get in my car and go. I had already loaded it and the garage door was already up. As I hooked my seatbelt, I turned and saw that he was on his knee right outside my open driver's side door. He held the most gorgeous diamond ring I had ever seen. Through his trembling tears, he asked me to marry him. Time stopped and I jumped out of the car to hug him as hard as I could. This was unreal but why now when I'm leaving for a party?

I knew why. He had it and he had to do it before he chickened out. We laughed and cried, and he put the ring on my finger. I then had to drive more than an hour to a party and try to stay focused instead of just staring at it like I wanted to.

The gorgeous ring didn't fix us though. Oh, how I wished it could. One day I realized that I was late getting my period. I couldn't be pregnant because I had my tubes tied right after Joe and I split up. A couple more days went by and still nothing. I was getting very scared at that point, so I took a pregnancy test. I was freaking pregnant! This was NOT my plan! I had my tubes tied for a reason and that reason was that I did not EVER want my children to feel like they were less. I believed if I had another child with Nick, they would be outsiders and I refused to let that happen. Nick already had 2 daughters and he was not financially sound. I was the breadwinner and I worked way too much to be pregnant. I had a big multi-regional training that coming weekend in Virginia, so I decided to not think about it until after that event was over.

I didn't tell anyone. I just focused. When I was alone, I cried. I would never ever abort a pregnancy, but how was I going to make it through this? There was no answer. As I did the closing speech for the weekend, I felt something in my belly. I finished my talk and ran to the ladies' room. I lost the baby right there. Now the tears were uncontrollable. Had I wished this on myself? Did my negative attitude cause this? I felt so guilty now and I was beating myself up. I cried all the way home and when I told Nick, he was so disappointed. It hurt me that I hurt him.

But at the same time, I was so relieved. I just had to forgive myself.

It wasn't much longer before our relationship ended. I don't remember exactly what happened, but I do remember that at one point after he moved out, he came into the house while I was in the bathtub, helped himself to some leftover spaghetti and meatballs, and brought his dish upstairs while he stood in the bathroom with me in the tub. I yelled at him to leave, so he tossed his bowl into the tub with me. I was now covered with meatballs. It wasn't funny then, but it is now.

Nicholas taught me so very much! Our intense talks over the years gave me so much introspection. He taught me that love isn't always given in the way you need it. Each person has a different love language. They give love a certain way and they want to receive love in a certain way. Our languages didn't work well together. I had become a super intense businesswoman in the years we were together and that often bled into my home life, unfortunately. We argued a lot and there was really no resolution. Our arguments were always the same. Our hearts always brought us back together, but I finally moved on. To this day, I love him, and I always will. I choose to remember our happy times and look back with gratefulness. I had wanted him so badly for so long and I gave it my best shot. I know he did too.

CHAPTER 81

Life Changer

Life on Running Brook Court without Nick and Nichole started to get comfortable, and everything was falling into place. I worked more, and my income kept growing. My region with PartyLite covered coast to coast, and I had more than 3,000 people in my lineage.

We had sprung new regions from ours. Cindy became a Regional Vice President, Debbie A. became a Senior Regional Vice President, she promoted out another region with Alissa, and Alissa promoted out another region with Tammy. There were more coming and more excited to grow, which was a fantastic time for us.

One day I got the call from Aunt Shirley telling me that my grandfather had passed away. It was Paul's Dad, and we all called him Daddy Paul. He had been failing for some time, so it wasn't a shock, but it was still sad. The last time I had seen him was at Paul's house on Thanksgiving a year before. Daddy Paul was upstairs in bed because he didn't feel well, so I went up to sit with him before leaving for the evening. He kept apologizing to me and telling me that he should have protected me. I didn't know what he knew, and I didn't want to get into it. I just needed to relieve him of the responsibility. I told him he did his best, and there was nothing more he could have done. Even though I knew there was. It was too late to discuss that, and I wanted his upcoming transition to be more comfortable for him.

I went to his funeral alone, and I tried to make my way around the family members to say hello to everyone. Since I wasn't involved with the family as an adult, some of my aunts and cousins believed that I was too full of myself to come around often. I didn't care what they thought. I had my life, and it didn't resemble my childhood in any way. I didn't want to be reminded of those years, so I kept my distance from the family.

At the funeral home, the tension was palpable, but I was there only to pay my respects to my grandfather. I sat down for a moment and just watched people walk up to the casket and then sit down. I had said my prayers, and now I was an observer. It was almost time for the viewing to end, and I saw Paul, Aunt Shirley, and Uncle Gene standing at the casket. They were deep in conversation, and they each kept looking over at me. That held my attention. What were they talking about?

Finally, Paul stood tall with his chest out and said, "It's time," and he started to walk toward me.

As he started to walk toward me, Uncle Gene quickly walked one way, and Aunt Shirley quickly walked the other. When Paul noticed they weren't by his side, he turned on his heels and headed in the opposite direction. What the hell was that? I knew this was not the place to get answers, but I would get answers.

A couple of weeks after the funeral, I finally called Aunt Shirley. I asked her what that was all about. She was vague and never gave me a straight answer. I begged her to be straight with me, but it was clear that she was very uncomfortable. I then called Uncle Gene and had the same conversation. He wasn't any more helpful.

After trying to get information from both of them, I started retracing conversations with Paul over recent years, and I remembered one cryptic slip he made at one point. A statement that should have shaken me, but I overlooked it. I remember being in the car with him, just him and me. I remember finally asking him face-to-face how he could have done the things he had done to me as a child. I didn't want to fight with him. I just wanted some answers. After some denials, he finally said, "In therapy, they told me it was probably because you weren't mine."

I remember asking him what that meant, and he backtracked and stuttered and ended the conversation. Maybe my psyche couldn't handle the idea that I had made all these excuses for him over all these years because he was my Dad, and I didn't want to accept that. It would make my whole life a lie. That couldn't be what he meant.

I needed to get answers on this now. Family members clearly were not going to help, but I had contacts from my years working in law firms. I called a previous coworker, who was a private detective. I shared the information I had, and he went to work. I waited patiently, and after a couple of months, he got back to me with news that would change my life forever.

Paul was NOT my father. Every story I had ever heard from him was a fabrication. He was NEVER married to my mother. He met her in Massachusetts either during her pregnancy or after I was born. Because my mother chose not to list my father's name on my birth certificate, and since she was deceased, there was no one alive who could tell me who my birth father was. All we knew was that it was definitely not Paul.

All those years of protecting him because I thought he was the only parent I had. All those years I'd made excuses for him and trying to be a good daughter. My whole life was a lie and a scandal!

I jumped in my car right away and drove to Paul's house. He was then married to his final wife, Darlene. She was inside the house, but his truck was gone. I went inside, and I was like a caged animal. I paced back and forth and told her I had to talk to him immediately. She said he was on his way home and tried to calm me down. Within minutes, his truck pulled up, and I went outside. Darlene followed me, and I asked her to go back inside to talk to him alone. She was visibly worried and getting angry.

As he got out of his truck, he could see there would be a problem, and I asked him to please tell Darlene to go inside. I told him I needed to speak to him alone NOW! Darlene went inside, and I continued my pacing until he was ready to talk.

I laid out the details of what I saw at the funeral home and hiring a private detective. He kept interrupting me and telling me that he did the best he could with me. I finally stopped him and said, "You can tell everyone else anything you want, but you can't say that to me. I was there. I know differently. Please be honest with me for the first time in your life!" Darlene came running out again because she saw me pointing at him in anger. She yelled at me to stop trying to cause trouble, and I kept calmly asking her to go back inside. I looked at Paul and asked him again to tell her to go inside. He refused. I asked him if he was sure, and he said yes. So, my rant continued and turned up a few volumes! I told him again that I wanted to know if he was really my father, after warning him that I already had information. He wouldn't give me a straight answer but kept saying he did his best.

Then I became furious and started yelling, "What kind of father makes his daughter sleep naked on her side in bed with him while he puts his dick between her legs. No penetration, but gliding it back and forth to give himself enjoyment? What kind of father puts his face between his daughter's legs and moves his tongue around in her vagina? What kind of father gets disgusted by pubic hair and then begins beating his daughter unmercifully since he can no longer enjoy molesting his child?"

At this point, Darlene was screaming and trying to hit me. He finally yelled at her and told her to go inside. I stood there, glaring at him. He paced back and forth and kept muttering about doing the best he could. I dared him to repeat it, or I would scream out more vivid memories. He then looked at me and said, "Do you want me to help you find him?"

I said, "Who?"

He said, "Your real father."

I shook my head and said, "That's all I needed."

As I strode back to my car, he yelled behind me, "I'm never going to see you again, am I?"

I responded, "Never."

CHAPTER 82

Marley

After Nick and I split up, I started spending time with my friends again—both old friends and new. The new friends from the neighborhood were showing me around town. They showed me where the cool stores were, the places to hang out, and they were introducing me to new people. One friend took me to a jewelry store close by, and I loved the designs. The store owner was the man who designed the jewelry. His name was Marley. I went into the store time and time again because I truly loved his designs, and I bought several pieces, little by little.

One day, Marley asked me out. Of course, I said yes because he was the sweetest, most talented man I had met. We started dating, and he was so good to me. I now had reasons to buy nice outfits from the local boutiques because Marley was connected and had lots of fabulous events to take me to. I felt like a million dollars when I was with him, especially when he took me to Vegas for a jewelry convention. He had me take several outfits into his store so his employees could dress me up in his jewelry so he could show off his collections on me.

Seriously? I felt like I was made for this! We stayed at a fantastic hotel, and we went to shows and fancy restaurants, and I was having the time of my life.

I focused on trying to be independent and not rely on a man for a change. I wanted to have fun with Marley, but I wanted to have my own space as well. I felt guilty for having brought two different men, Eddie and Nick, to live with me and the boys, and those relationships ended. I didn't want to spend all my time with another man yet.

Marley didn't get it. When I would need time with just me and the boys, he would try to find a way to get involved. I would stick to my guns, and in as pleasant a manner as possible, I would insist that I spend time with the boys. One time that happened, and I thought he understood. Then I looked out into my backyard and saw him out there clearing up a mess the boys had made. I was furious and felt utterly disrespected. Again, he did not understand.

While I enjoyed every minute with him, I was feeling claustrophobic. Something was missing, and I didn't want to hurt him, but I had to let him go. I couldn't put my finger on it, but I knew it. We ended as friends, and I returned all the jewelry he had let me wear. I kept the items I purchased, and I still treasure them today.

Marley brought me into social circles I had never known, and I created friendships with people I probably would have never met. He showed me the better side of life. He showed me that I was good enough. I treasure my memories with him, and I wished it would have worked with us. In the end, I was meant for someone else. I didn't know who yet.

CHAPTER 83

Scott

When I was dating Marley, I met a lot of his friends and acquaintances. He indeed traveled with some high-end people. I felt like I was living like the rich and famous, and I was getting quite used to it. On one of the many occasions, we were out, I met his friends, Jack, Sandy, and Scott. They were so much fun. After we stopped seeing each other, I would still run into Sandy. I just adored her. She was living with Jack, and they had several homes.

About a month or so after Marley and I split, I ran into Scott, and he asked me out. We were both concerned about how Marley would feel, so Scott called him to see if he was ok with it, and he was, so Scott and I started dating. He was in sales, just like me, only he traveled a lot. We dated for about 8 or 9 months, and we only saw each other on weekends. It was perfect!

Between his schedule and mine, that was all we had. The time we spent together was full of fun and laughs, and one day while we were driving to Jack & Sandy's place, he asked me to marry him. I said, yes. I adored his family and could see a future for us. A month later, we flew to Florida to visit with his parents, and I was thrilled that his stepmom was so happy that I was joining the family.

Upon reflection, I see now that we weren't learning about each other on a day-to-day basis, but instead, we had fun every weekend. That sounds great, but I'm living proof that it's not a great way to start a marriage. Here I was about to embark on my third marriage, and I still hadn't learned all the lessons I needed.

I didn't want Scott to move in until after the wedding. I had promised my boys that I would live by that choice after Nick and I split up. We focused on planning the wedding, which was to be held in my home and it was quite the party. We had a minister and a rabbi perform the service because Scott is Jewish. He wanted me to convert, but after taking classes to learn about Judaism, I realized that I am a "Jesus" girl. I believe whole-heartedly in Jesus, so I could not convert.

Sandy and Jack were there, and they both signed the marriage contract as our witnesses. Marley was there too and was supporting our marriage. That meant the world to both of us. The wedding was beautiful, and aside from the torrential downpour of rain outside, the party was perfect until the wedding toasts.

Scott's father spoke first, and he was so eloquent. It touched my heart. Then after he spoke, Scott took the microphone. He thanked everyone for coming, and then he looked at Ryan and Cameron and said, "Things are about to change around here."

You could have heard a pin drop after that.

What did that mean?

The boys' faces were as confused as mine, but the party went on. I never did find out what he meant when he said that.

Our honeymoon was free because we were going on a PartyLite trip to Paradise Island in the Bahamas a few days after the ceremony. It was perfect timing, and why not. Right?

Wrong.

The error was that Scott hadn't met many of my PartyLite friends due to our weekend-only dates for the past year. While he knew that I was successful, he clearly did not realize just how successful. When he found out the level of success I had, he wasn't amused.

Saying "I do" changed our relationship completely. I knew that the minute we landed in Florida and had to stand in line at customs. All my PartyLite friends surrounded me, and there was never a lack of conversation when we were all together. Maybe I made him feel left out? I don't know.

I tried to keep him involved in every conversation, but he told me he wasn't a good traveler. He was such a big guy and his back hurt while flying. When we got to the customs desk, I handed the man our paperwork, and he pointed out that I had forgotten to complete the questionnaires.

"Oops!" That was my reaction. We had to step out of line so I could complete them. I didn't think it was a big deal because we had a 2-hour layover before our next flight. Scott felt very differently. In his boisterous voice, he scolded me in front of everyone. He called me stupid and asked me if he would have to make all the decisions in our marriage because I couldn't do a simple thing like complete questionnaires.

I tried to slip away to avoid his rant and do the paperwork as he yelled after me. His words were, "You are MY wife now, and you WILL do as I say!"

Um, does he know me? I thought. To not create an even bigger scene, I stayed quiet and completed the paperwork without speaking to him. We went back through the line and met up with my friends and didn't say much to each other on the next flight. I had pretty much become an expert at what a honeymoon should look like since this was my third, and I could see clearly that this wasn't going as planned.

On the first night of any trip involving a flight, I'm tired when I get there. I always need to lie down in my room or go right out to the pool and relax. That was my plan. Scott planned to explore the resort and check out the casino. We had five days, and I needed a nap. He left the room aggravated, and I took my nap. Later he returned to the room in a fury.

He was screaming at me that these people were rude to him, and no one said hello. I calmly explained that no one knew him yet. That didn't stop him, the ranting and raving was crazy, and I couldn't seem to figure out what to say or do to calm him down. I ordered room service and told him we would stay in that night and just enjoy each other as a reminder that it was the first night of our honeymoon. I ate alone, dressed in a negligee. He kept ranting.

The next day we went out to the beach. I wanted the pool, but I was trying to keep the peace, so I went where he wanted. He found a secluded spot on the beach where none of my friends would find us. I tried to explain that this was a PartyLite trip and part of my job is to be there with my consultants and leaders. He trumped that theory with a reminder that I was his wife, and I would do what he said. This behavior was going to get old quick.

Day three brought the same as day two; in seclusion on the beach with no one to talk to because he was still pouting. At the end of the day, we went back to the room, got dressed, and went to dinner. We had to sit alone per his demand. After dinner, I just wanted to go back to the room. He had to go to the front desk to take care of something, so I would wait for him to come back. Again, he came back utterly furious. This time the ranting did not stop. I cried all night long. How could this be happening?

Day Four, he woke me up and said, let's go to the beach. I was exhausted from crying all night and told him no, I'm staying in the room. I told him I had a fierce headache because of all his yelling the night before. He didn't want to hear it. He threw a pill across the bed to me and told me to take it. I wanted to know what it was, and that infuriated him. He shouted, "It's something for the pain! Just take it like I said!" There were a few expletives in that statement, but I didn't want to include all that.

I took the pill and left with him for the beach. I have no memory of that entire day, but I would learn exactly what had happened upon my return.

Day five, and it was time to head home. At this point, I didn't know what I was going to. I was hoping there were some answers because this felt like the Twilight Zone. Our first flight took us to Florida again, and we headed to customs. This time I made sure I filled out all the paperwork. We then got to baggage claim, and it was packed. The luggage was coming around the carousel, and PartyLite friends were coming by to say they didn't see me all week. I just half smiled and nodded as I waited for Scott to grab the luggage as it came by on the carousel. I looked over to see if he had any of our bags yet, and I saw him grab a random woman's arm, and he screamed at her not to touch his bag. The bag in question was now in his hands, and she was stunned at his reaction.

I ran over and said, "Stop! She clearly didn't know it was your bag!"

His ranting started again, and I noticed that all eyes were on us. My PartyLite friends from all over the country were staring at this scene. Some I knew very well. Some I didn't. I was so embarrassed and frustrated from all of this, and through gritted teeth, I shoved his paperwork at his chest and said, you handle your stuff, and I'll handle mine. He then smacked my arm. All my paperwork went flying across the carousel—my passport, my customs document, my identification, the flight itinerary, everything found a spot between moving luggage. PartyLite husbands started jumping onto the belt and grabbing my things as Scott continued screaming at me.

My head was spinning, and all I could see were the looks of pity on my friends' faces. How dare he do this to me? I didn't deserve this; I didn't deserve any of it. I turned and saw my friend Yvette and I made eye contact with her and nodded as if to say, "Stay there."

She apparently got the message. I turned to Scott, who was still yelling, and I took off my wedding rings. I put them in his hand and said, "This is not what I bargained for."

I then turned to Yvette, grabbed both of her elbows, and stood nose to nose with her. I whispered to her to please not leave me, please stay here and stay close to me. He kept yelling, and he grabbed my luggage and told me to come on, or he would get rid of my stuff. I turned away from Yvette long enough to say to him there was nothing he could take from me that I couldn't replace. That felt so good to say! She and I then headed for the escalator to get to the boarding gate. He followed us for a while and then I didn't see him.

When we arrived at the gate, I went to the counter, and by this time, I was crying hysterically. I explained to the attendants that I was on my honeymoon and that my husband was acting erratically and being abusive, and I needed to move my seat quickly. They moved my seat, and all my local PartyLite friends circled me as I sat and cried. He tried to come over, and they wouldn't let him into the circle. He went to the counter and learned that I had moved my seat, and then he began yelling at them.

Shortly after that, the pilot came over to me, and my friends let him in. He got down on his knee and told me he was moving me to first class so he could keep an eye on me. He said that if Scott caused any more trouble, he would be arrested as soon as the plane landed.

At that point, the little girl who used to defend her dad's abuse came to the forefront of my psyche. I'm not saying I have multiple personalities, but that's how I felt. I asked the pilot to please let Scott know so he wouldn't act up and wouldn't get arrested. I could see my friends' disappointment after I spoke.

Once on the plane, my mind was swirling. What had I done to cause this? It had to be my fault somehow. Maybe I didn't understand him enough. Maybe there was a real issue behind all this that I wasn't seeing. I got up from my seat in first class and went to the coach section of the plane. He wasn't hard to find because he's so tall, so I saw him, and I stood over his seat, and I apologized to him. I cringe just thinking about it. I apologized and told him I loved him. My friends heard me. He heard me. He responded by saying, "You just need to grow up!"

Did you ever have that moment where you head just cocks off to the side, and you realize you're an idiot? Yeah, I had that moment. I said, "Never mind," and went back to my seat in First Class.

When the plane landed, they let me off first. I ran through the airport and to the baggage carousel. I found a spot where I could hide and catch my luggage before it came around the carousel. I saw Scott looking for me, but it was pretty crowded by then, so hiding was not an issue. I grabbed my bags and slipped out the door and into a cab. As soon as the taxi reached my home, I ran inside, locked all the doors, closed all the shades, and ran up to my bedroom closet.

I sat on the closet floor and called my friend, Debbie S. She had no idea about any of this because she wasn't on the trip. I sobbed and cried and told her everything. I then heard Scott beating on my front door and yelling from the driveway. He was calling me a slut, a whore, a child, and I don't even remember what else. I was sure he would break into the house, so I told Debbie that if he did, to please call the police immediately. I've never been so frightened in my entire life.

I honestly thought he was going to kill me.

He didn't break-in. He finally left. I got myself together and forced myself to make some decisions. I would have to face the embarrassment from PartyLite people and all my friends, family, and neighbors by having to end this marriage after just one week. None of this made sense, but I had vowed to myself years and years ago that no man would ever threaten me or physically hurt me and get away with it. I started packing up the wedding gifts to return.

Meanwhile, the boys were with their Dad and Vickie. I didn't tell them anything yet. I had to get my ducks in a row. Scott's stepmom called me, and that broke my heart. She pleaded that I give him another chance saying he had never done this before and that she wanted me to be part of her family. His daughters called me, and his friends called me. Every one of them found it so hard to believe. I felt like they thought I was making this all up.

As I ran errands that day to get groceries in the house before the boys got home, I dropped off my camera film to be processed. I wanted to see if there was anything in the pictures that could shed some light on this horrible trip. When the photos were ready, I sat on the grocery store bench and started leafing through them. To my horror, I learned what happened the day Scott gave me that pain pill.

On that day, rather than keep me secluded on the beach away from my friends, Scott decided to parade me around everyone. He took pictures of me trying to eat a cheeseburger beside one of my favorite PartyLite colleagues. I was unsuccessful at eating the cheeseburger because I was so high from that one pill that the cheeseburger was hanging out of my mouth, and my eyes were nearly rolled back in my head. He took pictures of me lying on the lounge chair at the pool, where it was clear that I was not aware of my surroundings. Then finally, there was a picture of me with Debbie A, one of my lifelong friends. She was smiling, but it wasn't a genuine smile. I was drooling.

I burst into tears in the grocery store and started heaving. When I could gain my composure, I drove home and called Debbie A. I told her what I saw, and she said to me that he was telling everyone that would listen that I had a severe drug addiction and he didn't know what to do to help me. Debbie knew better, but she also didn't know what to do.

I did!

One of Scott's closest friends, Harvey, was the most verbal about Scott not being abusive to women. I called Harvey and invited him over. I gave him the pictures. We both cried together. He left with the images in hand and said he was going to confront Scott. I didn't care. I just didn't want people believing I made it all up.

A week later, Scott stopped by the house. He had gentleness in his eyes, and he was apologizing. Then he told me that the pill he gave me was a Quaalude. He had a supply of them from years ago. He told me that he uses them for his back pain, and he thought it would help me. He had an answer to every question, and he was making sense. I was softening and reconsidering. Then I said, "But what about the boys?" and he said, "They'll just have to deal with our decision." My head cocked again, and I kicked him out of the house. This childhood habit of allowing abuse was going to stop NOW!

I didn't lay eyes on him again for a couple of years. But the scars were significant. I couldn't work for a month. I didn't trust myself to make decisions, and I was utterly humiliated. I didn't want to go out in public because I felt like everyone was shaking their heads at me. After the hurt subsided, the anger grew. I was angry at every man, not just Scott. My rampage would now begin.

So, what did I learn from Scott? Open my freaking eyes! Don't make excuses for bad behavior. If it happens once, it's likely to happen again and possibly again and again.

All I wanted was to feel loved and to feel safe—neither of those happened in this relationship. I had to be a "better picker," or I had to stay single.

CHAPTER 84

House of Cards

When the marriage to Scott ended so abruptly, nothing changed for me. I still lived in my house, it was still in my name only, and I went on with my life. I had lost nothing except a bit of my pride.

As I was taking a bath one day with a glass of wine next to the tub and bubbles surrounding me, I leaned back and closed my eyes to take in the relaxation. I listened to my breathing and took a mental picture of how good my life was and how I had escaped a tragic mistake by marrying him. As I opened my eyes, I saw a couple of flies in the skylight above me over the tub. I watched them as I wondered how they had gotten in there. I watched as more and more come through the ceiling light fixture. Suddenly there was a massive swarm of them, and they didn't look like flies after all! I jumped out of the tub, freaking out because this was like a bad horror movie!

What in the world was happening?

I hurried up and called our neighborhood handyman. He came right over and, after examination, shared with me that they were not flies. They were termites! How could that be? I had a termite treatment service every couple of months!

He told me to call them and let him know if I needed anything from him.

Great! I was already paying a $5,000 monthly mortgage. I had replaced all four heat pumps in the house, and had put in driveway lighting, had my lawn service weekly, my pool service weekly, and I had just finished placing lighting on the front of the house along with brand new landscaping. On top of that, I was still paying off some of the furniture Scott and I purchased, and I decided to keep. I was fit to be tied!

I called the termite service, and they told me that I explicitly told my service guy NOT to inspect that side of my house. What? Why would I do that? Did they have it in writing? No, but they didn't need it in writing! It was a verbal agreement. I called my attorney friends, and they told me it was nearly impossible to hold the termite company responsible, and it would be costly to pursue it in court. I called my insurance company, and they told me that they would come out to inspect, BUT that I should be aware that they would not pay for termite damage.

I was speechless, scared, and furious.

I was at my breaking point. It was too soon after this awful marriage, and I was not in the mood to be taken advantage of. I kept my cool until the insurance company came out to inspect and give me an estimate. The estimate was $45,000, and they weren't paying a dime. I called the insurance company again and shared my lack of funds to pay for this on my own. I explained my situation, single mother, blah, blah, blah. They had no compassion, and they just stuck to their guns, so I pulled out mine. I asked for the manager, and I waited. When the manager got on the phone, I was as calm and concise as I could be. I explained that I did not have $45,000 to fix the house. I also explained that I didn't come from money, but instead, I had built a business, and I was very proud of what I had. But I had come from nothing, and I wasn't afraid to have nothing again.

The ball was now in their court. They could step up and fix the house, or I would let it fall like the house of cards it was at that point.

I meant every word of it.

They had so much more to lose than I did. I would walk away and let it fall and then file bankruptcy. The manager heard me loud and clear. A few days later, I got the call that the repairs were being arranged and they would be paying for it.

As they pulled the stucco off the front of my house, I saw all the rot, and I cried like a baby. That could have fallen and killed us! Thank God for that bubble bath and thank God I wasn't afraid to stand my ground to have the repairs done.

As I watched them work each day, I knew that I needed to sell the house and get out as soon as they completed the work. The house's purpose was to give me the ability to sell it before the boys started college. This house was their college fund, and I had to get out before I lost it.

Three months later, I sold the house. I had purchased it for $459,000, and I sold it just seven years later for $650,000. I paid off the loans and pocketed $150,000. I then bought a townhouse in a gated community in Pikesville for $400,000. Now the boys were closer to their school, I had a low maintenance house on a corner lot with a gorgeous view of the Grey Rock Mansion, and I even had a community pool right behind my house. I loved this place and decided this would be my forever home.

CHAPTER 85

Sowing My Oats

When I first met and started dating Joe on my 21st birthday, he told me he was concerned about my age. He was seven years older than me, and he felt that I needed more time to "sow my oats." I considered it for a moment, but then I was afraid I would lose him. One evening while we were on the phone together, I told him I was considering seeing other people. He said, ok.

I wouldn't say I liked that.

There was a snowstorm that night, and I lived about four blocks away from him. I walked to his house in the snow, and he was shocked to see me at his door. I told him I didn't want to date anyone else, and I just wanted him. He was pleased and knew he already had me wrapped around his finger.

Here I was 25 years later, and it was finally time for me to explore my options. The problem was that I was now damaged goods. I loved the attention of men, but I hated the male species. In retrospect, I think I was trying to make them feel what men in my life had made me feel, with no regard for the fact that they weren't personally the culprits.

One of my friends started calling me a "black widow." I didn't kill anyone, but I purposely broke hearts. I hung out with my friend, Laura, on weekends. She was a single mom too, and while she didn't hate men, she didn't have time for a relationship, so we were pretty much in the same boat. We went out dancing often, and we had a great time. We traveled together a lot. She was my guest on PartyLite trips for years, and we created so many beautiful memories together. We also looked out for each other. I was much more aggressive when it came to strange guys trying to pick us up. She was always so lovely, so I became her "bodyguard" of sorts. I never raised my hand to them, but I scared them away with my aggressiveness. I could write a book just on stories about Laura and me, and maybe I will write it one day.

I joined dating websites too. I met several guys on Match.com but found that free websites bring all kinds of craziness out of the woodwork. I joined eHarmony.com and met some very nice guys there, but none that I wanted to keep around. I had a couple of dates that made comments when they saw my home. "What do you need me for?"

I responded each time with, "Not to pay my bills; that's for sure!" I knew right away that they weren't going to pass my tests.

I even joined It's Just Lunch, which is a website for professionals looking for love. In other words, it cost $2,500 to join for six months. I had plenty of money then, and I thought if I met men with money of their own, I would not have to worry about their intentions. While I wanted to meet someone, I wanted to be clear that I didn't want a significant commitment for quite some time. I had a mantra: If it's not fun anymore, I'm not doing it. That mantra, for sure, eliminated a few options. Some of them did not like that train of thought. My thoughts in return were…sucks to be them.

I dated a doctor from Johns Hopkins Hospital. He was very handsome and very accomplished in his work. He was also of Hispanic descent, which made him super-hot to me. That is until he would talk to his friends and family, both in-person and on the phone, in Spanish. I think that is one of the rudest things you can do. Why would you have a date in your car and then spend 15 minutes on a phone call speaking another language? Was he talking about me and didn't want me to know what he was saying? I don't know. That last call was the last time I saw him.

I had a date with a well-known millionaire in the area. We met for dinner, and upon sitting down, he asked me if I was going to go home with him. In my shock, I stared at him for a moment and said, "No." He said ok, and we ordered drinks. When the drinks arrived, his phone rang, and he said, "Do you mind if I take this?" I said, "No, that's fine." I had no idea who was calling, and I didn't think it was any of my business. It could have been his children, or it could have been work.

As I was trying not to eavesdrop on his conversation, I heard him ask the person on the phone if the person would be around later so he could drop by for a cocktail. When he hung up, I asked him if he had just made a date for after our dinner. He said, "Yes, you're not going home with me, so I'll go to her place." I smiled, got up, and left him sitting at the table at the restaurant.

I dated a man who owned a popular restaurant in the city. He was very conservative in his appearance, and I was not. He shared me with a couple of times that he would prefer if I dressed more conservatively. I shared with him that he would need to get used to who I am if he wanted to see me. We met one evening for happy hour, and I showed up in a low-cut blouse and a pair of snakeskin jeans. That was the end of our relationship.

I made a habit of catching up with old friends during this time too. One of my first contacts was Peggy Sue. She planned for us to meet at the Lighthouse, a bar in our old neighborhood. That sounded like fun. I met her there, and the place was full of old friends. I was so happy to see Barbara and Dani and other friends from the old days. When I was catching up with Barbara, she told me someone wanted to see me. She took me by the hand and led me to this little old lady sitting at the bar. When she turned to me, I could see she was crying, and it was Miss Doris!

I was so happy to see her!

I had felt so guilty my whole life for not telling her the truth and for not thanking her for her efforts. Here she was right in front of me after all these years. Her tears made me cry, and we hugged for the longest time. She pulled me back from her and looked in my eyes and said, "I knew you were strong enough to get out!" I felt my knees buckle. She knew all along, and she believed in me. She had always believed in me. I'll never forget that night.

Getting back to my dating life, I have to admit that I had so much fun putting men in their place. I was determined that no one would ever change me again. I would be true to myself, and never again would I put up with any unnecessary crap. The men available were all lessons to me—lessons of what I did NOT want. I would not accept spending time with anyone who showed the least bit of disrespect to me again.

My friends, neighbors and my PartyLite hosts were always trying to fix me up. I had no problem with a blind date. I stood my ground with each date, and they never lasted more than 2-3 dates before I stopped taking their calls. Yeah, I was that girl. I didn't feel the need to explore the drama of a break-up over such short relationships. They would get the message.

I had this group of friends that got together each weekend at the area hotspots. Sometimes Laura was with me, and sometimes she wasn't. Paul, Michelle, Reggie, Russ, Shannon, Jake, Shirelle, Scott, Kirsten, and many others were there. They were the core group, and there were often extras.

One evening we were at a popular bayfront bar, and it was just the guys and me that night. It was pretty crowded, but it usually was on a Friday night. We were assembled on a walkway just drinking our cocktails, telling stories, and laughing. A small group of guys walked up to us. One of them stopped next to me and went into a flurry of compliments about my appearance. He was charming and cute, and I was so surprised. He introduced himself to me, and then introduced his friends. There were 3 or 4 of them. The last friend he introduced was named Sid. Sid put out his hand to shake mine, held it, looked into my eyes, and said, "When you're done with the youngster, I'll be right here." Oh, that made me smile!! I put my other hand on top of his hand, still holding mine, and said, "Oh, I'm done with him already." There were fireworks!

He took me down to his boat and asked me if I wanted to get on. I said, "Sure!" I loved boats. As soon as I sat down, he grabbed a canister of whipped cream that was sitting nearby, and I stopped him right away. He just laughed and said he was kidding.

He did that a lot. Sid was fun, so very witty, and very charming, but he kept me at a distance. We hung out like buddies, with the occasional kissing sessions, but it went no farther.

I needed to get out of town one day, so I bought us both tickets to go to Jamaica for a week. We had a fantastic time, and I loved every minute of it. Still nothing more than kisses. When we returned, I think he was afraid that I was getting too close. I was, but I kept it to myself. I could tell that he didn't want more, so I just put him in my friend zone and spent as much time with him as he would let me.

One evening we went to dinner at a sushi restaurant and then went to a local bar for drinks. He drank too much that night, and I saw another side of him. For some reason, he started schooling me on how I had created mama's boys with my sons and told me that I was so desperate for love that I made sure my boys loved me more than any son should. His tirade continued as I drove him back to the sushi place to get his truck. When he noticed where we were, he looked at me and said, "I can't drive." I looked over at him and said, "Get the fuck out of my car." His shock was all over his face. He got out, and I left him there.

The next morning, I woke up to the phone ringing. It was Sid, and he didn't remember anything from the night before, but he knew if I left him there, he must have done something.

That was the end for us. We stayed friends, but with distance. I still love when I chat with him because he is so kind and so funny. He just was not the right one for me.

CHAPTER 86

Scott B.

Then there was another Scott. The Scott that hung out with us at the local spots. The one who was engaged to Kirsten. That ended, and there was sadness on his face. I had never really spoken intensely with him before, but when I did, I saw much more than I had ever seen before. There was something about him, and my hate for men was dwindling. One night outside of a bar, I kissed him. He was so nervous, and it made me laugh. About a month later, he called me, and we met for lunch. My next emotional roller coaster was in process.

Scott was a big kid. He loved video games. As luck would have it, so did my son, Cameron. Scott and Cameron became BFFs, and I let my guard down. He moved in with us, and so began the next four years of my life. He proposed to me with a gorgeous ring, and I said yes. Scott owned a car repair facility, and he was often stressed out between his employees and his bipolar. He could certainly be a mess at times. Scott would teach me patience and empathy. He would show me that there was so much more to a man than first impressions. The deeper we shared, the deeper I fell for him.

In the early stages of our relationship, we spent a lot of time at our favorite restaurant, Geckos. We knew the owner, and a lot of our friends hung out there too. It became the place we chose to spend our most memorable events, including our engagement and my 40th birthday. However, the most significant memory I have of us at Geckos was the night we stopped in for drinks on a weeknight.

The bar was packed, so we went downstairs to another area. We sat very close on our barstools facing each other, and we held hands, looking into each other's eyes. We were so in love at that point. As we chatted, our conversation became about how we each were feeling about our relationship. This incident is going to sound odd, but I'm sharing the memory exactly as it happened.

As Scott spoke, his body shook, and some type of energy burst came out of his chest and slammed into mine. Honestly! It took both of us by surprise, and we sat there staring with our eyes wide and saying, "What the HELL was that?" We never got an answer to that question, and I've tried to google it, but nothing came up. Whatever it was, it made us feel like we were meant to be together.

Another fond memory wasn't so fond at the time. I had gone for my annual breast exam, and this time it came back questionable. The doctor found a mass, and I needed to have a biopsy of my right breast. The doctor explained that before I could have the biopsy, I had to get an MRI, a CT scan, have blood work done, and then make another appointment with him to do the biopsy. This doctor was not prepared for the person I am. It was a 10 am appointment, and I knew that I could not sleep until that biopsy was over. I would completely stress out, and I needed to have it done that day. He laughed at me and told me that couldn't possibly happen because I had to make three other appointments to get these things done before I could get back to him. I asked him if he would squeeze me in later in the day, and he laughed again. I was serious. He then told me that while he knew it wouldn't happen, if I could get all of that done and be back in his office no later than 5 pm that day, he would do the biopsy. He then proceeded to tell me not to worry. Yeah right.

I went out to his secretary and asked her for the three referrals I needed. I also asked her in which order I should see each of these people. She said the first one should be the MRI. My cell phone wouldn't get reception in that office, so I asked if I could use her phone. She tried to explain that there was no hurry and that I could make the call when I got home. I briefly explained that I wanted to go directly to the MRI place and was sure I would need an appointment first. At this point, the doctor was standing beside me and nodded for the secretary to let me use the phone. They were having a little chuckle between the two of them at my expense, but I didn't care. I called the MRI office and explained my situation…I'm a single mother with two small boys at home, and I run a multi-million-dollar business on my own. I cannot possibly wait weeks or even days to get this resolved. They gave me an appointment for 45 minutes later. I was on a mission.

After the MRI, the nurse told me it would take a few days for the information to be processed and sent over to the doctor. I explained that I needed to take the information with me as I was having the biopsy that same day. She was stunned and said they couldn't do that. I asked her if she liked candles. I told her I would give her a stack of free candles if she could do this for me. I was happy to wait.

She caught on quickly and realized that I was camping out in that office until I got what I needed. I waited an hour, and she brought the information to me while I was in the waiting room, making the next two appointments. At each appointment, I had to explain again that I needed the information that day because the biopsy was scheduled for 4:30 pm. They each worked with me and got it done. At 4:15 pm that day, I walked back into my doctor's office with all the information he required. He was stunned and shook his head, laughing. He told me he needed someone like me to work for him and a promise was a promise. He took me right into his surgery center and did the biopsy, but now I had to wait a few days for the results. I had done as much as I could do, even when they didn't believe I could do it, but I still had to wait in the end.

I cried all the way home. I called Scott and told him what was happening, and he told me he would be over as soon as he could. When he got there, I was in bed sobbing. He looked helpless. He wasn't used to me being like this, and he didn't know what to do. He sat with me and tried to console me, but nothing was working. He then went into my bathroom and ran me a bubble bath. He came out and undressed me while I cried and then carried me into the bathroom and put me in the tub. I still sobbed. He took off his shoes and climbed into the tub with me, fully dressed, and held me for a very long time.

That's the kind of man he was.

He then scheduled a dinner for the night before the results were expected with all our friends so they could bring up my spirits. Everyone was there, and they were terrific. The biopsy came back as benign. It was a fibrous tumor, and there was no threat. Thank God!

We made so many memories during the time we were together, and we certainly had a lot of fun. Scott is a super caring, super sweet guy, and he treated me like a princess. He is a forever friend now, and we will always have a special place in our hearts for each other.

CHAPTER 87

Cameron

Back when I was with Nick, Nichole took part in the school play, "Bye Bye Birdie." Cameron was in the second grade at the time. He and I went to the show, and it was the first play he had ever seen. I noticed his captivation, and at some point, he turned to me and said, "I want to do this!" I was so excited to hear that. Cameron had no interest in sports and was only interested in video games. I had wracked my brain, trying to figure out how to get him involved in something. I jumped at the opportunity to make this happen for him.

After some research, I learned that the middle school Nichole attended offered a Saturday class just for theatre. I signed him up right away. He attended those classes every Saturday and performed in every show. When it came time for him to go to middle school, he applied and auditioned to be a full-time student. Of course, he was accepted.

After a year and a half there, he wanted to leave the school and attend his zoned middle school instead. As a child, Cameron had a hard time making friends. He was tiny and very bitter about it. His anger was easily triggered, and he became very dark. I allowed him to change schools, and I sent him to a therapist. Therapy did nothing for him because he refused to talk to the therapist.

He seemed to like the new school better and made friends, although many of them shared his darkness. I tried to pay extra attention to him, but I had no idea just how dark he really was.

Theatre was his outlet, and he soared with his talent at this school. Again, I never missed a show. He was building confidence, and I was so hopeful that the darkness in him was fading.

For high school, he decided he wanted to audition for the Baltimore School for the Arts. Tupak Shakur and Jada Pinkett Smith attended this school. I took him for his audition, and it was so crowded with applicants. I secretly worried he would be overlooked. I waited for his turn and worked on what I would say to dispel his disappointment if he was denied. There was no need. He was accepted.

He was growing. Perhaps not physically yet, but emotionally. He began making friends, many of whom remain his friends to this day. He was thriving in this atmosphere, and he developed a love for Shakespeare. After his second year at BSA, he was chosen by the Director of the school to perform at the Hippodrome Theatre in downtown Baltimore with the off-Broadway presentation of Evita. I just about lost my mind! Of course, I bought front row tickets on Opening Night!

At another time, he was invited to perform at the Baltimore Shakespeare Festival, which was huge. For a month, every night after an early dinner, I drove him to the theatre in the city, about 45 minutes away, so that he could rehearse. Then for two more weeks, we did the same for the actual show. I had to re-arrange my party schedule to accommodate the timing to be there to pick him up after each show, but we managed.

I attended opening night, and I found that my interest in Shakespeare was equivalent to needles in my eyeballs. Nonetheless, I supported his dreams and continue never to miss a show.

When graduation time came, all his college choices were in New York. We did college visits, and he chose SUNY Purchase. This college would be the catalyst for considerable changes in him and his plans for his life.

CHAPTER 88

Bay Drive

Scott B. didn't like the house in Pikesville. He wanted to live on the east side of town, where the boys and I lived initially. I didn't want to move because I loved our house, but we were now engaged, and I agreed that if we moved east, I had to be on the water. He was good with that. We drove around a lot and looked at lots of homes. I wasn't in a hurry, but I think he really wanted it done.

We found a home in the process of being built already, but there was no owner yet. It was right on the Chesapeake Bay, but it was across the street and not on the waterfront. In comparing the homes' prices on the water and the costs of the homes across the street, I decided this home would work just fine. We put in a contract to pay $500,000 for the new house, and I then needed to sell our home in Pikesville.

I was able to work with the builder to change a few things about his floor plan, and we picked out cabinets and flooring. We shopped for light fixtures and door handles too. I was able to have a hand in every decision being made, and it was awesome. The house was to be ready right around mid-November.

My house in Pikesville was up for sale for $500,000, and I started packing, in between working my PartyLite business. It was challenging because I had a lot of stuff, and I knew there was the possibility that the new house wouldn't be ready soon enough, but the builder convinced me otherwise. The home in Pikesville sold within the first two weeks of listing it, and the buyer was motivated to get in quickly. He agreed to settle in mid-November to make it an easy transition for us.

I shared with my builder that my house was sold and asked if we were still on target. He was confident he could make the deadline. Scott and I would drive to the new place at least once a week to watch everything unfold. We started noticing that the crews weren't showing up each day, and we were getting concerned. Our builder was trying not to worry, but I was doing enough worrying for all of us. When it was clear that it wouldn't be ready by mid-November, I decided to chat with one of our new neighbors about potentially renting their guest house. Tom and Lisa lived directly across the street from the new place, and it was their property that was sold to build my new home. They took an active interest in everything going on and had been very friendly whenever we saw them on our visits.

On one occasion, they had shown me the inside of their guest house, and it was adorable! I decided to see if they could help. Cameron and I knocked on their door one evening and asked if we could come in to chat. I explained that it was me, Scott and Cameron, and sometimes Scott's daughter, Lexi. It was only a 1-bedroom house, but the kids were small enough to camp out in the living room area. Tom and Lisa told me we could stay there, and they would only charge us for the electricity. That was amazing! The next issue was what I would do with all my furniture and boxes during this transition.

I met with the builder again and explained that I would be living in the guest house across the street until my new home was ready, so that should ease his frustrations a bit.

I had hired a mover, but we had to move our belongings before the new house was ready for it. We discussed the options and settled on me, signing an agreement not to hold him responsible for the property I needed to store in the lower-level space. Houses in this area had to be built 17 feet off the ground to allow for rising water from the Bay during bad storms. This area had a terrible hurricane just two years prior and wiped out the whole area. As our new neighbors told us, we were taking a risk; sometimes, when you live ON the water, you have to live IN the water!

I signed the agreement, and the builder agreed to make one of the four bedrooms in the house into an office for me. I needed that office-ready immediately with electricity and cable so I could do my job. He promised to have that ready, but I would have no running water yet. That was fine. The movers moved all our stuff into the lower level, and we packed necessities only to live in the guest house across the street. Each day, I would take Cameron to school, come back to feed the dog, and then I would walk over to the new house, which was still being built, and I would work in my new office all day. Whenever I needed to use the bathroom, I had to walk back across the street to do it. I used my cell phone for every call, and we made it work. It was a tiny little guest house, with the shower in the one-bedroom, so it was cramped. We were being patient and trying to make the best of it. After all, the builder PROMISED we would be in the new home by Christmas.

Meanwhile, Scott was going to work each day running his auto shop, and he carried a lot of stress from that job. He was often all over the place, and I didn't even try to keep up with his mind as it raced from one topic to another.

One day he came home from work with a brand new bright yellow Hummer. I knew his financial situation, and I knew that he was sitting on a bit of money, but he was supposed to be putting down $40,000 for the down-payment, along with my $100,000 down-payment. That way, the house would be easily affordable, and we wouldn't be house poor.

I asked him why he bought this truck instead, and he stated that I drove a Lexus, so he thought he deserved to drive a Hummer. That's true, of course. He had the right to buy any car he wanted, but what about the down-payment on the house. His response was, "Oh, you've got that." My head did that thing again—cocked over to one side, and I thought, Ok, I do have this.

The next day, I called our loan officer and told him to remove Scott's name from the mortgage and the deed because he wouldn't be making the down-payment with me after all. I didn't mention to Scott that I had made that call.

As Christmas got dangerously close, I mentioned to the builder that Scott's daughter was only five and we couldn't fit a tree in the guest house. I had done a lot of shopping for Christmas gifts and kept wrapping them immediately and hiding them amongst the other items in the new house's lower level. The builder and his wife came to me one day and said that since they were unable to meet their promised deadline, they wanted to put us up in a local hotel on Christmas Eve to spend the holiday with our family. I was so touched and so very grateful.

Since Ryan was living on campus with his friend, Eric, I called them and invited them to spend Christmas Eve with us at the hotel. We got a 2-bedroom suite, and it was an adventure getting set up for a 5-year-old.

Scott and I loaded the car with gifts and a small pre-lit Christmas tree we bought just for this occasion. We put everything in the back of my SUV under covers. Cameron and Lexi got in, and we drove to the hotel in the early afternoon of Christmas Eve. While Cameron kept Lexi busy in the hotel's lobby, Scott and I walked the stairs at the other end of the hotel to carry our decorations and gifts up to our suite and hide them before we brought Lexi in. It all went without a hitch.

After dinner with Ryan, Eric, Cameron, Lexi, Scott, and I, we put Lexi to bed and waited for her to fall asleep. We then got busy setting up the Christmas tree, decorating it, pulling out all the Christmas gifts, and finally, we were able to go to bed too. When Lexi woke up the next morning, she was so excited and so adorable. She believed that Santa had come and set it all up for us while we were sleeping. It was a beautiful Christmas, and we laughed so much! We made some beautiful memories that day. What could have been a disaster became one of my favorite Christmas memories.

We finally settled and moved in just before New Years' Eve. Scott was quite surprised at the settlement when he went to sign the documents that didn't require his signature. He was puzzled as he looked across the table at me, and I said, "No deposit, no name on the mortgage or the deed."

He said nothing more.

CHAPTER 89

I Just Can't

One big deal breaker with Scott and me was travel. I loved traveling, and he was terrified of being outside the ability to reach a hospital within 10 minutes. His panic attacks felt like heart attacks, and he was understandably neurotic about it. I begged him to try, and he refused. Finally, there was a PartyLite trip that I really wanted him to go on with me. He agreed to give it a shot. Long story short, we got on the plane, he sat, then he stood up, looked and me, and ran off the plane. I didn't get off the plane. I went without him, and I was so very disappointed. I could not and would not give up my love for travel. It was definitely a wake-up call that this was not going to work.

The other deal-breaker issue was Scott's relationship with Ryan. He loved Cameron, but Ryan was a different story. Ryan had moved back home for the last year of school, and I hadn't planned for that. He would have to set up space in the lower level to be his bedroom. It was often cold there, but I just told him to grab more blankets. We would learn years later that Scott had put pillows in the air vent downstairs so the heat would stay upstairs. No wonder it was so cold down there.

Ryan and Scott often argued and over the silliest things, like who drank the milk. The milk story took the cake for me. I worked diligently in my office each day and doing candle parties and meetings every night. I was exhausted, and I was annoyed by it all. One afternoon when both Ryan and Scott were in the kitchen, which is right off my office, they were loudly arguing about the milk. That was my final straw. I yelled out into the kitchen at both of them. They kept arguing. I got up and walked into the kitchen. I told Scott that he was an adult, and he should behave differently. He didn't see it that way. I made it clear that I did and that it was time for him to go. They both stood there, shocked as I pointed to the front door and told Scott to pack his stuff and leave. I would not have a man disrespect my son over drinking milk. He packed up and left, and Ryan was in awe. After Scott left, he kept calling and making promises. He wanted to come back. I told him he had to ask Ryan. He did, and Ryan said Ok. He came back, and they were on notice to not start that nonsense again.

After several more break-ups over issues unrelated to travel or milk, I was finally empty and had nothing left to make it work. It was heartbreaking because I knew it wasn't his fault. He didn't understand why I would break up with him if there wasn't another man in my life. I explained to him that I wasn't a cheater, and I believed the man meant for me was out there, but I wouldn't find him if I stayed in this relationship.

Scott and I are still friends, and I fixed him up with a woman he always admired, and we were both friends with. They are very happy together, and I'm glad for both of them.

CHAPTER 90

Zoey

A year went by, and I hadn't dated anyone. I was still crying and still depressed. I met a friend for drinks one evening, and she suggested that I get a dog. That sounded silly, especially since the last two dogs I had—a Husky and a Weimaraner were absolute nightmares. I was as bad at choosing dogs as I was choosing men.

I thought long and hard on it and realized I had a lot of love to give, and I decided to get a small dog to share all of that love. The boys and I drove to a puppy farm in Pennsylvania, and I picked a female Lhasa Apso. We named her Zoey, and she was perfect! She was EXACTLY what I needed.

Zoey showed me unconditional love, and she shared everything with me for over 15 years. I never knew a pet could make me a better person. She did. She helped me through some of the most challenging times in my life.

When Zoey was 15 ½, she started showing signs of failing. One evening she started crying, and she never cried. I thought she might have eaten something off the floor that didn't agree with her. I slept in the guest room with her that night, and she cried all night long. I was so worried about her.

The next day, I had a commitment to attend to, and she seemed ok, but she was tired the following day. As I walked out the door, I told her I would be right back.

My friend Juanita had broken her foot, and I had a scooter that I offered to lend to her to get around her home better. It was a 45-minute drive to her house, and I had convinced myself that when I got home, I would call the vet and see if they could see Zoey later that day. When I arrived at Juanita's house, I knocked on her door, and when she answered it, she said, "Where's the scooter?" In my worry about Zoey, I forgot to put the scooter in my car. I had driven all that way and didn't even have what I needed! Juanita saw my distress and offered me a glass of wine. I told her what was going on, we drank a glass of wine, and I headed back home.

When I got home, I went up the basement steps, and as I opened the basement door, I saw Jimmy standing in the kitchen crying. Jim rarely cries. Somehow, I knew. I just yelled, "No, no, no, no!!" He hugged me hard and told me he found her on the kitchen floor when he got home. She had passed. I was devastated! I didn't get to say goodbye! He had put her on the guest room bed, and I climbed into bed with her. I stayed there and held her until the next day. When I woke, she was stiff.

Anthony and Joe, our friends, came over to show their respects, and Ryan came over to take us to the vet for her final arrangements. Both Ryan and I cried on the drive there, and when we arrived and we walked to the door, with Zoey wrapped up in my arms, I slid down the outside wall of the vet's office and cried my heart out. Poor Ryan had no idea what to do. He got me up, and we took her inside. They cremated her, and I have her in my office. She was a massive impact on my life, and I'll never forget my baby girl.

CHAPTER 91

PartyLite – 2007

I lived and breathed PartyLite. I dreamed about doing parties and running meetings, and when I wasn't sleeping, I was doing parties and running meetings. The business was still thriving, but there was discontent brewing. Many other direct sales companies were popping up, and some of the older companies were getting deceitful in their practices in terms of scouting successful people from other companies.

I was always such a ridiculously loyal person that I would quickly end conversations when others tried to tempt me with leaving PartyLite to join them. I was sure I was in the right place and with the right people. I loved our region, and I felt like I had found my reason for being born. I was meant to be a salesperson, mentor, leader, and student. I was rigid in my training style, and some people liked that about me, and some didn't. I was comfortable that I always focused my efforts on helping them be better, so I didn't feel a need to change a thing.

There were many times when I should have listened more and dismissed less. Those times are regrettable, but they helped me learn many lessons. I loved my business; I loved my customers, hosts, consultants, leaders, colleagues, and home office staff. It was a family-like none I had known before. It had taken me three years to become a Regional Vice President, and I would hold that title for more than two decades.

I got awards constantly and felt so appreciated. I was asked to speak at our RVP meetings, and I earned the RVP Positive Influence Award, which was my proudest moment in business ever! I was asked to train at National Conference nearly every year. Several times those trainings were in front of up to 10,000 people. I was in dance routines with our company entertainers, so I achieved a hidden dream of being a professional dancer. Not exactly professional, but these guys were so good they made us look good.

I was once playing the role of a cheerleader, and my favorite dancer was Billy. He was beautiful and sweet, and I just adored him. He was married and had 4 or 5 kids, but I secretly dreamed that we would be a thing one day. It never happened, but it was a great dream. In this cheerleader role, I ran out onto the stage and threw my pom-poms to the floor before jumping into Billy's arm, and then he lifted me over his head and threw me behind him, into the arms of Kevin and Karl. I was a flying RVP! The move had the audience screaming, and I was so thrilled! Of course, the part where I had to jump into Billy's arms was a necessary retake often – hahaha!

The PartyLite memories are all recorded in my many, many albums of photos taken over the years; memories of trips, meetings, events, Leader Retreats, and every other opportunity we had to get together. I had worked my way up to being one of the top 10 RVPs in the entire country, out of 120 at the time. With a name like Bunny, everyone knew me, and I always had a smile for them.

Consultants and leaders across the country would reach out to me for advice, and I always helped them the best I could. I started doing Facebook parties and created a YouTube video so consultants and leaders worldwide could refer to it for ideas anytime they wanted. PartyLite gave me an opportunity, and I ran with it with everything I had.

I loved my life!

At one point, I remember there being a couple of phone conversations with Debbie A. about her region in PartyLite. She wasn't earning the same income as me, and she had issues with how the home office was handling different things. I would tell her to go around the problem and keep moving forward. I told her she got stuck in the negative too often, and all she needed was a better attitude. I would learn that these were not the words she needed to hear.

For every RVP meeting, Debbie A. and I would be roommates. We would go to the airport together, fly together, share a room, and hang out together the whole time. It was great for our friendship, and we always had a great time. The RVP meeting this time was in Boston again, and Debbie A. told me she would meet me at the airport. It was early February, and Debbie's birthday had just passed. I didn't get a chance to see her, so I brought her birthday gift with me to surprise her with it at the airport. I knew she would love it, and I was so excited to see her open it. I waited at the gate for her to arrive, and then they started boarding the plane. I called her cell phone, and it went right to voicemail. I tried a couple more times and still no answer. I thought she might be stuck in traffic, and her husband was probably driving her. I then remembered his phone number, and I called him. He picked up. I told him the plane was boarding and asked how far away they were. He stuttered and said, "Bunny, remember she loves you." And then he hung up.

What did that mean?

My mind was swimming, and fury was rising from my belly. She loves me? What the hell did she do? I remembered a recent conversation where she told me one of the other direct sales companies was trying to recruit her. She wouldn't really go there, would she? That company was known to be unethical, and there's no way she could make the same money there. She was smarter than that. As I waited for the last person to board, I had decided to throw away her birthday gift before I got on that plane.

After I arrived in Boston that day, my face was swollen and red from crying throughout the whole flight. Debbie A. had been one of my closest friends since we were 15 years old. I felt so betrayed. By the end of the RVP meeting, I had learned from the home office staff that not only did Debbie A. resign as an RVP, but her downline RVP, Alissa, did too. When the leader jumps in with another company, most of her people follow. Most of them did. In just one day, my income dropped by over $100,000. I was a single mother with two sons in college. I had no child support; I had no significant other, and I had my life lined up with the income I was earning at that time. How in God's name would I be able to keep my house with an income drop of that amount in just one day? I was devastated.

I talked to Debbie on the phone while I was at that meeting. She learned that I had learned the truth, and she kept telling me not to take it personally. How could I not? This had an enormous effect on my family and me. I spouted evil insults at her and told her she was dead to me.

We didn't speak for three years.

That one day shook me to the core. I had always struggled with trusting men, but I held all my female friends close to my heart. I was still secure that my female relationships were strong and knew we were always there for each other. At the time, I felt this betrayal was worse than anything a man had ever done to me. I was always strong enough to recover from emotional and even physical pain. Financial betrayal put my family at risk, especially since both boys were in college. I changed that day. I moved very friend to an arm's distance. I would never again allow a friendship to crush me.

CHAPTER 92

Female Friends

I remember way back when Joe and I were married. Once he knew about my childhood, he had questions. The biggest problem was how I could imagine a life away from the one I lived? How did I know things could be better? I told him my first memories of believing life could be better were watching the Brady Bunch and other TV shows I enjoyed. Their lives in no way resembled mine. I held onto the belief that I would live a life that in no way reminded me of the life I had lived.

I realized at some point that I was always a chameleon. I watched people closely, and I learned bits and pieces from everyone I got close to. My friends were my only link to a world without pain and torture. They had no idea what was going on at home, and I was getting quite the education.

Every person I've ever considered to be a close friend is a person I learned something from. Every one of them helped to shape the person I am. While we shared laughs and adventures and secrets and enjoyed our time together, my brain was creating the person I wanted to be. I know that I will forget someone by listing names, and I don't want to offend anyone at all. If you are reading this and you know I've told you "I love you," and you know that I consider you a close friend or one of my many BFFs, you helped create me. You helped me be better, and you helped me be stronger, and you helped me overcome the tragedy in my life. I could not be the person I am today without you. I would love to list the names and include what you taught me; however, this is too important for me, and my fear of leaving someone out outweighs my need to share those details at this point.

You know who you are! Some of you are school friends, some of you are neighbors, some of you are co-workers, some of you I met with PartyLite, some of you are family, some of you are bosses, some of you know deep down in your heart how much I love and appreciate you.

One friend I will mention is Anita. Anita was my neighbor at Running Brook, and after I moved away, we met each summer for lunch. Anita was a Baltimore City school teacher, which was the best time for us to catch up. It was an annual thing that we both looked forward to. On one such lunch date, Anita mentioned that she worked with an organization as a volunteer. This organization held a bingo at a local place called the Hope Lodge.

The Hope Lodge provides housing for adults who need a place to stay while getting cancer treatments. Anita actually shopped each month for small gifts from dollar stores or yard sales, personally wrapped them as gifts, and the patients win the gifts as rewards for winning bingo games. I loved this idea! I wanted to do volunteer work for some time, but I couldn't find the right fit. Unfortunately, this organization was for Jewish women only, and I'm not Jewish. However, Anita told me she would keep me in mind to fill in as needed. I was fine with that.

Not too long after that, I got a call from Anita asking me if I would like to come to the next bingo. I jumped on the opportunity! I attended not every month, but as often as I could. I'd chat with the patients and try to make them smile while I play bingo with them. Anita brought snacks and all the gifts she wrapped, and we'd leave there with smiles on their faces and big thank you' s as we'd walk out the door. It's incredible, and I'm so grateful to her for including me in this miracle she creates.

CHAPTER 93

Depression

I am a person that is continuously trying to be better. I wouldn't call myself a perfectionist, but I would say that I obsessed over every action I took, and I beat myself up terribly. My depressions were always fueled by relationships with men and/or flashbacks from childhood abuse.

There have been times that the depressions got so dark that I felt the only answer was for me to die. Since I refused to use my own hand to make that happen, during those times, I would pray each night and beg God to take me in my sleep. When I woke up the next morning, I was angry at God for not taking me, and then I had to make it through another day. When these depressions come over me, I was mixed with sadness, desperation, and guilt. My self-loathing made me angry because I had so much to be grateful for, yet I couldn't see through the darkness. I couldn't seem to talk my way out of it, and I would sink deeper and deeper.

After each breakup, even when it was my choice, I would berate myself for possibly making the wrong decision. Was the guy that bad, or was I too picky? I felt like my childhood should have been enough negative drama in my life.

Why were relationships so complicated for me? And yet, I yearned to be loved in the ways I needed. My last major depression happened after Scott, and I ended.

Six months later, I signed up for eHarmony again. This time, I met Michael. A lovely man who adored me. It was nice spending time with him, but there was no magic. I wasn't in a hurry to move on because who knows. Right?

I had just gotten signed up on Facebook against my children's demands. They did not want me on Facebook because then I might see what they were doing. I didn't sign up to stalk them, and I signed up because it seemed like a fun thing to do. Facebook would turn out to be a significant contributor to my life.

CHAPTER 94

Back in the Neighborhood

After signing onto Facebook, I found that many of my old friends were on there, and I had lost touch with so many. One that I had lost touch with was Peggy Sue, and I really missed her. We chatted one day after seeing each other on Facebook, and she asked me to join her and her husband, Wayne, at a luau at a local hall. She said there would be other people from the neighborhood there. I had promised myself long ago that I would stay away from that part of town because it held so many bad memories for me, but I wanted to see Peggy Sue, and I talked myself into it. It was so great seeing her. The luau was pretty lame, but we had fun anyway.

I looked around the hall and didn't see anyone I really knew, just a few people I recognized but were never really friends of mine. Then I heard someone yell, "Bunny!" I turned and saw the person was not speaking to me, but to another woman named Bunny. It's not common to run into another Bunny! I watched the other Bunny as she went up to grab a plate of food. I stepped up beside her and told her my name was Bunny too. She wasn't really impressed by that, haha! I then told her the only other Bunny I knew was Bunny K. She then said to me that she was Bunny K.! That got a laugh, and we posed for a picture together!

Bunny was one of the older sisters of the family that lived across the street from me. Her mom, Miss Doris, was the lady who wanted to turn my family into social services. I asked how her mom was, and she said she was great. All in all, it was a fun night, and I'm so glad I went. It would turn out to be a huge catalyst in my life.

About three weeks later, I noticed the picture of Bunny and me was posted on Facebook. I then saw that someone had commented on it. That, someone, was Brian K., Bunny's younger brother. He asked if I was the same Bunny that grew up across the street from him. I said, yes! We exchanged numbers, and we immediately chatted on the phone.

We had so much to share! How was his life? How was mine? Shortly into the conversation, I had to ask, "Do you ever see Jamesy?" He said, yes! He told me that Jamesy now went by the name Jim. That made sense. He was a grown-up now. Jim had a farm in another county about an hour from the neighborhood, but he stopped in at the Lighthouse, a bar/restaurant where Brian worked every Friday to have dinner before hitting the rush hour traffic to go home. I told Brian we had to arrange a reunion to see everyone again and I had to see Jamesy! He was on it! He set it up for the Friday night of Labor Day weekend. We had a plan that I would drive there and call him. He would come out and bring me in to surprise Jamesy. The plan was Perfect. So that's what we did.

On that evening, Brian brought me into the bar and told me to sit next to the guy in the white shirt, but don't look at him. Ok. I did as I was told. Once I was sitting next to the white shirt guy, I asked one of the bartenders for a Stoli O with cranberry. I then noticed that Brian went behind the bar and leaned over to the white shirt guy.

Brian said, "Hey, Jim! Do you remember the name of the little dark-haired girl that lived right across the street from me when we were kids?" At that moment, I froze, and time stood still.

CRAP! I only lived there for two years. He's not going to remember me. How in the world am I going to sneak out of here before I embarrass myself?

It was too late. I was stuck. I was going to have to handle it gracefully. Time started again, and Jim answered, "Do you mean Bunny?"

Oh, how thrilled I was! I poked him in the chest with my finger, and he turned with a confused look on his face to see who it was. His face glowed as he recognized me, and he hugged me so hard I couldn't move! He pushed me back and moved my hair off my forehead to make sure I still had a scar there. I was shocked that he remembered that. He repeatedly said that he had always tried to find me, and he didn't know where to start. It was absolutely overwhelming!

I would later learn the side of the story about how Brian got him there. Brian invited him, and he said no. He said he had work to do at the farm and couldn't get away. Then Brian told him that one of the guys they had grown up with had a sex change operation, and that person would be there. Jim decided to go to see who it was! I asked Brian later why he would say that, and he told me I was one of the guys back then, so it wasn't really a lie!

The night was hectic, and I saw lots of old friends. I danced with Tommy, and I laughed with Barbara and Donna and Brian and all my old friends. It was a fantastic night! It got so crowded; you could barely move. I found myself at the other end of the bar, and Jim was with me. We were trying to catch up on everything in between interruptions from everyone else.

As we stood at that bar, I noticed an old lady standing near us, and she was staring at me. Jim was talking, so I held up a finger for him to wait a minute, and I asked the lady if I could help her. She told me she needed to call someone to pick her up, and her phone wouldn't work. I pulled out my phone and asked her for the number. I dialed as she waited and then told her no one was answering. She smiled a sweet smile and said thank you. I turned back to look at Jim, and he had tears in his eyes. He said, "You're the same person you've always been. You still care about other people." We looked back to the old lady, and she was gone. The odd thing is that no one we knew saw that old lady. She was not a regular, and why would she be there by herself? Was she a spirit helping us to see each other for who we really are?

At the end of the night, we all exchanged numbers and promised to stay in touch. Yeah right. I was sure that wasn't going to happen, but I was sure glad I had gone.

I don't remember who called who first, but Jim and I started playing phone tag. We kept leaving messages on each other's voicemails, but it was all just friendly stuff. I knew that he was in a long-term relationship with a woman from the area, and they had two children together. I also knew that he was miserable, but he refused to leave because he didn't want to abandon his children the way his father had abandoned him. I could truly appreciate that. It made me respect him, especially since they weren't even married. I was dating Michael, so I wasn't trying to steal him away, and I felt like he just wanted to be friends again.

Then one day, the phone rang, and we actually got to speak to each other. He was stuttering. He said that he had a dangerous job, and he couldn't think straight. He said he really needed to talk to me in person and asked if I would meet him at the Lighthouse again so we could talk. I heard something in his voice. I wasn't sure if he just wanted friendship anymore. I needed to find out what was on his mind. I called Michael and asked him if he remembered me going to the reunion a couple of weeks before that. He said yes. I asked him if he remembered that I had run into my childhood sweetheart that night. He said yes. I told him that I had just spoken to Jim, and he asked me to meet him to talk. I told him that I'm not sure what this is all about, but I need to tell you that I might have to explore this, and I wanted to give him a heads up. He was silent for a moment, and then he said, "To say that you need time is one thing, but to tell me that you want to pursue a childhood infatuation is unacceptable!" My eyebrows went up, my head cocked to the side, and I said, "Ok. Good luck with that!" I hung up, and I never spoke to him again.

Meanwhile, that Friday night, I headed to the Lighthouse to meet Jim. He called me while I was on my way and told me he was running late. "That's fine," I said. "I'll just wait in my car until you get there." I arrived and parked on the corner in front of the Lighthouse. From where I was parked, I could see the houses where we grew up. I could see Jamesy's house, and I could see the house of horrors that I lived in with my parents. Suddenly, I couldn't breathe!

What the hell was I doing? I swore I would never come back to this part of town! Why am I here? What am I trying to do, end up here again?

As I noticed I wasn't breathing, I paused and caught the song on the radio. Bon Jovi's "Who Says You Can't Go Home" was playing. I burst into tears—big slobbery, nasty face tears, and I was heaving! Just then, there was a knock on the passenger side door, and there was Jim's beaming face on the other side of the window. Oh, my God! His face went from joy to serious concern as he opened the car door and asked, "What's wrong?" He held me, even though he did not understand, and he was probably thinking, "What have I started?"

I pulled myself together, and he told me to drive. He had a plan. We went to Fort McHenry, which I learned is one of his favorite places to visit. It was part of our neighborhood, and I had been there many times, but it didn't stand out. It was closed. Then we drove to Federal Hill, parked, and walked across the park to the top of a hill overlooking the Baltimore Inner Harbor. The date was September 18, 2009. It was Cameron's birthday, but Cameron was away in New York at college. I had left him a message earlier in the day, but he hadn't called me back yet.

We sat on that hill for 4 hours, just talking. Cameron called while we spoke, and I chatted with him for a moment. After hanging up the phone, I noticed my hands were hurting from leaning on them on the grass. Jim scooted behind me and said, lean back. So, I did. When I did, he put his arms around me, and I quite literally melted. Seriously, all of my fears faded away. I was safe. Just sitting there in his arms had transformed me.

All my inhibitions were gone. We talked all those hours about our lives and our undeniable connection. Jim was the one and only. He was the one the psychic told me about all those years ago. All my anger towards men, all my painful history, none of it mattered anymore.

This was IT!

CHAPTER 95

IT Happened Fast!

After our fabulous evening on Federal Hill that Friday night, I spoke to Jim again on Saturday afternoon. He put his son, James, who was 14 years old, on the phone with me. James said hello and asked me if I was his dad's girlfriend now. I didn't know what to say, so I just told him to ask his dad. Awkward! Jim got back on the phone, laughing, and asked me what I was doing on Sunday. My only plan was to watch the Ravens' football game because I was an avid fan. He said he planned to do the same, so I invited him to my house to watch with me. He said, yes!

It occurred to me then, just how many Jimmys have been in and out of my life. Jay was a Jimmy, Jimmy R, Jimmy S. and now Jimmy W. Were all the other Jimmys just reminders that my childhood sweetheart was the true love of my life?

On Sunday, I was in a flurry to clean up the house and make some football snacks. This day would be a day to remember because it would be just the two of us all day, with none of our old friends chiming in as we caught up with each other's lives some more.

It was a beautiful day. It was a late game, though, and when the game finally ended, it was pretty late at night. He had to get up for work at 4 am, and I felt so bad for him. Not knowing the particulars of his life at home, but knowing that his son now knew about me, I asked if he wanted to stay. He said, sure! I was shocked! He went out to his car and brought in a small bag of work clothes. I had to laugh. It was almost as though he knew exactly how this was going to go down!

We slept in the same bed that night, but nothing happened between us. I knew his head had to be spinning because he was still living with the mother of his children, and now, he was in my bed. I wasn't going to make any demands or have any expectations. I just wanted to see where this would go. In the morning, he got up for work, and as he was about to leave, I asked him if he would come back. He looked at me for a moment and smiled. He then said, "I'll tell you what, if you have a toothbrush for me by the time I get off work today, I'll come back tonight."

I jumped out of bed and ran into the bathroom and came back with a family-size pack of toothbrushes, and I exclaimed, "I shop in bulk!" We both laughed, and he came back that night.

Finally, on Thursday of that week, he shared with me that he would have to face the music at his house with his children's mother. He was disturbed that she never once called him to see if he was ok or what was going on during these few days. He was angry about that. When he left for work that morning, I knew he would be going home to her rather than coming back to me. I also knew that I would cherish this time I had with him, even if I could have no more. I had no reason to be ashamed. We did not get intimate, and he had not cheated on her. This choice was up to him, and I would respect whatever decision he made.

To my surprise, in the early evening hours of that Thursday, he called me and told me that he went home, waited for her and the kids to come in, saw no reaction to his arrival, then he grabbed a basket of work clothes and told her he was leaving. She said, "Ok." He was on his way back!

WOW! I didn't expect that! I expected drama and a potential back and forth situation. I was thrilled, and I was nervous. THIS was my childhood, sweetheart! This was the little boy with blonde curls, and big blue eyes loved by every girl in the neighborhood! He was choosing me!

One concern I had was Ryan. He was on campus, at work, and at the school library most of the time, so I rarely saw him. I needed to tell him what was happening before Jim got there. My sweet Ryan, bless his soul, always wanted me to be happy. He was so tired of men disappointing me, and he was cautiously supportive, as I knew he would be. Ryan always knew that no matter what, I would choose him and his brother over any man. Ryan had gotten a chance to meet Jim over the last few days, and he liked him. He especially liked the change in me when I was around him.

CHAPTER 96

Family Answers

Jimmy W. was the perfect fit in our home! He was the FINAL Jimmy for me! He was so fun, so sweet with Ryan, so wonderful with me, and we fell head over heels in love. The running joke about us was that I invited him to watch football, and he never left. It was a very, very happy truth. Suddenly, everything made sense. All my struggles with men, all my trust issues, and all my pros and cons lists; there was none of that with him. He knew me at my core, and I knew him at his. While I knew we were in for some drama because of his ex and his children, I was ready to take it on, by his side. And boy, did we have a ride to take!

We tried to spend every possible moment together, just learning about each other and sharing our life journeys up to this point. We had both been through so much, and our experiences were very, very different. It was an unwrapping of each other's lives so we could know everything about each other. Unwrapping my life for him was a bit problematic for me, but he was easy to talk to. Joe had been the first person I ever shared my childhood horrors with. After some time, I was able to talk about it more with people I cared about, but without much detail. Jimmy W. (from now on referred to as "Jimmy") had known Paul and Debbie, and he was shocked and horrified by the stories I had to tell. We learned that while we only lived five doors away from each other as children, our lives inside those walls were utterly different.

I shared with him the stories of finding my brother David in Worcester and then losing touch with him after just one year of communicating. I never knew why he stopped writing, and I never understood why he never returned my phone calls each Christmas. I figured he had his own life, and it didn't involve me, so I moved on with mine as well. It had been 26 years since I had spoken to him. Jimmy asked me if I ever tried to reach my other brother, Dale, who was away in Japan when I visited in 1982. I told him no. He never reached out to me, and since David had stopped communicating, I figured Dale didn't want to either. Jimmy asked me if I had ever checked Facebook to see if they were there. I said no. I felt silly now because I had indeed done nothing to search them out after that visit. I think it was my pride. I didn't want to be seen as needy or make them feel like that had to include me in their lives. I knew that my grandparents and my moms' sisters were in Worcester too, and none of them had tried to reach me. It was their loss—that was my attitude.

I was a great person and by them not reaching out to me, they would never know that. I had enough to do at home with my children, and I didn't let it bother me. But now that Jimmy had asked about Facebook, I had to try it. I typed in my brother Dale's name, and his picture popped up! Oh my God, it was that easy! I got all panicky and nervous, and Jimmy laughed at me. Dale and I looked a lot alike, but I didn't even know if the family had told him about my visit. I bit the bullet and sent him a message. In the message, I told him I was his "sort of" sister and that I wasn't trying to bring any drama into his life, but I thought I would pop in and say hello. I knew for sure I would never hear from him, so at least I tried.

The next morning, I got up and saw that I had a message on Facebook from Dale. My heart was beating so fast as I opened the message, and I was so hopeful it would be something good.

And it was! He was excited to hear from me! He had checked out my Facebook account and saw my recent posts. He noticed that I had posted that I would be in Boston the following week. I had an RVP meeting with PartyLite every fall and every spring, and most of the time, those meetings were in Boston since our home office was in Plymouth. Dale told me in his response that he would love to meet me when I got to Boston!

I CANNOT EXPLAIN how elated I was! I jumped up and down and kissed Jimmy all over his face with thanks! I was now going to meet my other biological brother—one I had never met, and I was 45 years old. I wrote back to him, and we made plans for him to meet me at the hotel the following week.

When I arrived at the hotel in Boston, I settled in my room and then went down to the lobby to wait for my brother. What would I say? Should I hug him when I see him, or should I shake his hand? Will I know what to do when I see him? As I waited in the lobby, a few of my PartyLite RVP friends stopped to say hello and ask why I was there alone. I shared with them what a special day this was about to be. No one wanted to leave. They all wanted to see this play out. Valerie, one of my friends, even videotaped it for me, although I never got a copy of the video.

I knew Dale drove a Harley Davidson motorcycle, and I didn't think there would be many biker dudes walking into this hotel. As we waited, we heard the sound of a Harley approaching. My heart stopped, and I couldn't breathe. I decided I wouldn't determine if I would run to him or walk, hug him, shake his hand, or anything. I would follow my instincts. As he walked in the door, my friends were admiring his beauty! I could hear them behind me making sounds, but I just wanted to get close to him and see him. We caught eyes and were immediately in sync. We smiled big and walked fast and fell into each other's arms! I cried like a baby! My friends were cheering, and I introduced him to them.

We decided to go to the hotel bar/restaurant and chat. We sat across from each other, and I grabbed both of his hands and looked into his eyes. He was honestly so handsome, with his red bandana on his head and wearing his leather Harley jacket. It made me giggle that my brother was a member of a famous motorcycle club, the name of which I was told not to discuss in print! There are quite a few rules for motorcycle club members and their families.

To my surprise, Dale told me that his father had passed away just a month before. Ugh! Bad timing on my part. I had questions for him, and now I wouldn't be able to ask. I shared my condolences but didn't go into a lot about my visit to his family home all those years ago, simply out of respect for him mourning the passing of his Dad.

At this point, I had known for years that Paul wasn't my birth father, and the only candidate I could find was my mother's ex-husband, who happened to be my brothers' father. While Dale and I chatted and shared stories, I asked him if his Dad might have been my Dad, and he said he thought it was possible, based on the conversations he had with his Dad and conversations he heard between his Dad and Mona. We promised to stay in touch, and I had a meeting to attend, so our first date had to end. I was so thrilled this had come together.

I left there believing that Big Dale had been my Dad all along. Maybe there was a time before he married Mona that he ended up with my Mom again, for a minute. Perhaps that's why she took off to Baltimore with me. Why else would she give me his name?

CHAPTER 97

The Grave – 2009

Oddly enough, after meeting Dale in Boston in early October, I learned that he was planning a Baltimore trip for Halloween. His motorcycle club was invited to a Baltimore motorcycle club for a big party. I told him that he must stay with us if he was coming to Baltimore, and he did. He drove his bike down from Worcester and came to our home to meet my family. Right away, he and Jimmy got along great. Ryan loved him too. I called Laura to see if she wanted to join us in going to the biker Halloween party with Dale, and she said yes.

The craziest part of this event is that the bar holding the party that Dale was going to was right down the street from our home! Of all the places in Maryland, he was coming to my neighborhood! If I hadn't met him already, my brother would have been that close, and I wouldn't have known it!

Crazy!

Anyway, Dale had lots of rules to share with me. I couldn't touch the leather, I couldn't hug his friends, and I definitely couldn't take any pictures. Ok, got it. He rode down to the bar with Laura, and Jim and I got into our car. When we arrived, he and Laura were already chatting with other bikers outside the bar. We walked over to join them, and this large biker dude came over and told me he was so happy to meet Dale's little sister. He then hugged me. I panicked and held up my arms in front of my chest and realized I was touching the leather. I couldn't see Dale's face, but he had to know this wasn't my fault. When the biker dude released me, I just looked up at him and said, "Dale told me not to touch the leather." Then I rubbed both hands in circles on his chest and said, "But it feels really good!" The biker dude and I cracked up, and when I looked over at Dale, he was shaking his head!

We had a great night that evening, and Dale would spend a couple of days with us. I had a lot to share.

One of the things he wanted to do most was to visit our mother's grave. I was happy I had put that gravestone up because he wouldn't see an empty plot of dirt like I did the first time I saw it. Of course, now I had so much more information than I had when I put that marker on my mom's grave. I knew now that the last name on that marker was Paul's last name. I knew now that she was never Paul's wife. I also knew now that I had been fed lots and lots of lies, and I still didn't know for sure who my birth father was.

When Dale got to the gravesite, he was very emotional. He had spent most of his life, not knowing that he had a mother who had died. He and David were raised believing that Mona was their mother. This would be the first time he would truly be able to acknowledge his birth mother. I left him alone at the gravesite and watched him cry. It broke my heart. As he turned to me with tears in his eyes, he told me we had to get the gravestone changed to remove her last name. I agreed. We decided she should be buried with her maiden name, and we walked into the cemetery office to sign new paperwork. We did it, and she is now resting in peace with her birth name.

CHAPTER 98

Cameron's Adventure – 2010

When Cameron came home for the wedding, he announced that he had quit after two years of college. I was disappointed. He explained that he had been in schools focused on acting since 6th grade, and he wanted to learn differently now. He wanted to learn about the world and people through experience rather than school.

When the boys were young, I took the money and put it into savings accounts for them whenever anyone gave them monetary gifts. Their father's parents, their aunts, and uncles often gave them savings bonds. I saved those too. I always told them that when they were adults, I would release the money to them. Cameron was ready for his money, and he was going to fly to Amsterdam and begin a walking trip, alone, across Europe.

Cameron was now 20 years old, and I struggled with my role in his decision. I couldn't forbid it; he was an adult. I was so afraid for him. It was such a dangerous choice, and so many bad things could happen, but I knew my son, and I knew this was something he had to do.

He lived at home with us for a year. He worked and saved money and made all his own arrangements. I told him that if he had to do this, I would support him emotionally, but not financially. I couldn't let him take his phone, because there would be roaming charges, etc. He was going to have to do this by himself. I did make it clear, though, that if and when he ever decided to come home, I would buy the plane ticket. That way, he was never stuck. He always had a way home.

We dropped him off at the airport, and I feared I would never see him again. He knew how afraid I was, but he had no fear. His life was about to begin. Because he had no phone, sometimes I would have to wait months to hear from him. I could send him notes on Facebook, but he didn't have access to Facebook unless he was at a library and could get on the internet. I cried a lot, and I prayed a lot. The time between calls was painful. The fact that he celebrated his 21st birthday in another part of the world, and I couldn't even call him, was excruciating. But with each passing month, it got easier. When he did call, he shared his stories and adventures with me. He was living a life I could never imagine, but he was truly flourishing. He would share the kind acts of strangers and his ability to make friends with every person he saw, young or old. He was such an old soul, and he was making his mark. He had a journal that he wrote in to keep track of his adventures. He promised to let me read it when I saw him.

As that first Christmas approached, I knew I could not get through the holiday season without seeing him. We made plans to meet in Barcelona, Spain, two weeks before Christmas that year. I flew out, and he met me at the airport. I booked a hotel in the area, and he would stay with me, on real beds, rather than the conditions he was living in, like sleeping outside and on cots. That was the very best trip ever. We spent a week together, getting to know each other again. We explored Barcelona, we ate, we drank, we walked, and we shared.

One evening in the hotel room, he let me read his journal from cover to cover. I was so proud of the man he was becoming. I took him shopping before I left and bought him a much-needed new pair of shoes. I couldn't load him up with too many gifts because he carried everything he owned in a backpack. He saw me off at the airport as he continued his journey, and I flew back home to finish the holiday season with the rest of our family.

For nearly two years, Cameron continued this adventure, all while traveling alone, on foot, or on a bicycle given to him by a stranger. He took many odd jobs along the way, including but not limited to working on farms, building things, and teaching Italian children how to speak English. He made friends along the way that would be friends for the rest of his life. He would never be the same person again.

CHAPTER 99

David – Round Two – 2010

I have to admit that I was a bit hurt that my brother David had quickly stopped corresponding with me after our first meeting, but I didn't let it harden me in my resolve to get to know him. I was getting to know Dale now, and I would ask questions about David to learn more about him from someone who knew him well. Dale and David weren't very close, and they were very opposite people.

When the next RVP meeting came around that following February, I planned to go to Boston 2 days early and spend it with Dale and his girlfriend before my meetings began. When I arrived at their place, Dale told me that he had invited David over and he was coming. I was pleased to hear that. When David arrived, it was not like the way our previous had ended. He was wary of me, mistrustful, nervous, and deep down, he felt like he was disappointing Mona by being there. It was a very odd meeting, and while we were there,

Mona called Dale to see what was going on. She did not want me to have relationships with them. She thought I was after something. In her defense, it is very coincidental that Big Dale died, and I showed up just a month later, but that's exactly how it happened. I had no idea he had died, and what could I possibly want? I just wanted to establish a relationship with my brothers. I was annoyed but chose to focus on making the best of it.

David left as uncomfortable as he arrived, but at least I got to see him, and we had exchanged phone numbers. We would see where that would lead.

Not too long after this meeting, Mona passed away. I guess she died of a broken heart. I couldn't imagine the pain my brothers were feeling. First, their Dad and then the woman they believed was their mother.

Sometime later, maybe a year, maybe more, David called me. I was shocked to see his name on my phone, and I answered quickly. He didn't sound great, and he asked me what I take for the pain. I didn't take anything for pain. I was nervous about medication because that's what my mom used to take her life. He agreed with me about the fear. We bonded over CMT/Muscular Dystrophy and started having calls here and there. Something was beginning.

CHAPTER 100

Creating a Life Together – 2009

My favorite memory of introducing Jimmy to my friends was with Laura. Laura had been with me through so many relationships and so many break-ups. She would sometimes get frustrated with me that I would fall so quickly for guys, and then just as soon as I fell in, I fell out. It exhausted her, and it made me laugh. It was time for her to meet Jimmy because THIS WAS IT!

We met at a local restaurant, the Wild Duck, for dinner. Jim and I walked in to find her waiting. We sat, we ate, we drank, we shared, and she burst into tears. She kept saying, "This really is it for you!" It affected me so much that she was so emotionally involved in this. She was truly happy for me.

With the fact that Ryan still basically lived at home with us and now Jim's children, James and Taylor, would be spending time with us, we had some prep work to do. I started preparing the room that was once Cameron's to be a place for the two of them, and I tried to clear out everything so they would feel like they had their own place in our home. I expected that Jim and his ex would feel the same way about visitation as Joe and I had. Children needed both parents, and the goal was to keep everything as peaceful as possible for them.

Unfortunately, his ex, Kim, did not feel that way. Just as I reserved nasty details regarding the end of my marriage, I will not share the ugly details regarding the end of his relationship, either. All four of our children are amazing human beings, and they should not ever have to read details of those events. Instead, let's say that it took until Taylor graduated college (and she was 11 when we met) for the drama to end.

Jimmy kept teasing me and asking when I would be his wife. I kept answering that I would be his wife when he asked me. As February approached, we started making a plan. He had a fantastic job and earned an excellent income, but a good portion of that income was being spent on the mortgage on the home the ex and kids lived in, car insurance for both him and his ex, child support, and lots of other expenses that Kim kept passing on to him. Fortunately, my income was sufficient, and I didn't care.

We wanted to plan a small, inexpensive wedding, but there would be no engagement ring because it wasn't in the cards. I was totally fine with that. I had many engagement rings over the years, and none of them brought the kind of marriage I wanted. This time, I didn't need a ring. I just needed him to be my husband forever.

We decided to get married at the Wild Duck, our favorite neighborhood restaurant. The owner had become a friend, and we were regulars. We arranged for hot dogs and hamburgers and an open bar. My first great idea was to reach out to Peggy Sue. I asked her if she would consider becoming ordained to perform marriages so she could do our wedding for us. After all the years of having her as the go-between for us and since it was her invitation to the luau that set this reunion in motion, I wanted her to have an integral part in our special day. Of course, she agreed, and it was the best decision we had made, aside from the wedding itself.

We did cake tastings when Cameron was in town, and we began tying up all the details. Laura picked up the flowers, and Jessi, another dear friend from PartyLite, set up the arch and helped us cut the cake. My BFF at the time was Kim G., and she would not only be my maid of honor, but her husband would videotape the whole thing.

I wanted a real wedding dress, but since we were getting married at a beach restaurant, I didn't wear shoes. I just had foot jewelry. Kim G., Jim's sister, Jenny, and Taylor were standing with me, and James, Ryan, and Cameron were standing with Jim. We invited 120 people, and we had a large part of the outside area of the venue sectioned off for just our wedding party. I asked all of my PartyLite leaders to bring a candle centerpiece with a beach theme, and they were beautiful. The owner hired a reggae band, per our request, and did not charge us because the venue was still open for other guests.

Just a day or so before the wedding, we reached out to my friend, Bonita, and she lined up a yacht to pick up my girls and me at a marina down the street and drive us up to the pier at the Wild Duck for our grand entrance. Jessi rolled out a red carpet on the pier, so it didn't ruin my dress, and best of all, my brother Dale came in to give me away!

Because all of this happened just seven months after Jim and I re-met at the Lighthouse, I hadn't met most of his family and hardly any of his friends. He hadn't met most of my friends either. For years after our wedding, we ran into people who told us they were in the other section of the bar area when our wedding was held. They watched from afar, and we found that to be so very cool.

CHAPTER 101

True Partners

With each passing day, I became more and more grateful. Jim was indeed my other half. He was unlike any man I had ever known. We did everything together, we respected each other, we loved each other, we loved each other's children, and they loved each other too. THIS was finally where I belonged.

I finally got it right!

Jimmy went to nearly every candle party I did and attended every meeting. He went to National Conference with me each year and, of course, he was on every PartyLite trip. Everyone that met him loved him. Everyone close to me adored him because they saw how happy we were. It was the most incredible feeling in the world.

One-year, National Conference was in Orlando, Florida. We decided to bring Taylor with us, and she and Jim could do the amusement parks while I was in meetings. They had a blast, and I was a teeny bit jealous in the happiest way! They also knew about a secret that I didn't yet know. On the last evening of the Conference, Taylor and Jim came into the hall to watch the secret be unveiled. Apparently, PartyLite had reached out to Jim. They wanted to do a special video with some of the RVP children sharing how the business affected their lives. Jim then arranged to have Ryan and Cameron get together to make a video and send it to PartyLite. He hadn't seen it yet, but he knew it was coming that evening.

As he and Taylor sat on the floor at the back of the hall, and I sat with my region, the video started, and I wasn't paying attention. Until I heard Ryan's voice, I quickly looked up at the screen and saw both of my beautiful boys on the video, sharing their memories of their Mom, the SRVP. One of my friends videoed the shock on my face and my reactions throughout the video. I was in tears. I was so very proud that my boys were so proud of me!

We lived each day and went through hurdles like every other married couple, but we had taken advice from his mother before getting married. Her advice was to wake up each morning and think of what you can do to make the other happy. As long as we both lived by that mantra, our happiness would grow, and neither of us would be taken for granted. We took it seriously because we both wanted this to last forever.

We had challenges, though—most of them from his ex. I was supportive and tried to be helpful, and I stood by his side throughout it. His children grew past the mistrust of our initial meeting and began to love me. I certainly loved them. Just as my kids were my world, his kids were his world. Now we had four, and it was terrific.

We certainly knew how to have fun together. Jim immediately loved our home and met all the neighbors. I had lived in the house for four years before Jim moved in, and I knew only three neighbors, all directly across the street. I learned that I had a nickname in the neighborhood. They called me the phantom because they never saw me outside. I stayed in the house, and when I had to go out, I walked down my basement stairs, into my garage, and drove from there. They never really saw me.

In no time at all, Jim knew everyone. I wasn't pleased about that at first because I had terrible experiences with neighbors when I was married to Joe. I didn't want people getting involved in our lives, and I didn't want that kind of drama again. I realized the neighbors didn't cause the drama; it was caused by what we shared with our neighbors. Jim and I didn't have any bad stuff to share, and therefore, there was no drama. He opened a new door for me, and I was so happy he did!

CHAPTER 102

Taylor and James

From the first time I met them, I knew I would love them. I did, however, believe it would go more smoothly than it did. I had a lot to learn about teenagers raised by another woman with entirely different parenting skills than I had. I tried so hard to make the transition easy, but they were young enough to be influenced by their mother's intense dislike for me, and there were struggles. I did not doubt that the love Jim and I shared would get us through this, and I knew it wouldn't happen overnight. It was a slow process.

I am a strong-minded parent. I believe that children should be allowed to be children and not made to carry adult issues. I think children shouldn't curse – especially in their family home. I believe in respect on both ends. I believe you do as you're told when you're told. I was the only person in the house now that thought these things.

James cussed like a sailor. The F-bomb was his every other word. They were both so loud, and they argued so much. Taylor always wanted to bring her friends over, and I was okay with it. The issue was the hour and a half car rides from their mother's home to ours was deafening with the sounds of the high-pitched voices in the back seat. It made my head hurt. Jim thought I was silly, and he laughed. I wasn't kidding.

They both played sports every season of the year. Jim had to be at every single game. Those games again were an hour and a half away. I joined in when I could, depending on my work schedule, and I didn't mind it at all, but there were times when James wasn't speaking to his father. It broke my heart when we would attend his games, and James wouldn't acknowledge his dad in the bleachers. These kids were so caught up in the drama between their mom and dad, and I wished I knew how to make it end for them.

James graduated from high school and went into the Marines. He traveled to the most dangerous parts of the world, and he served his four years. When he came back from the Marines, he moved in with us instead of his mom. That was huge for Jim. My sweet husband didn't want to compete with his ex for the love of his children, but this was a sign that James loved him and wanted to be a regular part of his life.

Taylor grew to be gorgeous and a driven scholar, even though she talked like a sailor too as she grew older. I made a habit of asking them repeatedly to watch their language.

Taylor chose to attend college at George Mason in Virginia, and she did so well that she earned a full-ride scholarship to the University of Maryland for her master's and Ph.D. They even gave her a $2,000 a month living expense stipend. She chose to move home with us, too, while she went to the University of Maryland, and I never thought it would be so easy to live with her 24/7. She's an absolute dream roomie.

As they became adults, we got very close. They became my children too, and I took great pride in everything they accomplished. I don't look at myself as a mom of 2 boys anymore. I'm a proud mom of 4.

CHAPTER 103

Billy As An Adult

As my little brother Billy grew, he didn't follow the same path I did. I would visit him as a teenager and try to coach him into hanging out with better people and working on his anger issues but to no avail. As an older teen, he got into trouble so much that the judge told him he could choose between jail and the Army when he went to court. He chose the Army. After graduating from boot camp, he didn't get the job with the Army that he wanted, so he got out. He went back to his same old friends and the same old behaviors. Finally, he landed in prison.

I wouldn't help him with anything while he was there. I visited him a couple of times, but I wouldn't give him money, and I told him he would have to figure it out for himself now.

When he was released from prison, he had a new girlfriend, Shannon. She was the ex of one of his friends, and she had visited him quite a bit while he was in prison. He brought her to my home, and she seemed lovely. As I visited with them more and spent time with them, I thought this was an excellent shot for him to grow up and become responsible. I wanted to help solidify that option for him. They were talking about getting married and wanting to buy a house. That was huge because Dad never bought homes. He just rented. Billy wanted more for himself.

I invited Billy and Shannon over one day and made them an offer. I told them I would help them look for a home, I would make the down payment, and I would pay half the mortgage for the first 2-3 years until they got on their feet. They were elated. I was too! I felt like this was the right thing to do, and maybe it was just what they needed to make changes in their lives for the better.

We found a great little house, and everything went as planned. They made that house their home, and they had a beautiful baby girl named Sarah. Shannon already had two children from a previous marriage, and they made such a great family.

After three years, I told them it was time for them to take over the mortgage because I needed to start putting away money for the boys' college funds. They weren't pleased, but they did it. What I didn't know was that things were going as well at home for them as I thought. Within a year after taking over the mortgage, they lost the house in foreclosure. I was so angry that I had spent so much money helping them, and they blew it, but I kept that to myself. I had decided to help, and it was a decision I didn't regret. I would learn later that they were both doing drugs and cheating on each other. They rented another house, and shortly after they moved in, the major drama began, and they split up. My heart broke for them.

Their relationship became a circus of love and hate, together and not, one or the other going to jail, one or the other going to the hospital, one or the other beating up someone, and I could go on and on. I stepped out and could no longer be a part of any of it.

Meanwhile, Billy and his anger wound up in prison again. I think he went to prison three times. I decided to focus on my life and let them figure out theirs. I needed to stay focused on positivity, and this was dragging me down.

CHAPTER 104

Billy in Vegas

When Billy got out of prison for the last time, he convinced Shannon to let him take Sarah to Vegas to stay with his mother. He wanted a new start without the friends that kept dragging him down. While he had been in prison, Shannon's life spiraled out of control. They were homeless half the time and staying with other people the other half of the time. It was not a healthy environment for any of them. He made Shannon believe he would be in Vegas, setting up a good life for them, and she could follow when it was all set up. He never intended to bring her to Vegas. This was Billy's way of getting his daughter out of those situations, without having to deal with fighting for custody because they were both a hot mess, and Sarah would have probably been taken away from them both.

When Billy arrived in Vegas, he quickly met another woman. They moved in with her, and Shannon was having a fit. She couldn't afford an attorney, and she couldn't afford a flight to Vegas, so there wasn't a whole lot she could do. She talked to Sarah constantly on the phone and was still able to manipulate her into begging her father to let her fly home for visits. He would send her on a plane periodically, and then there was usually drama trying to get her back. It was all such a ridiculous game.

To complicate matters even more, the new woman announced that she was pregnant. All I could do was shake my head. They fought like crazy, and Billy and Sarah eventually moved out and into a home of their own. They became inseparable, and Billy spoiled her with every material item she wanted. I tried to coach him through proper parenting, but he didn't want to hear it. Sarah was demanding, she was mouthy, and he thought it was funny.

Jim and I were planning a trip to Vegas soon. His Army buddies wanted to have a reunion there and would bring their wives. Our friends Joey & Dennis in New York were going as well, to celebrate Joey's 50th birthday. It was also the week of Halloween. We chatted with our closest friends, Ricky and Leslie, and they decided to join us. This was one packed week of fun.

Jim and I got there first, and he had found the perfect hotel for us! It was a massive room with a gorgeous view of the Bellagio fountain!

Our first item on the agenda was meeting up with Billy and Sarah. We went to their home, and I saw that they barely had furniture. They had no kitchen table. I sat down on the small sofa and did some online shopping right then and there. They had a new dining room set arriving within the next 2-3 days. The next day, the four of us drove to the Grand Canyon in Billy's truck. We had such a fantastic day! We were taking photos of us pretending to call into the canyon. At times it was scary.

We went to the In & Out Burger joint. We laughed, Sarah and I played Miss Mary Mack in the back of the truck on the way back. It was a blast!

The next day, a few of the Army guys were arriving. We met up with them, and Jim was in his glory. Then Joey &

Dennis and their crew arrived. Now it was time for a fancy dinner and more laughs. Finally, Ricky and Leslie came, and we were in full swing. There was lots of laughing, lots of drinking, plenty of gambling, we went to a strip club, and the Army guys bought me a lap dance. I was not a fan! Leslie and I joined Joey & Dennis to see a drag show. That was fantastic! We ate more, we drank more, and then it was Halloween.

By this time, the Army guys were gone. Joey & Dennis had a Halloween theme of the Wizard of Oz. Ricky, Leslie, Jim, and I were prepared. We were part of their theme, and we all headed to a drag club for the evening. Boy, was that a hoot! We didn't win the costume contest, but we did make it into the finals!

This was one of the best vacations of my life. It wasn't about a beach or lots of tanning; it was purely about having a great time with three different groups of friends and my brother and his daughter.

CHAPTER 105

Sarah

Billy was calling me and sharing that he was having issues with Sarah. They had moved back in with the woman with his baby, and apparently, she didn't like Sarah. That reminded me of Billy's mother, Debbie. I tried to convince him to back up and understand that he had created a monster, and he now had to work through it with her. He disagreed. He got annoyed with my advice and stopped calling me.

About a year later, I was at a candle party, doing my thing, when my cell phone rang. It was Sarah. Even though I was in the middle of the party, I thought it was very odd for her to call me. I answered, and she asked me to order her a pizza. What? I told her I was working, and I would finish in 30 minutes, and I would call her back. When I called her back, I had questions.

Why would she ask me to send her a pizza in Vegas?

She wasn't in Vegas. Where was she? She was in Baltimore. When had she arrived? Three months ago. I got the address, sent her a pizza, and told her I would call her from the road on my drive home.

Sarah shared the story with me the next day when I picked her up at Craig's house, where she was currently staying.

Billy and Sarah argued, and Sarah got mouthy. There was no surprise there. The surprise was how Billy handled it. He was highly offended by the things she said, so he took her phone and put her on a plane. She was 12 years old at the time, by herself, with no one notified to pick her up. When she arrived in Baltimore, she asked a stranger to let her use their phone, and she called her mother's cousin to pick her up. They lived out in the boondocks, and Sarah felt she was too far away from her family. She couldn't stay with her mom because she was in jail again. She reached out to Craig and his wife, Lori, and they took her in.

Billy was not paying a dime to help with raising his child. He had wholly dismissed her and walked away. I was horrified. This was Paul's behavior, and now Billy was repeating it!

While Sarah was visiting us that day, she said there was drama at Craig's house and that he and Lori were splitting up. There were many arguments, and they had kids, and she felt like she was in the middle of it all. Sarah asked if she could stay with us. I told her we would discuss it, but she needed to know that she would have to live by our rules—no cussing, no drugs, a curfew, etc. She flat out said, "No! No one is ever going to tell me what to do again!"

That was a deal-breaker. I explained to Sarah that this wasn't my first rodeo, and I was happy to help, but she would not turn our world upside down. I expected respect, and I promised to respect her as well, but these conditions were not negotiable. She said, "No, thanks." I took her back to Craig and Lori's, and when I got home, I called Billy.

I was very upset with him, and he was very defensive. He didn't want to hear anything I had to say, and how dare I judge him. I told him I wasn't judging him; I was trying to get through to him. A child is not something you toss away when it gets difficult. He went into a barrage of insults and told me he was done with me too. He blocked me from his phone, and we've never spoken again.

Meanwhile, Lori and I began chatting about Sarah and what needed to be done. She couldn't keep her there with her situation, and I wouldn't take her because of her attitude. We decided our only option was to involve Social Services. Lori and I were by Sarah's side every step of the way, and Sarah was not happy. Sarah was put into foster care with a trained professional. Lori and I both felt bad about it, but we promised to stay in her life. Sarah would end that too. She would only call me when she wanted money, and I was smarter than that.

Eventually, Sarah stopped calling me. I check her Facebook account every once in a while, to see if she's ok. It's hard to tell, but there's nothing I can do about it. I hate to admit this, but my attitude had become, "Not my circus, not my monkeys."

CHAPTER 106

50th Birthday

Jim and I share a birthday week. I was born five days before him! He called me a "cougar!" For our 50th birthdays, he planned a trip for us to Key West. This amazing man took care of everything. We flew to Ft. Lauderdale, rented a convertible, and drove through the keys. He planned a stop at a beautiful small hotel called "Dove Creek" for a night, and then we continued our drive. We were in no hurry and stopped along the way to have a beignet and drinks and just had a great time driving in the beautiful weather.

When we arrived in Key West, he took me to the sailboat he had chartered for the week for us. How awesome was that?

We had the most magical vacation EVER! We slept on the sailboat each night and played around town each day. We had a crew make us dinner a couple of times, and they even planned a day on the water with us. Unfortunately for me, there had recently been a storm in the area, and the seas were rough. As we proceeded into the area where the ocean meets the bay, the water was churning, and so was my belly! The captain noticed my green face and told me to throw up, but I didn't want to. I had to! And it didn't stop. There was a beautiful sunset coming, and I didn't want to ruin Jim's arrangements for us completely. They asked if I wanted to go back in, and I asked if we could just sit still long enough to watch the sunset and then go back in. That's what we did.

While I knew it wasn't everything Jim had hoped for, he understood.

I want to make this trip again! Jimmy, are you reading this?

CHAPTER 107

Charcot-Marie-Tooth – 2014

I noticed my toes were curling so much that I was having trouble getting shoes on and off. They were shaped like claws. The knuckles curled upward, and the toes curled under. They would almost flatten when I stood, but I got blisters on the tops of the knuckles from walking in shoes. I refused to go back to Hopkins, so I decided to search for a podiatrist. I found a great guy, Dr. Adelberg, and he was just 20 minutes away. He was a great doctor with an excellent bed-side manner. He and I worked closely together to plan a surgery that might help me. I didn't want my tendons replaced by having leg surgery as David did. I didn't want fusion to stop the foot drop like David did. David had shared with me all his nightmare issues with the many, many surgeries he had gone through. All I wanted to do was remove the knuckles in my toes so the curling would stop.

Dr. Adelberg scheduled the surgery after many conversations, drawings, and research. We had a plan. He told me to do just one foot at a time so that I wouldn't be completely immobile during the healing process. After the surgery, I woke up with the nastiest feet ever! Every toe was straight on my left foot, but every toe had a metal pin coming out of the top of it. It was a bloody mess!

I was prescribed Dilaudid and immediately hated it! It made me scratch like crazy, and I couldn't take it after the first two days of recovery. I was in so much pain, and Jimmy took such great care of me. I knew the only way to really recover would be to get back to work, so he brought my laptop, office phone, calendar, and paperwork into the family room, and I worked from my sofa with wine at my fingertips!

I had known all these years I was the role model for the boys for how to accept and work through issues with CMT. If they had it, I wanted them to know it was manageable. They were always aware that they had a 50/50 shot, and chances were at least 1 of them would have it. It turned out to be Cameron.

CHAPTER 108

Surprise!

I was patiently waiting for the pins to be removed from my toes. It took much longer than I had expected, and I wanted to move onto the next foot. Dr. Adelberg kept me in line and was very patient with me. I had several follow up appointments and x-rays, and I just had to wait until it was finished healing. On one afternoon, Jim came home early to take me to the doctor's appointment for the next follow-up. As we sat in the waiting room, my cell phone rang. I saw that it was our friends from the neighborhood, Anthony and Joey. They were our closest friends in the neighborhood, and they probably wanted to have dinner together or something. I sent the call to voicemail and decided I would call them back when we were done.

When we got into the examination room, they called again. This time I answered and whispered into the phone that I was at the doctor's and would call them back. Anthony spoke up and said, "When will you be home?" I didn't have an answer, so I told him again that I would call as soon as it was over. I then went into the room for the x-ray, and my phone rang again—goodness! I sent it to voicemail again and told Jimmy that something must be going on over there. We spent the next few minutes sharing ideas of what it was. I thought they bought a new car. Jimmy thought they got a new dog. I agreed. Their dog had recently passed away, and we were sure that was it.

As I was about to get into the car, the phone rang again. I answered it and said, "What are you doing?" Anthony said he got something, and he really, really wanted us to see it. I told him we were going to the movies, and then we would come over to see it—whatever it was. He was panicky and said, "No, you need to come right now! Please!" The call was on speaker, so Jimmy heard every word. We looked at each other and nodded. The movie could wait. We had never heard Anthony like this, and we needed to find out what was up.

We arrived at their home about 20 minutes later, and I needed help walking across their stone driveway. I used a cane to walk, and I still couldn't put all my weight on the left foot. Anthony came down and asked if I wanted to use the elevator. Yes, of course, I did. As we got into the elevator, Anthony shared with us that an old friend had stopped by, and he rolled his eyes. I didn't think anything of it. I was more worried about the two small dogs I knew he had. I was concerned they would cause me to trip or fall and told Jimmy to hold on tight to me.

As the elevator door opened on the main floor, I kept my eyes on the dogs, and I stepped gingerly onto the solid floor. I looked up and saw Joey in the kitchen, and I saw a male figure in the living room. I looked back down at the dogs, and then it suddenly registered that the male figure was familiar. I looked back over and saw that it was Cameron! My mouth dropped open, my eyes were like saucers, and my legs went numb.

I heard Anthony yell, "Catch her!" and Jimmy's arms were around me, trying to help me stand. All I could do was cry! Cameron came running and held me so tight, and I cried and cried. What was he doing here? I didn't know he was coming home! He said it was a secret and he wanted to surprise us and well, he certainly did that! Once I stopped touching his face and crying, I called Ryan and told him to get to Joe and Anthony's right away, but I wouldn't tell him why. When he got there, he got to be surprised too. Both of my boys were here, and my baby was home!

The next day was Thanksgiving, and the surprise was now headed to Joe and Vickie's house. Fortunately, Kristen video-taped it, and I was so touched when I saw and heard his grandparents' reaction to seeing him again. Everyone was happy he was home and safe.

Cameron was only home for a short time. He was heading to NYC to work on a project with his college friends. Cameron had rewritten Hamlet and produced the play and took the leading role in an off-Broadway show. He was ready to get to work in his profession.

As for the surgery results, the knuckles are gone on my left foot toes, but that didn't stop the shoe issue. Now, instead of my toes curling, they stand up straight. I did not have the same surgery on the right foot. I'll live with it.

CHAPTER 109

South Carolina

As the four kids grew, they established their life plans. Ryan became a paralegal with one of the largest law firms in Baltimore. Cameron created Hamlet, and it was a success. He then got roles in several other plays and kept himself busy. He had found a small apartment, and he stayed with his friends when he needed to be closer to a particular area of town.

When James went into the Marines, we decided that we would be there to support him when he graduated from boot camp. We decided to make a full week vacation out of it by spending the first part of the week in the Myrtle Beach area of South Carolina before driving to Parris Island for James' graduation. When we checked into our hotel in Myrtle Beach, we posted a pic on Facebook. My brother, David, saw the post and texted me to tell me he and his wife were there too! We made plans to catch up and have dinner together the next night.

We had a blast driving around Myrtle Beach, and we couldn't help but check out areas for retirement. This was a great area, and we both were intrigued. I was looking forward to meeting up with David and Rosemary, and I was very nervous. Our last meeting wasn't so great, but our conversations by phone seemed to be warming him up. This time was so very different! He was open, he smiled a lot, and he gave me the biggest, warmest hug ever! I loved Rosemary immediately, and I knew this was the beginning of something extraordinary.

David and Rosemary were actually in Myrtle Beach to put in a contract on a home in a neighboring area. After signing the contract, they would go home, pack everything up, and move to the Conway area. Now I had even more reason to want to retire there.

CHAPTER 110

Mobility Issues

As time went on and I got older, it became apparent that the CMT was advancing. I was falling more often and sometimes even at people's homes while I was doing candle parties. It was quite embarrassing because to look at me; you would have no idea. I think people often thought I was drinking too much, and a few were concerned that I would file a lawsuit for falling down their front steps. When I would explain that I have a form of Muscular Dystrophy, I saw that dreaded pity on their faces. I hated it!

One day during the holiday season, I saw the UPS man unloading a bunch of PartyLite boxes. I knew the driver because he was at our house often. I clicked the button to open the garage door, and he knew that meant to put the boxes into the lower level. I also realized I hadn't given him his Christmas gift yet, so I walked down the outside stairs to hand him his gift. He was very appreciative, and I thanked him for bringing the boxes inside. I looked at my watch and realized I was supposed to be on a conference call with all the RVPs at that very minute. Crap! I said my goodbyes and proceeded to run up the outside steps to my first level.

As I ran up the stairs, I tripped and experienced the most excruciating pain since childbirth. I didn't want the UPS driver to know I had hurt myself. He had a hectic route, and I was so embarrassed. I held my breath and turned to sit on the stairs right in the middle range of the stairs and waved goodbye to the driver. I saw a puzzled look on his face, like what is she doing sitting there? Luckily, he kept driving, and then I struggled to get to the top step. Tears were streaming, and I had no idea what I had done. I just needed to get onto that conference call!

Once I got to the top of the stairs, I tried to step on that foot, of course, the left foot again, and down I went! Oh, this was not good! Still focused on the conference call, I crawled through the house to the office, climbed into my chair, dialed into the call, muted my line, and sobbed like an infant.

Once I could breathe again, I texted my husband while I stayed in the conference call. I told him by text that I thought I had broken my foot. He panicked and tried to call me, but I sent his call to voicemail and texted him back that I was on a PartyLite conference call. I told him I would call him as soon as the meeting was over. When I returned his call, he was so confused. I broke my foot, yet I was still on a conference call. I tried to chuckle but just said, "I need to know what's going on with my business, and I can't go anywhere right now with a broken foot, so why not?"

I told him not to hurry home, but I would wait for him so he could take me to the emergency care center for an x-ray. When he got home, he just kept shaking his head at me.

Then I told him that I had a 3 pm manicure appointment to go to before we went to the urgent care. He thought I was kidding. I have a standing appointment every two weeks, and I can't miss it. Still shaking his head, he took me to get my nails done, and then he took me to the urgent care.

My foot was definitely broken. The bone that runs down the outer part of my left foot was broken at an angle. The doctor told me to see my podiatrist and get the foot wrapped. He put me in a boot before I left. I never went to see my doctor. I just kept my foot wrapped and stayed off my feet for a bit. Because of this, it took a very, very long time for that foot to heal completely. I'm talking years.

Since this was not the first time I had fallen down the stairs at my house, I decided it was time to make some life changes since I was falling more and more frequently. I had to stop pretending I didn't have this disease and that I would be just fine. I was getting older, and it was only going to get worse as I aged.

I had some serious thinking to do.

CHAPTER 111

Forgiveness

As the years passed since Debbie A.'s betrayal with PartyLite, she had tried several times to reach me, and I wouldn't accept her calls. Our mutual friend, Jessi, passed on the message to me that Debbie's mother had passed away. I did not react at all. I had eliminated her from my life. I had no intention of speaking to her ever again. But who was I kidding? She had been an integral part of my life for so long. Neither of us was perfect, and we had always worked around our differences. But this one was so cutthroat, in my opinion. In her opinion, it wasn't personal. It was business, and she felt that it was the best business decision for her.

Wasn't it personal?

Giving me zero notice of a mutiny that caused me to immediately have my income cut in half while I was paying a mortgage and putting two boys through college at the same time? How is that not personal? In her opinion, I ended our lifelong friendship over money. In my opinion, it was a huge betrayal, and I would never trust her again. I've always believed that trust was the most significant factor in any relationship.

The problem was that my sleeping self-made me think of her way too often. I had dreams constantly about her and including her. One day she called again, and I answered the phone. She was surprised, and she was grateful. She was very nervous and very sweet. I told her I had to let the hate go. It wasn't healthy to hold on to it, and I wasn't doing either of us any favors. I would open up communication again, but I would never be as close to her as we once were. We agreed to meet for a cocktail near her office in the city. Jim and Ryan went with me, and she brought her husband, Dan. It was weird and so uncomfortable for both of us. When she got there, she had a wrapped gift for me. I was puzzled because this wasn't a gift-giving event, but I accepted it graciously. It was a lovely polka dot make-up travel bag with my name stitched into it. She then asked me to go to the ladies' room with her. When we got inside, she told me she knew I was confused about the gift. She had learned through other people that I held her birthday gift on that terrible day at the airport and then threw it in the trash before I got on the plane. She knew then how hurt I was. She felt so guilty and had carried that guilt for all those years. We both cried and embraced, and some of the discomfort passed.

It took a few more years for us to feel close again, but we did it. I can't deny that I love her like a sister. Life is about love; it's about sharing this world and your heart with others. It's about forgiveness. It's about understanding each other's shortcomings and accepting people for who they are. Honestly, I can walk away from almost anyone, and I have, but apparently, she was a lifer for me, and I for her.

More times were ahead for us. The times she needed support concerning the ending of her nearly 30-year marriage, the times we just chatted about old times, the times we shared photos, the times we just thought of each other and dropped a text. We were friends again, and I was glad.

CHAPTER 112

Stepping Down

Things had not been going well with PartyLite for several years. Home office members and executives were being fired and replaced with strangers. Our product line was not as appealing, they continuously made changes, and it didn't feel like we had the same "family" attitude as we had always had. There were discussions with the RVPs about changing the profit program. There was a lot of fear.

Meanwhile, established RVPs were leaving the company and joining other companies. Consultants and leaders across the country were getting scared that their mentors were jumping ship, and they followed. Most of us in the field were scared but hopeful. We kept pushing through. We kept answering all the fears and offering words we didn't honestly believe ourselves. Our jobs became less about growing and more about saving. It wasn't a pretty transition.

I watched many of my mentors leave, and I watched the size of our RVP gatherings dwindle from filling a double banquet hall to just barely needing ten tables for us. The gifts were getting smaller, the recognition was decreasing, and the sharing of yearly incomes nearly stopped. It just was not good news. Meanwhile, the company was sold, and there were fears that we would be broken up and sold off. It got to the point where I knew less than a handful of home office people, and my clout of being an SRVP for so many years was gone. Most of them at the home office didn't even know my history with this company, and the family feel was truly gone.

Aside from these facts, I was ready to stop doing live candle parties. It had become so challenging carrying my products in and out of people's houses. Jimmy didn't go to my parties anymore because most of them were in the evenings, and after he worked all day installing elevators, he was just too tired. I had to do it myself. I was fearful with every step I took when walking into my hosts' homes and walking out. I was afraid when I lit a candle and held it up to show the beautiful glow. I was always fearful that I would fall in front of people. My fear was justified because it happened often. Once I fell carrying a large piece of product as I walked into my host's home. The front door rug slid as I stepped inside, and my body went one way, and my feet went the other as I fell on my face half in and half out of her home!

There were several times that as I held a burning candle holder in my hand, my hand would go numb, and the burning piece would drop from my hands onto my host's floor, smashing glass and liquid wax going everywhere. I fell in driveways, streets, kitchens, family rooms, and backyards. I always had bruises and aches and pains but rarely got seriously hurt.

I went to my last RVP meeting in November of 2017. All of my upline leaders had either retired or stepped down, and most of my close friends on the RVP team had done the same. For the first time, I had to search for a roommate amongst those that were left. It felt so lonely. I took the position during those few days to sit back and watch. If I walked away, would I miss it? I listened intently to everything being shared, but I kept to myself, just taking it all in. At the end of the trainings, I went up to the Vice President and told her that I wanted to step down as of December 1st. I'm sure she thought I was leaving for another company, but that was of no interest to me. I never wanted to rebuild again. I just wanted to sell my products online, no longer hold meetings, and no longer do live parties. She accommodated me and assigned our region to another RVP.

CHAPTER 113

Urban Axes – April 2018

I stepped down as SRVP in December, and by April, I was bored! I was still working my PartyLite business online and by phone. This new way of life provided plenty of time to spend with my family, but I needed something else to fill my days. I considered joining the community groups in our neighborhood, but I just wasn't inspired enough. I had lunches with friends more and shopped more, but I needed something fulfilling. I started a job search for a part-time gig working at home doing some customer service job.

I expected some response with each application I submitted, but never got a single one! I wouldn't say I liked the new way the hiring process worked in this new world of ours.

Meanwhile, Cameron had taken a part-time job in Philly working for a company called "Urban Axes," and it sounded like a blast! He loved it, and I was so happy he found something to do between his acting gigs.

One day Cameron told me that Urban Axes was opening a venue in Baltimore. I told him I had to be part of it. He reached out to the owners, and we had a friendly phone chat. They weren't quite ready because there was still red tape with opening the venue, but they wanted to know what I wanted to do. I shared my extensive experience with working with customers and coaching my hosts to have successful parties. I planned to book events, do consistent follow-up, and create a comfortable, fun atmosphere for everyone attending. My forte has always been about building relationships with my customers to be loyal to my company and me. I knew this would benefit Urban Axes too!

By September, I had given up and was sure my age was the issue. I was surprised to get the call for an interview after that long. The venue had now been open for two months, but they were still ironing out details. I was interviewed twice by phone, and then I had to go to the venue to meet the manager and be interviewed by him. I always feel so much better when I can meet someone face to face, and I loved Eli the moment I met him. I could tell that he cared about his crew and that he had a great sense of humor. I was going to enjoy this!

I got the job and began training right away. This turned out to be the perfect part-time job for me. Urban Axes gave me a laptop, and I created a new working desk in my office—PartyLite on one desk, Urban Axes on the other. I spent my days working at home, bouncing back and forth between the two, and neither of these jobs required me to punch in or punch out, and they both allow me to work on my own terms. Absolute perfection! I get to show up at the venue whenever I need to meet a client, and I'm met with hugs from the staff each time. It's incredible, and I adore these people! I'm so glad they found a place for me to do what I love to do.

CHAPTER 114

Bella

It might seem strange that this book is about my life and those that molded the person I am, and I include my dogs, but they really did influence me as a person. Even my friend, Reggie, knew that when Zoey passed, I would NEED another dog. I had become so attached to Zoey, and she gave me a comfort I had never known before. I finally understood what unconditional love was.

But after she died, Jimmy said he didn't want another dog in the house. In his defense, Zoey had never been properly trained, and she relieved herself wherever and whenever she felt like it. I wasn't ready right away because I knew I had to mourn her passing.

As the months went by, I found myself to be so needy of Jim's affections. I realized it was because I didn't have a little dog anymore. He would get annoyed with me and then start laughing when I would tell him to get me a dog, and I would leave him alone.

One evening when we went to Reggie's 50th birthday party, Reggie kept telling him to get me a dog. He was telling him over and over and explaining that it would make his life so much better because I just had too much love to give. A year after Zoey passed, Jimmy told me to get a dog.

Taylor and I drove to different places to see dogs needing adoption. We could only find big dogs, and I did not want a big dog. There were commercials that week on television about no adoption fees for a whole weekend. I decided that on Sunday I would find my new dog. Jimmy would not go with me, and Taylor wasn't home. I went by myself. I went to different rescue places and could not find what I was looking for. I needed something small because I fall so much, and I didn't want a dog to be able to knock me down. I wasn't picky about a particular breed or anything; it was just an issue of safety for me. I had no luck and was about to go home when I realized that I had enough time to check another place. It was an hour in the opposite direction from where I was, but there was time.

When I got to the Fallston Animal Rescue Movement, I had 20 minutes before they closed. I wasn't even hopeful at that point; I was marking off my list of places to check.

It was a small place, and they only dealt with small animals. They only had about a dozen cages, and the employees took the dogs home with them each night to be fostered until they found their forever home. The FARM (as it's called) has an older couple as the owners. The wife was working the register when I arrived, and the husband was brushing a small, scrawny, ratty-looking dog with fleas jumping off her like crazy. I was kind of cringing as I watched him with her. They told me she had been dropped off just 10 minutes before by her owner, who said she was moving and couldn't take her with her. The poor thing was infested with fleas! You could tell she was not being taken care of previously by her owner. She was also six years old, and I was concerned about how long she would last.

My Zoey had passed at 15 ½. I don't know what I expected, but I wanted to be sure I had plenty of time with my next baby.

As he brushed her out, I checked out the other dogs, and I kept being drawn back to her. They were gracious enough to let me stay past closing time to make my decision. The wife told me that she knew someone would snatch this little girl up if I didn't want her. I wasn't sure yet. I had to keep watching her personality. When her brushing was over, and she was partially dry, I asked if I could take her out on a leash to the grass patch beside the building. They said yes. I took her out and let her pee, and then I loosened the leash enough for her to run a bit. She was adorable, even though she was so skinny.

She had wandered a bit too far for me, and I stooped down and said, "Come here, Bella!" She came running back to me and then lay down on her back for me to rub her belly. I was done.

That made me giggle so hard, and I could see just how precious she really was. I went inside and completed the contract. I had to wait a couple of days so they could check my previous vet's records on Zoey, and they would get back to me.

Jimmy went with me to pick her up the following week. Bella is the most precious dog I have ever known. She has a personality that suits mine perfectly! She snuggles with me and loves me and everyone else in the home. I thank the Lord each day for leading me to her. There's no other answer for how I met her. I am forever grateful to this day.

CHAPTER 115

Ancestry.com

It was Father's Day, and Jim didn't want to do a thing. He wanted to stay home and relax. I had no father to visit, the boys went to their Dad's house, and I was bored silly. Jimmy was playing on his iPad and watching "Man TV." A commercial came on for Ancestry.com, and I thought I would check it out. I picked up my iPad and googled it. The membership was on sale for Father's Day, and it promised great results. At this point, I had met both of my brothers and may have met my Dad, but I didn't know for sure. I also had my mom's obituary from the newspaper in 1964, and it listed that she had two sisters that I had never met. I had never really tried to find them because I figured that they probably weren't interested in me finding them since they had never searched for me. I was going to put away negative thoughts for the day and see what I could find.

I signed up and started inputting information. I had my mom's sisters' names, so I put them in there. Their pictures popped up! I now had faces to go with the names. I expected them to be much older than they were, or these were old pictures. Regardless, since I could see their faces, I decided to check Facebook. They were both there! I shared my news with Jimmy, and he was excited for me! He told me to send them messages like I had done when I searched for Dale. Ok, it worked last time. Maybe it will work again. I typed individual messages to both, saying the same thing.

Something like this ... "My name is Bunny. I just found you on Ancestry.com, and I believe you're my mother's sister. My mother was Gail, and she passed away when I was a baby. I'm not a drama person; I just thought I would pop in and say hello. If you're interested, I would love to chat."

Within an hour, they had both reached out to me with their phone numbers, and they were thrilled to hear from me! It was so exciting to hear their voices! First, it was Aunt Paula, and she was only ten years older than me. Aunt Cheryle was a few years older than her. That's why they never searched for me. They were just children when their sister died. I felt guilty for thinking they didn't care, but now we could fix it. It was a whirlwind of excitement, and I knew I had to make a trip to Worcester ASAP! I had cousins and second cousins to meet too!

A month later, Jim and I planned our trip and he drove me to Worcester to meet my mother's family for the first time. As we went, I felt like I did when I was meeting Dale the first time. Nervous, not sure how I would react, yet excited. It was an 8-hour drive, and I was beat when we arrived at our hotel. The plan was that we would settle in and then call the family and see where they wanted to meet. As we parked at the hotel, I looked out my passenger side window and saw two women standing next to us, looking at us. I had no idea who they were, so I opened my door and asked, "Can I help you?" Aunt Paula and my cousin Lauren had been waiting for us! I had no idea they would be there, and I was so caught off guard.

I recognized Aunt Paula from her Facebook photo, and I hugged her so hard! She introduced me to Lauren, and I hugged her hard too! They had gifts in their hands, and we brought them into the hotel and our room so we could chat. I was so overwhelmed at that point because I expected to have some downtime before I saw them, yet I didn't want anything but to talk to them right then and there.

They gave me my mother's bible, photos, and a framed wedding picture of my mom and Big Dale. It was absolutely beautiful! I finally had things that belonged to my mother! Not just an old obituary from a newspaper, but real things that belonged to her. I now had her sisters to tell me everything about her. I could not get enough!

Later that day, we met with Aunt Cheryle at her home and drove to a park where the rest of her side of the family would meet us. My family was growing right in front of me. All these new people were part of me. It was insane! Throughout the next couple of days, I spent time with as many of them as I could as often as I could. It was so much to take in, and I was starting to worry. I had gotten used to the fact that our children were our whole family. Could I keep up now that I really had a family of my own? I didn't want to disappoint anyone, and I knew I wasn't a master at communicating by phone. I let myself off the hook to allow it all to sink in. I would figure it out BECAUSE it meant the world to me!

CHAPTER 116

Ryan's Scariest Day

I had always told the boys that they didn't have 12 years of school. They had 16. I was determined that they would both go to college. Ryan wanted to go to college in Florida, but I was not having that. He was a bit too fond of alcohol, and I would be a nervous wreck if he were far away, and I couldn't be there to help him if anything were to happen. Ryan went to Towson University instead, and his college years were interesting, at best. I'll just say he definitely enjoyed his college years. He graduated with a degree in Criminal Justice, and he made the Dean's List during his last semester. He then became a paralegal at one of the biggest firms in Baltimore. In 2018, he purchased his first home on his own. I was so very proud of the man he had become, and I looked forward to seeing how his future would wind up.

In 2018, right after he signed the papers to buy his home, he started having seizures. We didn't know what triggered them, but it turns out they were caused by repeated damage to his head. He had been in a few fights, and he had been jumped in the city when he was renting an apartment there. The seizures were terrifying at first because we didn't know what caused them for quite some time. He was put on anti-seizure meds, but then in February of 2019, he had another one. This time his neurologist told him to continue taking the anti-seizure meds and added another medication, Lamictal. Since seizures require the person to not drive for three months, he was getting pretty annoyed with being so needy for rides to and from work, etc.

One Sunday evening, he called me and told me he had a fever and needed to go to the urgent care center the next day. I told him I would be there to take him. When I picked him up, he got in the car with a hoodie on, and I couldn't see his face. I drove him to the urgent care, and we got him signed in. I looked over at him and still couldn't see his face, so I reached over and pulled the hoodie down. What I saw made me jump out of my seat! He was covered in a heavy red rash! I pulled his shirt open, and it was everywhere! I yelled for someone to help and insisted that this was not normal, and he needed help right away.

The staff came running and took him to an examination room. His fever was 105! The doctor asked questions and took tests, and she was in a hurry to find out what was wrong. She brought in a television with another doctor on the screen so she could get another opinion. They had no idea! They sent for an ambulance and took him to the closest hospital, Franklin Square. I was not happy about this choice because this was the hospital that mistreated Cameron as a baby. But I had no choice.

I followed him to the hospital and stayed by his side. He was very annoyed by being there and especially annoyed that he couldn't have any liquids. He was very thirsty. I noticed a few times that he wasn't acting like himself and was saying odd things, but I just let that slip by. His girlfriend at the time was there too, and she said he had been having issues with facts. He was saying things happened that didn't happen, and he was argumentative. I just figured it was part of the high fever, and he was in the right place now to recuperate. He spent the night there that night.

The next morning, I arrived at the hospital before he had gotten out of bed. When the nurse checked on him, she advised us that he had another seizure in his sleep. Crap! They sent him for a CT scan, and he had another seizure while he was in the machine. Things were getting really scary, and Ryan was getting more annoyed.

Ryan insisted that I go home, and he would keep me up to date. His ex-girlfriend was there with him instead.

The following day, which was Wednesday, started with a frantic phone call from Ryan telling me that the hospital was transferring him to another hospital in Virginia. He was irate and insistent that he wasn't going to Virginia. I tried my best to calm him down, but he was not having it. He was leaving the hospital and choosing the hospital he wanted to go to. I quickly called his ex and asked her how far she was from the hospital. One of us had to get there soon to stop him from leaving. She was farther away than me, so I flew over there as quickly as I could.

When I arrived, he wasn't in his bed. I panicked that he had already left. Then I noticed his bookbag was sitting on the sofa, and his bathroom door was closed. He was in there. I sat down and crossed my arms to wait for him to come out. He wasn't happy to see me, especially when I told him I was there to keep him from leaving. He was so angry.

After maybe 5 minutes, the door flew open to his room, and a barrage of hospital staff came busting in. They had a helicopter waiting! The other hospital, Georgetown, needed them to take blood before he left, and they were grabbing him and poking him with needles as I grabbed his clothes and tried to talk them into letting me get on the helicopter too. They were adamant that I could not get on that helicopter, but I could meet them at Georgetown. Ryan was frantic and yelling at everyone, but they were not stopping. They tied him down on the stretcher as he freaked out about getting on a helicopter and leaving Maryland. I was simply speechless!

All I could do was cry. I got in my car and cried even harder. Georgetown was at least an hour and a half away. I wouldn't be there when he arrived. So much could happen, and I had to drive down I-95 and onto the DC beltway, which was always a nightmare of traffic. I then noticed that it was 5 pm! Oh my God, that meant I wouldn't get there for at least 2 hours. I cried, and I prayed so hard! I begged God to let me get there as quickly as possible. I shouldn't have been driving in the state I was in, but I had no choice. Jim was at work, and I couldn't even reach him to let him know what was going on.

So, I just drove.

When I hit the DC beltway, the roads were clear. I drove and kept watching, and there was seriously no traffic at rush hour on a Wednesday afternoon. This never, ever happened. Finally, as I reached the exit off the beltway and saw that I was less than 20 minutes from the hospital, I looked up to the heavens and said, "I know that was you! That had to be you! Thank you so much, and please get me there quick!" Within 1 hour from leaving Franklin Square, I was at the hospital!

This hospital was huge! There were so many entrances, and I had no idea where to go. I pulled into an area with an entrance and saw an exhausted nurse walking out. I opened my passenger side window and yelled out to her. She could see how frantic I was and could hear the panic in my voice. She came to my window and told her my son was rushed there by helicopter with a seizure disorder, and I had no idea where they took him. She gave me directions, but I couldn't process them. She showed me where to park and told me she would wait and explain once I parked. I did, and when I saw her outside the parking lot, she didn't explain how to find him. She took me there, personally. Who does that? She was exhausted, and I told her I didn't want to bother her like that. She insisted, and she took me directly to him. I told her I knew she was an angel. God had helped me get there, and she had taken me to him.

When I saw him, he was already hooked up to all kinds of machines, and he was so happy to see me. Right away, he was asking me for water and a cigarette. I couldn't get him either. He wasn't glad to see me anymore. I stayed by his side from that Wednesday, March 20th, until he was finally discharged two weeks later.

The nurses told me I couldn't stay in his room with him. I didn't respond. I knew I was staying in his room with him, regardless of what they had to say. After several hours there, the nurse brought me a blanket and a pillow and told me I could take the chair in the corner to sleep. I did. At this point, Ryan was sharing the room with an older man. The older man talked and laughed with his children throughout the night over the speaker on his phone. The nurses noticed, too, and made arrangements to move Ryan to his own room.

I had called Joe when I was driving to the hospital to give him a heads up so he could get there too. He thought I was exaggerating, so he wasn't in a big hurry. When he got there the next day, Ryan had started hallucinating. He was amusing, though. Whatever medication they had given him made him hysterical. He was flirting with the nurses, which Ryan didn't normally do. He kept trying to pull the IV's out, and I kept moving his hands away. He was getting very annoyed and told me he had to get it off him. I gently argued that he couldn't, and it was there for a reason. He continued to ask his father and me to sneak him a cigarette, which he thought he could smoke without anyone noticing. As we both laughed at him and with him, he nodded off to sleep. Joe went home and said he would be back the next day.

The next day turned out to be one of the worst days of my life. When I woke up, I thought Ryan was sleeping. When the nurse came in, she told me he had slipped into a coma. She told me not to worry, that this wasn't an unusual thing based on his situation. One of the doctors came in and began talking quickly and loudly, telling me that I had to sign paperwork right away for Ryan to have a liver transplant! What? I hadn't even had coffee yet! She had a laptop in her hands, put it on my lap, and told me to watch the video so I would understand what I had to do. I sat up and did as I was told. The video was all about how transplants work and the side effects, and it freaked me out. She stood there while I watched the video and then put papers in my face to sign. I couldn't think straight! I told her I had to go to the bathroom and I really needed a cup of coffee so I could understand all this so quickly. She went to get me coffee, and I went to the bathroom and called Joe. I tried my best not to get hysterical, but it was a struggle. Joe was coming as quickly as he could get there. I walked back into the room, and several doctors were there, all waiting for me to sign that paperwork. I asked more questions, and they were anxious to get moving. They kept saying they needed it right now! I signed it. Now Ryan would be on the list for a liver transplant, and he would be moved to the top of the list because of his dire situation. The doctor walked out, and I burst into tears!

I must have been sobbing hard because Ryan's nurse fell to his knees in front of me and was so sweetly trying to console me. I was heaving, and I was out of breath! He asked me if I was a person of faith. I said, yes. He asked me what I believed. I told him I was a Christian. He ran out and asked the nurse's desk to find the Pastor of the hospital immediately. He came back in and kept talking to me as I stood next to Ryan, crying my eyes out. How bad was this going to get? I couldn't do this! I needed Ryan to wake up and be ok!

The Pastor came to the room, and I chased him out because he had a white-collar. And I didn't know what Ryan could see from his coma-state, and I was terrified he would think he was getting his last rights or something. I followed the Pastor out of the room, and he took me to a private room and closed the door. He talked to me calmly, and I was like a caged animal. I paced, cried, screamed, and yelled at God and told him he couldn't do this to me. Then I took it back because, of course, he could. The Pastor asked me if I wanted to pray with him. I said yes and sat in front of him, throwing out my hands to his quickly. I held my head down and waited. When I looked up again, the Pastor told me to start. Ughhh! I wasn't good at this! I took a deep breath and told the Pastor that I had begun talking to God every day over the last couple of years, from my home alone. I didn't go to church because I found too many hypocritical situations that turned me away. When I talked to God, I didn't use the right words like I've heard others use. I talk to Him like He's my friend. The Pastor said, fine. So, I put my head down again, and I began my conversation with God while holding the Pastor's hands. I told God everything I was feeling, and I cried like a baby begging Him to save my son's life. When I ended my prayer, I looked up at the Pastor, and he was crying. He told me he had never cried, listening to someone else pray before. It broke his heart to hear my pain. He then said his own prayer to support me. He gave me a bible, and I asked him to sign it. He did. I felt a sense of relief and went back to Ryan's room.

As soon as I got there, another woman was looking for me. She was a social worker, and she needed to discuss exactly why I believed my son deserved a new liver. Huh? Um, the doctors said so! This woman told me that she had done her research, and she was questioning whether or not Ryan "deserved" that new liver! My legs almost went out from under me. As I was walking out to follow the social worker into yet another room for a conversation, I saw that Ryan's ex had shown up, and his sister, Kristen, and her husband, Ross, had shown up too. I introduced them to the social worker and asked if they could come with me. She said yes.

The 5 of us sat in the waiting room alone. The social worker spoke directly to me, and Kristen, Ross, and Ali listened and watched in horror. She knew that Ryan had been expelled in high school for drinking on school property. She knew that he had several DUIs. She asked me what kind of car he crashed headfirst on I95. She had way too much information about his misuse of alcohol, including that it had begun at the age of 14. I sat in horror, listening to her share her records and trying to answer questions without making matters worse. Finally, she closed her book and said, "I do not believe your son deserves this liver, but I'm going to give you a chance to tell me why you think he does."

All 4 of us had eyes the size of a golf ball! I can honestly say that I have no idea what came out of my mouth! I know I kept my composure as much as I could. I know that I told her that Ryan has the biggest heart I've ever known and while he didn't respect his own body and he thought he was invincible. WHEN he woke up with a stranger's liver, he would treasure that gift like no other, and he would take care of it because it had been a gift from someone else.

I couldn't deny the facts that she shared, but I could show his human side. I shared that he had purchased his own home on his own. That he was successful in his career, and he was loved by so many. I don't know what else I said, but I know that all 5 of us were crying when I was finished. I held my breath waiting for her response. She looked down at her lap for a minute and then looked up and said, "From one mother to another, you just bought your son a liver." I ran to her, and she stood for the biggest, hardest hug I've ever given in my life! When she left the room, the 4 of us sobbed and were shaken to our core! Now what?

We each took a deep breath, and I took them back into Ryan's room so they could see him.

As the doctors explained to us that he was going to have a liver transplant within the next two days, another doctor came running into the room and told them to stop. She said he couldn't have a transplant until she eliminated the possibility of a rare disease—HLH caused by Lamictal. I had never heard of that, and I began asking rapid-fire questions. They said he would die if he didn't have a transplant within two days. She said she could work around that and that if he had the transplant and this turned out to be HLH caused by Lamictal, he would infect the new liver with the disease, and we would be back to square one. There were so many unanswered questions, and so many "what ifs!" This doctor was now in charge, and she had lots more tests to run and days to wait for results. I have to admit, I was hoping for a quick fix to get him back home healthy and happy, but that was no longer on the agenda. We would now go through nearly a week of doctors coming and going, tests being continuously run and waiting while Ryan remained in a coma.

Because the liver was so badly damaged, the kidneys were now struggling too. He had to go on 24-hour dialysis. When he was initially intubated, the tube cut the top inside of his mouth pretty severely. Because the kidneys were not working correctly, his blood was thinning, and his mouth would not stop bleeding. He was so helpless, lying there in that hospital bed on life support and plugged into so many things! It took several days for the blood to start to thicken and the constant bleeding to stop. I was so relieved when we could finally take that off the list of his issues.

The silence in the room with just him and me was deafening. I talked to him and prayed by his side. I cried constantly and begged for updated information, which no one had yet. Several of my friends came to visit and brought me goodie bags of snacks and gifts. Angela even brought me several outfits she purchased for me so I would be comfortable. I couldn't post anything on Facebook because Ryan is so extremely private, so I created a Facebook group page for people who were reaching out to keep them updated.

At night, it was a different story in that room of ours. I was constantly trying to get them to stop doping him up, but he would get very active and increasingly angrier each night. He would bolt up in the bed and fight to get out of the restraints they had him in. He would try to pull the IV's out and try to get out of the bed. He was angry and uncontrollable and had to be held down until he calmed down. At first, he would hear my voice and would stop, but after a few days, that didn't work either. I would wake up in the middle of the night with nurses trying to restrain him, and I would jump up to help. The male nurses were the best with him. They were strong enough to keep him in place. Two older nurses were afraid of him, and they just kept dosing him to put him back down. It was so frustrating to watch. Every night got worse. Toward the end of the episodes, one of the nurses climbed on top of him and was yelling in his face for him to stop. I could see the fury in his eyes, and she wouldn't let me talk to him. She said it made him worse. All I could do was cry.

Finally, the doctor in charge came in to let me know that it was HLH caused by Lamictal. Only eight other people in the world have ever been diagnosed with this, and it's a disease caused by an interaction of Lamictal with the body, and its goal is to kill the victim by shutting down the liver, the kidney, and then the rest of the organs. The only treatment that had been found to work was chemotherapy. She then began giving him chemo through the IV's each day while he was still in a coma. Then we just had to wait and wait and wait for tests to show that his body was responding to the chemo.

The days rolled into one another as we waited for results. The late-night episodes were lessening once the chemo started kicking in, so there weren't so many interruptions to his sleep at night. Each morning, I would walk across the street to get coffee, and I would go to the ladies' room to wash up with my wet wipes. Jimmy came down twice and insisted that I go with him to take a shower. I wouldn't go home. It was too far away. He made arrangements with Taylor's friend to let me shower at her place, and then they took me out to eat. I was so uncomfortable being away from the hospital that I couldn't enjoy it like I should have. I just wanted to be there in case he woke up. I did not want him to wake up alone under any circumstances.

The number of doctors visiting began slowing down since they now had a diagnosis, and they had a routine set up for him. His main doctor came in once a day and gave me an update, but it wasn't much most of the time. She then began seeing that his liver was beginning to repair itself! That was huge! We focused on the positive, and I just kept talking to him and begging him to come back to me!

I could not bear the idea of him not making it. Just the thought of that would make my breath stop. I was trying so hard to be strong, and I was focused on getting all the information correct so I could share it with those that love him. I had a job to do, and I would not forgive myself if I messed anything up. In my tears one evening when his ex-girlfriend was visiting, I told her that if he died, I would too. I simply could not live in this world without him. I meant it.

Each day the news was getting better; he was showing signs of improvement. One day they told me they were going to try to remove the intubation tube to see if he could breathe on his own. They told me I had to leave the room. I didn't want to leave the room. I wanted to be there for that. They then said that if he didn't respond positively, they would need to intubate him again, and it would get very messy. They didn't want me there for that. The nurse on duty promised to come out to the hallway to get me as soon as she could. I walked back and forth and back and forth, waiting.

Finally, the nurse came out and waved for me to come in. I ran! When I got to the doorway, Ryan was sitting up without the intubation tube. He opened his eyes, turned, and looked right at me, and in the sweetest voice, he said, "Hi." My knees went weak, but I ran to his bed and hugged him gently with tears streaming down my face! I told him right away that he had done nothing wrong! This wasn't his fault! He nodded and was grateful to hear that. I had my baby back!

Two days later, they moved him out of the ICU and put him in a regular room on another floor. His nurses came to visit him, and they were amazed that he lived through all that! But since he was now awake, he was also in a hurry to get out. I had to keep trying to get him to relax and let them do what they needed to do. He wanted a cigarette and swore to me that he had been sneaking cigarettes the whole time he was there. We knew that wasn't true, but he kept insisting. It was then Opening Day for the Baltimore Orioles, and Ryan never missed an opening day. He kept insisting that I take him to the game and that the doctors wouldn't mind because we would come right back. There was no convincing him, so I just had to be patient. He then wanted to see a movie and again insisted no one would care. It was exhausting, but I was so grateful he was no longer in that coma. He was so impatient with me, with the nurses, and with the doctors. He kept getting out of bed, and the alarm would go off. Then he figured out where the alarm was and tried to turn it off himself, but he stumbled into the chair I was sleeping in, and that made me jump and scream, and then he fell on the floor because I scared him. The nurses were continually reprimanding him, and he was constantly annoyed.

Finally, after 2.5 weeks, he was discharged, and I took him home. He insisted on going to his place and not mine, which I hated, but I respected. We then had a weekly date on Mondays to drive back to Georgetown for his chemo treatments. It was uneventful most of the time, but a few times, he would be vomiting in bags all the way home. He lost his hair, and he gained about 50 lbs., but six months later, he was told he no longer needed chemo. He would need to have his blood drawn and sent to them once a month to keep track of his numbers, but there would be rare visits back to the hospital.

Thank God!

Ryan got his hair back, but it came back curly. He lost the weight he had gained, and he got his life back. The seizure disorder would remain, and the fears of relapse would always crowd my mind, but my faith gave me hope.

CHAPTER 117

Keeping My Promise

During all of those days in the hospital, I prayed constantly. When Ryan was released from the hospital with a good prognosis, I went to church for the first time in many years. My friend Lois was always inviting me to her church, so I reached out to her and asked her to take me. That first Sunday after getting home, I was there, and I've been there nearly every Sunday since. Ryan went with me a few times, but it wasn't for him.

My faith in Jesus is stronger than it's ever been, and I genuinely believe that God brought my son back to me. A few weeks after my first visit to Mountain Christian, I was baptized. This time it meant something to me, and it instilled in me a sense of belonging like I've never known before. I didn't make friends right away, and I went to church alone most of the time. I go to church to hear the message and learn how to be a better person based on the bible stories shared. It has made a massive difference in my life.

CHAPTER 118

Who's My Daddy?

After meeting Dale, I went back to Ancestry.com and decided that his and David's father, Big Dale, had to be my Dad. It was the only answer I could find. Why else would my Mom give me his last name? I knew that Paul was not my Dad, and Big Dale was the only other option. I put Big Dale's name in as my Dad and Ancestry pulled up all his relatives. I thought I finally had the answers.

However, Big Dale and Mona had children together too. One of their daughters, Lynn, was highly offended, and I mean HIGHLY, and she insisted that I remove a photo of my Mom and Big Dale's wedding from my Facebook account. She refused to believe that he was my Dad, and she was livid that I was telling people otherwise. My brother Dale even got angry with me because Lynn was upset about it, and he demanded I remove the photo from my Facebook. I was so upset that he was so callous about this and went to her defense. I removed the picture, but I won't forget the way he made me feel.

In late September/early October of 2019, Lynn sent me a message through Ancestry.com that told me that she had done her DNA and that there was no link between her and me.

She then insisted that I remove HER FAMILY from my tree. I cried for days. Now I was back to square one yet again, and I didn't have any way to find out who my father was. I wrote back asking her why she found pleasure in being so mean to me. Of course, she didn't answer. So, I made one last-ditch effort.

I went back to Ancestry.com and deleted Big Dale as my Dad. I then ran my search for family members related by DNA, and I sent messages to the top 5 people with the most DNA links to me. I had done this previously and didn't get a response from anyone. This time I made my contact stronger. I wrote to each of those five people and asked them to please let me know how we were connected regarding our DNA. I told them I didn't want anything from them, but I was desperately searching for my Dad. I expected no response.

Meanwhile, Ryan was telling me over and over to drop it. He felt that I was causing myself more pain, and at this point in my life, it didn't matter who my Dad was. No one understood. As time went by, I dropped it and decided to move on with my life.

On November 15th, the day after my 56th birthday, I was up early because I had taken on a part-time job for the holiday season, and I had to get to work. My cell phone beeped, and I saw that it was a message from someone on Ancestry.com. I opened it up quickly to see what it said. It was from someone named Rob, and all he said was, "You're my first cousin." I quickly responded with, "Ok, how?" He responded by saying that he would rather chat by phone than text, and he gave me his phone number. I told him I had to leave for work, and I would call him later. By this time, I had run into so many dead ends with this search, and I wasn't in a hurry to hit another one. I went to work, came home, made dinner, and as I sat next to my husband to watch TV, I remembered that I needed to call Rob. I quickly shared with Jimmy what had transpired, and he became anxious for me to make the call. I took a deep breath and dialed the number. Rob was very friendly, and when I asked him again how we were related, he said he had three questions for me first. Ok.

The first question he asked was about my real first name. Yes, my name was Bunita and not Bunny.

His next question was if I lived in Baltimore. Yes.

His third question was if my mother was still alive. I told him no, and that she had passed when I was ten months old.

He was quiet for a moment, and then he said, "Oh my God, you're Uncle Tony's daughter.

I said, "Ok, and who is Uncle Tony?"

He replied, "He was my favorite uncle."

I knew that meant I was too late. I said, "Was? Really?"

Rob told me that his Uncle Tony had just passed away the previous March, only eight months prior. It figured! I was still unsure of what to do with this information and whether it was completely accurate. Rob started telling me a few things, and then he asked me if he could add his Mom to the call because she knew a lot more than he did. I agreed. The puzzle of my life was about to be completely solved FINALLY.

Rob's Mom was Aunt Dee, and she was the youngest of 9 children. When Aunt Dee got on the phone, she was full of answers, and I was in shock! I looked over at Jimmy, and he was in tears! I couldn't cry. I was just frozen and listening to what she had to say. The first thing she said to me was that my family had been looking for me my whole life! I had always wanted to hear those words! They loved me! They wanted me, but they couldn't find me!

As she was speaking to me, my Facebook was blowing up with people sending me friend requests. They were all family members that Aunt Dee was texting while she was chatting with me. With each friend request, I would ask who that person was, and she would tell me. In between the friend requests, she was giving me more and more information. I had a stepmother, a sister, and two more brothers! All I could repeat was, "I have a sister?"

The next thing I knew, my baby pictures were coming through on Facebook from the relatives. They had the same baby pictures that I have in my photo albums! This was insane! These weren't just pictures of a baby that looked like me. These were my pictures! I asked Aunt Dee how they had these pictures. She told me that my Mom's mother sent photos to their mother to see what her granddaughter looked like. This was really it! This was my father's family.

We talked for quite a while, and I was completely overwhelmed. I still didn't cry. I was taking it all in. Before I hung up with Aunt Dee, I asked for my sister's phone number. She had already sent me a friend request, so I knew she knew about me now. When I called, I just kept saying, "I have a sister?" My sister, Linda, was as sweet as she could be. She was 51, married with two adult children, and she lived in Connecticut. Neither of us knew what to say, but she said something so wonderful to me. She told me that she and my brothers, Bill and Michael, always knew about me. She told me that my Dad and their Mom never stopped searching. When they were growing up, she told me that whenever someone asked them how many siblings they had, they always included me in that count by saying and a sister we've never met. Oh, my God!

This was so unlike when I met my brother, David. I had turned his world upside down and felt so bad for it afterward. This time, I was the one with the world upside down! I told Linda that I wanted to talk to her Mom, and she said her Mom was hysterical at the moment! She couldn't wait to talk to me, but she wanted to take it all in first. I understood completely! It was getting late, so I decided to sleep on it and follow up the next day.

The next day I chatted with "Mama." That was my new name for her, and she loved it! She had so much information to share, and I couldn't get enough! She and my brother, Bill, lived in Rhode Island. My brother, Mike, lived in Texas. I told them that I had to meet them very soon and I would plan a trip.

Just three weeks later, Cameron and I got into my car and drove to Connecticut! Mama and Bill would drive from Rhode Island to Linda's place, and we would all meet there. I reserved a room at a local hotel for Cameron and me. As we drove for 8 hours, we had plenty of time to chat. It was a nice ride for us, but I got more anxious as we got closer. The next morning, we had a 5-minute drive to Linda's place, and I turned around to go back to the hotel. I don't know what was going on in my head, but I was freaking out inside. Cameron calmed me down. I'm so glad he went with me!

We pulled up to the apartment complex, and I called Linda to tell me which floor she was on. Instead, she told me she would meet me outside. Here I was again, like when I met Dale at the hotel in Boston. Will I shake her hand or hug her?

I saw her and ran to her to hug her! We were in the street, hugging and crying! She took me inside the building, and Mama was in the lobby waiting for me. She was the sweetest little lady, and she was beyond excited to meet me. She kept telling me that she had loved me from the moment she found out about me, and couldn't believe she was finally meeting me!

We went up in the elevator and walked into the apartment, and oddly, I felt completely at home! I met Linda's husband, Angel, and their daughter, Anna Leah. We sat together for hours and hours, talking about our lives, and telling our stories. I learned so much about what really happened back in 1964. Finally, I had the truth.

My Mom met my Dad, Tony, in a local bar in Worcester, where they both hung out. They both had drinking issues. They dated, and I was conceived. My Dad knew about me all along, but my Mom didn't know what she wanted. Her main issue was getting her boys, Dale and David, back. She had no money to hire an attorney, and neither did my Dad. There are different opinions on whether my Dad ever met me, but he paid child support regardless. When my Mom met Paul, a stranger in town, he told her he would help her get her kids back but only if she left Worcester with me and joined him in Baltimore and they were married. She thought this was the only way she was going to get the boys back. She agreed, and without saying a word to my Dad, she packed us up, and we headed to Baltimore. I was nine months old.

When we arrived in Baltimore, it wouldn't take a brain surgeon to figure out that Paul had no money and had entirely led her on. He demanded that the wedding go as planned, and my Mom got dressed and went to the courthouse with him. However, she confronted him when they got there, and she refused to marry him because he had lied to her. There was no money to help her get her boys. In the end, she agreed to wear the wedding ring and tell his family they had gotten married so that he wouldn't be embarrassed. He was furious, though. After they got back to their house, Paul beat her terribly. She went to her room and swallowed a bottle of pills. That was the end of her struggles. It was just three weeks since we had moved there.

Meanwhile, word got back to Worcester that my Mom had passed. My Dad found out and went to court to get custody of me. I was so happy to hear that. However, he was denied custody because my Mom hadn't put my father's name on my birth certificate, so he couldn't prove he was my Dad. In the Judge's opinion, since my Mom was living with Paul and claiming he was my father, the Judge believed him instead. My Dad had no way to win.

My Dad knew that I was born with my Mom's ex-husband's last name. When he searched for me, he always searched for that name. But I wasn't raised to believe that was my name, and therefore he was never able to find me.

Four years before this meeting with my family, when my Dad was diagnosed with cancer, he and Mama turned their efforts to find me. He really wanted to meet me before he died. Mama had posted the baby pictures on Facebook and asked for help circulating them so they could find me. It didn't work. She told me he never stopped talking about me. His only hope was that I had a better life than he could have given me.

It would have broken his heart to know the truth.

That evening, we went out to dinner, and I met Linda's son, David. It was a sweet time to spend with the family I never knew I had. When we got back to the hotel that evening, Cameron and I talked for hours! We were both so overwhelmed with all of it!

The next day, we went back to Linda's, and this time Bill and his daughters were there. I had taken small gifts up for everyone since Christmas was coming. I thought I would surprise them. They surprised me because they did the same thing! Everyone was wonderful, and I immediately fell in love with every one of them. We had an incredible weekend, and I didn't want it to end. But that evening, Cameron and I drove back home to Baltimore and shared our thoughts all the way home.

Cameron has planned for years to make my story into a screenplay. He told me on that ride home that I needed to finish my book finally. He was right. This was the chapter that would ultimately bring the puzzle together. As my new family and I grew closer, and my relationship with my mother's family had solidified, I was finally where I was supposed to be. With the biological family that loves me! At the same time, there are members of my childhood family that I will always consider family: Uncle Gene and his family, Aunt Shirley and her family, Aunt Patsy and her family, Aunt Dot, my cousin Lee, my cousin Linda, Aunt Sharon, and the girls, my cousin Steve, Nikki, and Sirah.

Who Says You Can't Go Home?

I thought the book was done. I sent the full draft to Peggy Sue because, of course, she was my mentor with this whole thing. As an established working author in her own right, I looked to her for advice and helped with the process. But just after sending her that draft, as Jimmy and I watched television one Monday evening in May 2020, my phone rang. It wasn't over yet!

CHAPTER 119

Nicky

The call was from a Baltimore County detective. He told me he was investigating Paul. I lost my breath and broke out into a cold sweat! I had hoped that the horrors of my childhood were enough and that I would never have to rehash all of it in a court of law. I had made the decision many times over that I would not do it. His death would be my closure. But as they say, "Man makes plans, and God laughs." There was one more chapter to close this story.

Paul's youngest daughter, Melissa, had several children and was clearly not the maternal type. Her first two children, Nicky and Sirah, were from a man she dated, and then I understand she had at least two more children from 2 other men. There may be more, I've never had a relationship with her, so I lost count. Her first child, Nicky, was born with cerebral palsy and was restricted to a wheelchair. Before the children became teenagers, Melissa asked Paul and his wife, Darlene, to babysit so she could go out for the evening.

She never came back!

Paul and Darlene stepped up and became legal guardians, and they raised the two kids into adulthood. I was always very nervous about this situation, and when Billy and I were close, I would always ask him how the kids were and if Paul was bothering them. Billy never believed my claims, and he would scoff at me and say they were just fine.

At one time, I visited Billy when he was married to Shannon, and Siriah was there staying. I was so happy to see her, but she didn't respond to me in any way. I guessed that she had been told stories about me and didn't like me. I was okay with that. But I watched her play and interact, and shivers went down my back. I could see the darkness in her eyes, the slumped shoulders, the shyness, and I saw myself at that age. Paul WAS bothering her. I felt it in my soul. I talked to Billy later about it, and he angrily denied it. There was nothing I could do. No one believed me, and I was no longer a member of that family anyway.

I had heard that in November 2018, Nicky reported Paul for molesting him for years! I didn't suspect that one! This horrible monster was molesting a boy in a wheelchair—his own grandson, who could not defend himself.

I was livid! I heard Paul was on the run and in hiding. His sister, Daisy, was helping him! This is the same sister whose son, Michael, went to prison for molesting his daughter! Michael learned what he did from Paul, and now Daisy was helping the man who ruined her son's life!

Unbelievable!!

When the detective called me that evening, I knew it was time to face the music. Due to the coronavirus pandemic, he wanted to take a recorded statement from me over the phone. I agreed. It was a 2-hour conversation. He wanted details of everything. I cried. I shook. I was a wreck. Each question brought back painful memories and extreme embarrassment. I had never done the right thing and tried to prosecute him. He had continued molesting children, and I could have tried to stop it. Instead, I put my head in the sand

and moved forward with my life, all while attempting to forget the past.

It never completely worked.

I would have flashbacks often when I was married to Joe. I couldn't watch movies that had anything to do with child molestation because I would be having night terrors again, and it was always in the back of my head whenever I saw a man alone with a child. The detective was so very gentle and understanding. At the end of our call, he told me that the court system was different back then and that I did what I had to do for myself. I spent the next two days crying in my bed. I knew I needed to let it out, and I needed to forgive the child version of me, as well as the adult version of me. I made decisions for reasons, and my biggest motivation was to escape and create a better life. I did that. Now I had to do something. On the third day after the call, I called the detective and asked him to file charges on my behalf.

I was committed to supporting Nicky, and I will do whatever needs to be done to make that monster pay.

ABOUT THE AUTHOR

B. Loren was a transplant from Worcester, Massachusetts to Baltimore, Maryland in the first year of her life. She was kidnapped and raised by a man she thought was her father, after her young mother's untimely death. She worked as a legal secretary/paralegal for 10 years and then moved onto a direct sales business, which changed everything about her life circumstances. Out of this endeavor, she would grow a multi-million-dollar business and raise her two sons to be independent, strong, loving men. She was fixated her entire adult life on giving them the best life she could, as a single parent.

This book is the only book she is planning to write because she has just one story to tell - the story of her life. She believes this story needed to be told and now that it's done, she plans to retire with her husband and spend her golden years traveling and continuing to make happy, wonderful memories.

Made in the USA
Middletown, DE
21 January 2022

59323035R00215